Comrades against Apartheid

 The ANC
the South African
Communist Party
in Exile

Nkosi
sikelel'i Afrika

God
bless Africa

Comrades against Apartheid

The ANC
& the South African
Communist Party
in Exile

& STEPHEN ELLIS
& TSEPO SECHABA

James Currey
LONDON
 Indiana University Press
BLOOMINGTON & INDIANAPOLIS

James Currey Ltd
54b Thornhill Square, Islington, London N1 1BE

Indiana University Press
601 North Morton Street
Bloomington, Indiana 47404-3797

*We are grateful to those scholars who have read drafts of this manuscript but who
do not wish their names to be mentioned.*

The photographs are reproduced with the permission of IDAF.

British Library Cataloguing in Publication Data
Ellis, Stephen
   Comrades against apartheid : the ANC and the
   South African Communist Party in Exile.
   I. Title. II. Sechaba, Tsepo
   322.420968

ISBN 0-85255-353-6 (cloth)
ISBN 0-85255-352-8 (paper)

Library of Congress Cataloging in Publication Data
Ellis, Stephen, 1992.
      Comrades against apartheid : the ANC and the South African
   Communist Party in exile / Stephen Ellis and Tsepo Sechaba
         p.   cm.
      Includes bibliographical references.
      ISBN 0-253-31838-6 (cloth) — ISBN 0-253-21062-3 (pbk.)
      I. South African Communist Party. 2. African national
Congress. 3. South Africa - Politics and government --1961-1978
4. South Africa — Politics and government — 1978–   I. Sechaba,
Tsepo, 1992.   II. Title,
JQ1998.C64E45   1992
324.268'083—dc20   91-18439

Typeset in 10/11 Plantin and with Gill display
by Opus 43, Cumbria
Printed in Great Britain
for Villiers Publications London N6

Contents

Joe Slovo at the microphone of an SACP meeting in London to celebrate the 65th anniversary of the Party's foundation, 1986

Joe Slovo

Oliver Tambo in his younger days

Alfred Nzo at Kabwe, 1985

John Nkadimeng at Kabwe, 1985

Mac Maharaj speaking with Chris Hani behind him, Kabwe, 1985

The leaders of Umkhonto we Sizwe: left to right, Joe Slovo, Chris Hani and Joe Modise

Introduction

It is too soon to write a definitive history of the South African Communist Party (SACP) since 1953, when it was established in its modern form, or since 1961, when it took up arms in its struggle against the South African state.

In many ways, there is no such thing as a definitive history of anything. Any human experience, especially one which takes place over a period of years and which directly affects thousands of lives, is impossible to reconstruct in all its detail. Some important events are never recorded in writing. Memories of meetings and conversations become blurred by time or distorted by later feelings. In any case, every history is partly a reflection of the people writing it and of the times they live in. A history of the South African Communist Party and of its relationship with the African National Congress (ANC) which might appear full and satisfactory now, would seem dated in a few years' time. Even if it gave full and satisfying answers, it might well appear to have asked the wrong questions.

Quite apart from these considerations, which apply to all writing of history, the SACP poses very special problems of sources. Communism was banned by law in South Africa in 1950. It was not unbanned until February 1990. In the intervening period no loyal Party member – and, on the whole, they were immensely loyal – would willingly impart information about the Party for fear of committing himself or his comrades to gaol or exposing them to the risk of assassination. This pressing need for secrecy was grafted on to habits of discretion and clandestinity which the Party had assumed since its inaugural congress in Cape Town in 1921.

Despite the Party's meticulous secrecy, written material is publicly available for an investigation of its history. Much of this material falls into two main categories. First there is information published by the Party about itself. Like any political party, it has felt a need to propagate information – including manifestos, resolutions, appeals, polemical writings and so on – which in its case were designed to keep the image of an illegal and beleaguered organisation alive in the public mind. In addition to these basic political communiqués, the Party's leadership, which was composed essentially of intellectuals during the years of underground existence, has shown itself to be preoccupied with a sense of history. Perhaps this is normal for any group threatened with extinction. It is certainly to be expected in people holding deep-seated Marxist beliefs, who are convinced that politics is not just the product of individual human action and of chance, but is governed by profound laws of historical development which Marxists can aim to understand. Party journals such as *The African Communist* and *Umsebenzi* are valuable sources of information on the Party during the period covered by this book. Also of great usefulness are books by official Party historians such as Brian Bunting, who has written a biography of the veteran South African communist Moses Kotane, the Party's General Secretary for almost forty years.[1] Other Party members who have written on the history of the Party, or of the socialist movement in South Africa, include Jack and Ray Simons[2] and Michael Harmel.[3] Edwin Mofutsanyana has given extensive interviews on the early history of the Party to academic researchers. There exist sympathetic biographies of Party leaders Bill Andrews[4] and S.P. Bunting.[5]

The second main source of information on the Party is the attacks made on it by its political enemies. The South African public may know little of a political party whose very name was banned from public mention for so many years, as though it were tainted by some strange form of leprosy communicable only through thought. But sections of the South African state, and most notably the Security Police, made it their business to gather information about the Communist Party by reading its published information, by detaining, interrogating and sometimes torturing its members, and by sending spies to infiltrate it. Much of whatever information it was able to glean by these means the Security Police has kept to itself. Some details it has made public, no doubt often adding a good deal of disinformation for public consumption. Anti-communism has been a constant theme on the right of South African politics, and has often been carried to extremes which make right-wing attacks on the SACP hard, or impossible, to swallow. The *Aida Parker Newsletter*, for example, has for years thrived on lurid anti-communist writing in which there are many shades between the seemingly true and the clearly unlikely. Curiously, perhaps, even this school of robust anti-communism has produced only one full-length history of communism in South Africa, that by Henry Pike, a right-wing American clergyman, first published in 1985. It is an extremely polemical work replete with anti-communist

1   Brian Bunting, *Moses Kotane, South African Revolutionary* (Inkululeko Publications, London, revised edition, 1986).
2. H.J. & R.E. Simons, *Class and Colour in South Africa, 1850–1950* (Penguin, Harmondsworth, 1969).
3. A. Lerumo (Michael Harmel), *Fifty Fighting Years* (Inkululeko Publications, London, 3rd revised edition, 1987).
4. R.K. Cope, *Comrade Bill: The Life and Times of W.H. Andrews, Workers' Leader* (Stewart Printing Company, Cape Town, 1943).
5. Edward Roux, *S.P. Bunting, a Political Biography*, (published by the author, Cape Town, 1944).

diatribes of the most vitriolic type. It was compiled from a wide range of published sources and interviews with top security officers including Gerard Ludi, one of the most successful of Pretoria's spies, and Hendrik van den Bergh, the former head of the now-defunct BOSS, the Bureau of State Security.[6]

In addition to these primary sources of information – the Party itself and its sworn enemy, the South African state with its apologists – there are other sources which could be considered less partisan. These include testimonies by former Party members or sympathisers who have renounced their beliefs and given accounts of their experiences to the public. Such sources could be said to include Dr Eddie Roux, the early communist who grew disillusioned with the Party and later published extensive criticisms of it,[7] and Bartholomew Hlapane, a member of the South African Communist Party Central Committee who turned state witness, testifying in this capacity in several trials and later giving evidence to an American Senate sub-committee conducting hearings on Soviet bloc influence in the affairs of southern Africa.[8] There was the so-called 'Gang of Eight', which included several communists who publicly split with the Party and with the ANC, accusing the Party of manipulating the Congress. In these and similar cases it might be argued that former communists or fellow-travellers gave information about those who had previously been their comrades because they had been coerced into doing so by the state, or that they were embittered individuals whose motives were not disinterested; or that, like converts to any cause, their intellectual conversion to anti-communism had required such an emotional wrench as to cause them to become unbalanced in their judgement. There may be some truth in these criticisms in some cases, especially evidence supplied by a state witness such as Hlapane. Former political prisoners in South Africa have described the pressure put on them and their colleagues to give false testimony. Nevertheless, to discount everything said about the Party by former members hardly suggests objectivity or aids understanding. Such an attitude leads to the position that nothing said about the Party is true unless it is officially stated by the Party itself, which would be naïve in the extreme.

All of these and similar sources – official Party histories, court records, memoirs and so on – have been used by academic historians such as Baruch Hirson and Tom Lodge who have made a speciality

6. Henry Pike, *A History of Communism in South Afrca* (Christian Mission International, Germiston, 1985).
7. Eddie Roux, *Time Longer than Rope. A History of the Black Man's Struggle for Freedom in South Africa* (University of Wisconsin Press, Madison, 2nd edition, 1964); Eddie & Win Roux, *Rebel Pity* (Penguin Books, Harmondsworth, 1972).
8. *The Role of the Soviet Union, Cuba and East Germany in Fomenting Terrorism in Southern Africa.* Hearings before the Subcommittee on Security and Terrorism of the Committee of the Judiciary, United States Senate (2 vols, Government Printing Office, Washington, 1982).

of writing on the history of black and trade union politics in South Africa, and have already done much to uncover or illuminate the Party's history at least until its suppression in 1950.[9]

One of the reasons why observers of South African politics have tended to be either virulently anti-communist or rather indulgent in discounting evidence unfavourable to the Communist Party has to do with the nature of the Party's arch-enemy, the South African state. South Africa has been witness over the centuries to some of the worst depradations of colonialism, meaning the conquest and settling of the land by peoples of foreign origin, and of imperialism, meaning government by a foreign power. It has also had experience of capitalism, in the form of capital-intensive industry and mineral extraction accompanied by untold exploitation and misery. Most notoriously, South Africa has been the home of apartheid, a policy of racial separation condemned the world over and rejected now by the political party which first enunciated the concept, the National Party. Hatred of, or distaste for, the South African government and all its works has caused many writers of liberal or socialist inclination to pass over in silence some evidence concerning the SACP because to write anything critical of the Party can be seen as helpful to its enemy. It is a measure of the intensity of the political struggle in South Africa, which has engaged the attention of the entire world, and has made objectivity appear an almost quaint ideal.

The events of the last five years, however, have changed the political landscape and the intellectual climate. The end of the Cold War, in which South Africa had become quite centrally involved, now makes it easier to write about the South African situation without being labelled either pro-capitalist or pro-communist. The Soviet government itself, held to be at the very centre of Marxist intrigue in Cold War polemics, now has quite warm relations with the government in Pretoria and no longer seeks its overthrow. The SACP can no longer be portrayed intelligently as its tool or its shadow. The South African government has abandoned its determination to exclude from national politics all persons of colour and anyone it deems to be a communist. It has unbanned the Party itself, allowing it to go public to whatever degree it wishes. The struggle has ceased to be primarily military, although the use of violence remains one of the most striking features of South African political life.

The unbanning of the ANC and of the Communist Party, and their suspension of the armed struggle, has opened up a vast space for argument and legitimate persuasion: in short, for politics. This has already had its effect among adherents of the democratic movement in South Africa, the great numbers of people who have struggled

9. Baruch Hirson, *Yours For the Union. Class and Community Struggles in South Africa, 1930–1947* (Zed Books, London, 1989); Tom Lodge, *Black Politics in South Africa Since 1945* (Longman, England, 1983).

4

against the apartheid government and who have not been willing to countenance any criticism of its principal enemies. Since mid-1990 the South African left has been in the throes of a debate, almost certain to be protracted, on issues which include the ideology and methods of the South African Communist Party. One of the leading proponents of this debate has been Pallo Jordan, the information chief of the ANC. Himself a socialist, he has on several occasions attacked the Party's Stalinist past and, by implication at least, the less engaging features which it continues to display.[10] The Party itself, in spite of its formidable reputation as a monolith, has been affected by the new atmosphere. Although it still has a tendency to regard all criticism with acute suspicion rather than in a spirit of tolerant debate, it has to deal carefully with critics from within the South African left or trade union movement, for these are its own constituency. It can no longer dismiss critics of obvious sincerity as mere lackeys of the apartheid system. And, competing for the political allegiance of South Africans, it has to think long and hard about its own programme. The Soviet model of socialism, the Party's guiding light for seventy years, has been found wanting. In 1990 the Party published a pamphlet written by its General Secretary, Joe Slovo, entitled *Has Socialism Failed?* In it, Slovo accepts that communism has been thoroughly discredited by its failure in Eastern Europe but contends that the Marxist model itself remains uncorrupt. It is not Marxism which is at fault, but the methods by which it was applied. This analysis itself gives rise to theoretical debate which is outside the scope of this book. It also raises the question of whether, irrespective of its theory, the Party can change its modes of operating and the core of its belief, developed over decades. Time alone will tell.

It is in this context that we offer the present book on the history of the SACP and its relationship with the African National Congress in exile from 1960, the year when the ANC was banned, until 1990, the year when both the Party and the ANC were unbanned. We would emphasise that the book does not seek to go beyond February 1990, when the two organisations were unbanned and Nelson Mandela was released from prison. South African politics changed enormously at that moment, and the relationship which we describe between the two allied organisations in their exile years was transformed. The character of both the ANC and the Party changed, since unbanning and return from exile put them back in touch with their real constituents, the people of South Africa.

It seems important to publish this book now, despite the fact that it does not even pretend to be a complete or definitive history of the

---

10. The main vehicle for this debate has been *Work in Progress*, which published an abridged version of an article by Jordan, 'The crisis of confidence in the SACP'. The debate has also been conducted in the *South African Labour Bulletin* and has also spilled over into the mainstream press.

Party and its relationship with the ANC, because South Africa is at a crucial stage of its history. Both the Party and the ANC are leading players on the political stage. For 40 years South Africans were forbidden by law to be members of the Party or even to read freely about it in their newspapers. For 30 years the same was true of the ANC. Now they are able to do both, and yet the history of the Communist Party especially is relatively little known, for reasons we have already mentioned.

When writing about the period 1960–90, it is impossible to separate completely the histories of the Party, of the ANC, and of the organisation formed by both in 1961 under the command of Nelson Mandela, the guerrilla army Umkhonto we Sizwe. The relationship between these three organisations is not a simple one. In the early days, the Party and the ANC were indeed separate organisations, with their own lists of members and their own leaders, who formed an alliance to fight their common enemy. Umkhonto we Sizwe too had its own membership and its own leaders, drawn from both organisations. In the circumstances of the underground struggle the identity of all three became blurred. The Party, the ANC and Umkhonto we Sizwe effectively merged to the point that it became difficult to define the three separately. In most respects except for sheer numbers, the Party came to dominate the ANC. So many prominent members of the ANC in exile over the past three decades were also members of the Party that, at times, it became impossible to know on whose behalf they were speaking. They could choose to speak wearing either their Party hat or their ANC hat, depending on circumstances. The same was true of the other organisation which was officially part of the grand anti-apartheid triple alliance, the South African Congress of Trade Unions (SACTU). Since the late 1960s almost every Party member, and almost every SACTU member, has also been a member of the ANC. For much of that time the Party regarded the ANC, which can truthfully claim to be the main representative of the black people of South Africa, as a pool from which to recruit the best and the brightest to its own ranks.

This book is a collaboration between a participant, a black South African, and a white, British academic. Tsepo Sechaba is the pen-name of a man who joined the ANC illegally inside South Africa, left the country after 1976 and was recruited to the South African Communist Party. He worked in sensitive positions in the ANC's underground, and had access to highly confidential information, some of which is the basis for what is published here. He left southern Africa shortly before the ANC and the Party were unbanned. He has neither resigned nor been expelled from the ANC or the Communist Party. His writing and the information he has supplied in this book are motivated by a sincere belief that it is important that the South African public should know the broad outlines of what happened in exile for the sake of their country's political future. Much of what we have written about events in exile since the late 1970s is the result of things he did, heard and saw himself. He is himself a source and we would ask the reader's indulgence for the fact that, contrary to academic convention, there are few footnotes. He remains faithful to the ideals of the ANC. He also believes that it is important for a book to be written about the South African struggle, the ANC and the Communist Party by a participant, a black South African. Virtually all the other books on the subject have been written by whites, with rare exceptions such as the history of the ANC by the late Francis Meli. But that is a highly sanitised version.

The other author, Stephen Ellis, was a journalist from 1986 to 1991 and had occasion to travel throughout southern Africa, to interview people both inside and outside government throughout the region, and to observe from a distance. So the book is more than the personal memoir of a black South African who was a revolutionary during the 1980s. We have tried to put one man's personal experience into context using published sources and some interviews with others, although not as extensively as if we had been indeed trying to write a definitive history of the SACP in this period. But, in any case, the published sources are sparse when it comes to revealing the inner history of the Party and of its alliance with the ANC.

To some extent the nature of the collaboration of the two authors leads to an unavoidable contradiction – between one author who is attempting to remain detached, and another who remains committed to a political cause. On some things it is easy to agree. On other matters, differences of approach are difficult to resolve. When treating such organisations as the Angolan rebel movement UNITA, or the Mozambican RENAMO, for example, there is a clash between the academic aspiration to describe them scientifically and in neutral terms, and the activist's instinct to describe them politically, as bandits and counter-revolutionaries. To some extent we must find a compromise, so in this particular instance what we can easily agree on is that both UNITA and RENAMO were enlisted in the service of apartheid and the defence of white South Africa. RENAMO, which was originally created by the Rhodesian intelligence services, made particularly extensive use of terror and made little effort to govern justly or, for example, to establish schools and clinics in the zones it controlled.

This book is an interim report. It will be superseded by others which have been longer in the making, researched from a wider range of sources, and written with the help of ANC and Party members who may become more inclined to speak of the past as time goes by. Other books will also benefit from the enormous advantage of hindsight as the changing fortunes of South Africa adjust our perceptions of the past. It concerns the Party and the ANC in exile, for that is where their active membership mostly was in the period 1960–1990. The story of what was happening inside South Africa itself during those years – including the Soweto insurrection of 1976, the risings of the mid-1980s, the emergence of the United Democratic Front and of the Congress of South African Trade Unions – fall outside our scope. We mention them only inasmuch as they make our story easier to follow. The history of the Party and the ANC before 1960 are described only as a general introduction. Again, we emphasise that we do not attempt to describe the ANC and the Party since February 1990, when they were free to return home.

Readers will make up their own minds whether people were right or wrong to act as they did in the circumstances then obtaining. But any judgement which may be made on the armed struggle, a central theme of the period, must bear in mind the fact so forcefully underlined by Nelson Mandela in his statement from the dock in Pretoria's Supreme Court on 20 April 1964:

> All lawful modes of expressing opposition [to the principle of white supremacy] had been closed by legislation, and we were placed in a position in which we had either to accept a permanent state of inferiority, or to defy the Government. We chose to defy the law. We first broke the law in a way which avoided any recourse to violence; when this form was legislated against, and then the Government resorted to a show of force to crush opposition to its policies, only then did we decide to answer violence with violence.[11]

The banning of political organisations including the ANC, and the denial of any voting right to people of colour, excluded the black, coloured and Indian population of South Africa from any form of organised political expression.

Similarly, any judgment on the methods used by the ANC and the Communist Party must bear in mind also the atrocious methods used by elements of the South African security forces and their allies both inside and outside the country.

Although Umkhonto we Sizwe was ultimately unsuccessful in its aim of bringing about the downfall of the South African government by force, the armed struggle, as it is called, was instrumental in bringing about the changes which South Africa is now witnessing. The South African Communist Party and its alliance with the ANC were central to the conception and execution of that struggle. Beyond making these observations, we leave it to readers to decide what they think.

Stephen Ellis, Amsterdam, Netherlands

---

11. Nelson Mandela, *I am Prepared to Die* (International Defence and Aid Fund for Southern Africa, London, 1979), p. 29.

I

The Communist Party
of South Africa
1921-50

The esteem in which the South African Communist Party[1] is held by many people in South Africa today may seem bizarre in a world which has seen the transformation of Soviet and East European communism and the abandonment of old dogmas. To put it bluntly, communism has become unfashionable in the world, and it seems strange to many outside South Africa that any group of people, especially if they are trying to build a new politics and a new society, should be interested in a discredited system. So grave is the crisis of communism that many commentators wonder what, if anything, can be salvaged of the socialist ideal once the errors and flaws of Marxism-Leninism, as it developed in Eastern Europe, have been admitted.

The South African Communist Party has throughout its history identified itself closely, at times almost totally, with the brand of Marxism-Leninism applied by the government of the Soviet Union and in other states of Eastern Europe. South African communists were among the most loyal devotees of Stalin and Stalinism. The Party successively supported the Soviet invasions of Hungary in 1956, Czechoslovakia in 1968 and Afghanistan in 1979. For years, South African communists despised the positions adopted by reformist communist parties, such as Italy's, who argued that socialism could come about through negotiation or participation in an existing constitutional framework. Even after the appointment of Mikhail Gorbachev as General Secretary of the Communist Party of the Soviet Union, and later as President of the USSR, the South African Communist Party exalted the achievements of Stalin and showed little sign of the public self-criticism and the new thinking then in vogue in the USSR. South African communists continued to place their faith in both the doctrines and the methods of classical Marxism-Leninism. Some cynics have gone as far as to wonder whether South Africa is such an odd place that, having adopted an internationally discredited national socialism when the National Party came to power in 1948, it is now destined to repeat the mistake by clinging to the equally discredited ideology of Soviet-style communism.

1. From its foundation in 1921 until its suppression in 1950, the Party was known as the Communist Party of South Africa (CPSA). In 1953 it re-established itself as the South African Communist Party (SACP). We have tried to respect these titles according to the period under discussion.

9

As recently as June 1989, the SACP was still setting its face against the changes sweeping the communist world. At its Seventh Congress held in Havana, Cuba, the Party approved a new programme, *The Path to Power*, which continued to speak of socialism as a force sweeping the world. Only in January 1990 did the South African Communist Party, still illegal but aware of the rapid changes taking place in South Africa and internationally, publicly question its basic commitment to this traditional, orthodox ideology.

Very few South Africans know the Communist Party well. It was illegal from 1950 to 1990 and, as its General Secretary, Joe Slovo, has pointed out, for years South Africans were bombarded with anti-Party information or propaganda which it had no power to counter in the columns of the press or on the air-waves of radio and television. Even before its suppression over four decades ago, the Communist Party was represented by successive governments as the most terrible of all the devils in the official South African demonology. That condemnation has been a part of the Party's strength. If communism is such an implacable foe of apartheid governments then, in the minds of the many South Africans who loathe apartheid, it cannot be bad. A large part of the Party's appeal is based not on its size and power, and not on the intellectual force of its political programme, but on the mystique of being the ultimate foe of apartheid. It is also an important asset that the Party has been non-racial in its membership and its policies since 1924. Although its critics have argued with some truth that whites, and to a lesser extent, coloureds and Indians, have tended to dominate the Party's leadership throughout its history, it is also true that Africans of the stature of Moses Kotane, J.B. Marks, Moses Mabhida and Chris Hani have been major forces in the Party, none of these four being mere tokens or figureheads. The Party can congratulate itself on the hard work and foresight which have helped it to gain a reputation as the foremost enemy of apartheid. In as much as the South African Communist Party is proving itself to be a dynamic organisation with a degree of popular appeal, it is reaping the reward for decades of dedicated underground work, the courage of generations of militants, and a good dose of single-minded ruthlessness.

During its time underground, the Party made the cornerstone of its strategy the effective takeover of the ANC. In three decades of joint underground activity, the Party succeeded in acquiring a dominant influence over the leadership of the ANC and in changing its character, making it less of a broad 'umbrella' organisation which represented every strain of black nationalism, and changing it into something more closely resembling a socialist party. These processes have been reversed only since February 1990. During the early years of their association, which goes back to the 1920s, it was quite correct to describe the Party and the ANC separately. They were distinct and autonomous organisations, although their paths sometimes crossed and a few prominent individuals were members of both organisations simultaneously. Only after the banning of the ANC in 1960 did it become increasingly difficult to separate the two. After their flight into exile they came to appear almost as Siamese twins, inseparable without causing the death of one or both.

Both the ANC, founded in 1912, and the Communist Party, founded in 1921, arose during a period of exceptionally rapid change in South Africa. The earlier pattern of South African history – largely a story of migration and land disputes between black and white farmers, both trying to escape control by the British imperial administration based in Cape Town – was transformed in the late nineteenth century by the discovery of gold and diamonds on the Rand and at Kimberley and by the full exposure of the country to British capitalism, then the most advanced in the world. The owners of the mining houses, the Randlords whose descendants and companies still dominate South African business, became a fixture in South African life. Before the gold rush, there had been only one city worthy of the name, and that was Cape Town. There now sprang up mining camps, market towns and seaports which became modern cities in a few years.

Unable to exercise control over the interior of South Africa, including the independent republics established by Afrikaner migrants in the Transvaal and the Orange Free State, the British colonial administration concentrated on keeping hold of the ports and transport routes of southern Africa, a strategy which was revived with devastating effect in the 1970s and 1980s by governments in Pretoria, becoming a part of the policy known as 'destabilisation'.

Throughout the nineteenth century the tendency of the British imperial administration, based in Cape Town, was to attempt to dominate the interior of the region with the minimum expense in British money and British lives. All the peoples of South Africa were affected to some extent: some were overcome by military means, others in other ways. After the discoveries of gold and diamonds, and South Africa's conversion into a coveted reserve of mineral wealth, it became a matter of urgency for British business and strategic interests to subjugate the independent Afrikaner republics. The Afrikaners of the north fought a full-scale war against the might of the British empire, the world's first super-power, in defence of what they claimed as their right of self-determination. Their cause attracted worldwide sympathy from rivals of Britain and upholders of the rights of small nations. Even a contingent of Russian volunteers came to fight on their side in the Anglo-Boer War (1899–1902), during which neither the British nor the Afrikaners gave much thought to the country's black majority.

Even before the war, the mineral discoveries had led to the establishment of that central feature of modern South Africa, the mining industry. The rapid building of mining settlements and of new towns sucked in both blacks and whites from the farms. In the aftermath of the war, in the early years of this century, there were plenty of poor Afrikaner farm boys ready to work for low wages in the mines or in town. There they mixed with the flood of new immigrants coming from Europe to escape unemployment or, in the case of the many Jews among them, to escape the pogroms of Eastern Europe. Another wave of newcomers arrived to escape the conditions in Europe at the end of the First World War. They joined the steady stream of black Africans leaving their villages and farms for wage labour in the towns and mines.

South Africa acquired an urban working class, or perhaps we should say it acquired two: a black one and a white one. Their circumstances were quite different. The white workers included new immigrants with no knowledge of Africa but imbued with the culture and politics of Europe, Afrikaners leaving their farms in search of wages, and English-speaking South Africans from the Cape and Natal. For many blacks the memory of their own political freedom was still strong. Many took wage employment only for short periods, leaving their families in the country. Few were literate. There was already a long history of racism in South Africa, and in these circumstances solidarity between white and black workers was well-nigh impossible, or so absurd as to be almost unthinkable. The competing claims of class and race on the political allegiance of South African workers posed a problem for the first trade unionists and socialists who began to recruit in the late nineteenth century, and the succeeding 90 years have not resolved the matter.

Immigrants from Europe, arriving in the industrial jungle of the Rand mining towns, found conditions of exploitation surpassing even those they had been used to in the old continent. The earliest South African socialists included men like David Ivon Jones, a Welsh radical and admirer of Lloyd George. His socialism was so steeped in the tradition of the Chapel that his fiercest hatred seemed to be reserved for the grip of Mammon in South Africa. Bill Andrews was another founding father of South African socialism whose outlook was conditioned by his upbringing and early manhood in Britain, in his case most especially by trade unionism. Andrews arrived in South Africa in 1893 and commenced trade union activity almost at once. Perhaps as important as Andrews was Sidney Bunting, an English gentleman who first came to South Africa as an army officer during the Anglo-Boer War and later returned to settle as a lawyer. Bunting frequented the same gentlemen's clubs as the mining magnates, but, a passionate defender of the rights of the powerless, he frequently took on legal defence work on behalf of socialists. These people and others who were active in the politics of the labour movement in South Africa in 1915 formed the International Socialist League in Johannesburg, splitting with the mainstream Labour Party on the issue of the World War then raging. The ISL was one of the forerunners of the Communist Party of South Africa.

South Africa's burgeoning towns provided fertile ground for trade unionists and labour activists. Conditions in the mines of the Rand in the 1920s were very poor, and were worse for black workers than for whites. Government brutality against workers who demonstrated in support of demands for better conditions compounded the outrage felt by the early socialists. In 1913–14, troops were called out to put down a series of strikes.

The small band of white South African socialists opposed the First World War from the start. Like comrades in Europe who took the same line, they found that this made them unpopular with the white working class, and generally increased their isolation during the war years. Partly for this reason some of them tried to cultivate a following among black workers, although social and cultural circumstances made this difficult, not least because the African mine workers were migrants housed in secure compounds policed by the mining companies. Nevertheless, there is some evidence that socialist activists may have managed to spread pamphlets in black mining compounds that helped precipitate a wave of strikes in the mines in 1918–20.

The Russian Revolution of 1917 and the end of the World War in 1918 had their effect in South Africa as elsewhere in the industrialised world. A group of Johannesburg workers even formed a council which they labelled a soviet, in imitation of the Russian model. Bunting and Jones discounted the value of the Johannesburg soviet, partly because it was composed solely of whites. Bill Andrews, whose roots were in the politics of the white working class and who did not see blacks as a real constituency for socialism in the circumstances of the time, thought it an interesting development worth encouraging. Throughout these early years Bunting showed himself more sympathetic than many of his colleagues to the possibility of political organisation among black workers, although most African workers remained rooted in the countryside, coming to town only as migrant workers and returning to their villages at the end of their contracts. It was difficult to imagine them living permanently in the towns, let alone belonging to the same political organisations or trade unions as white workers. In the course of time the government was to confirm this pattern by legislation which it put into effect from the 1930s, making it illegal for blacks to live in the white towns for longer than they were required as employees and creating the basis for the later Group Areas Act. Even in the view of Bunting, who appears in some respects to have been the most far-sighted of the first generation of white socialists or revolutionaries, the best that could be envisaged in the medium term was for black and white workers to make the South African revolution together, and then for land to be returned to blacks so they could develop in their rural economy. The towns seemed destined to remain in the hands of the mostly white proletariat.

These early socialists founded the CPSA in 1921, and immediately affiliated the new party to the Moscow-based Communist International, the Comintern. Like socialists throughout the world, they believed that the Soviet Union after the Bolshevik revolution represented the prototype of a new type of workers' state, in which national and ethnic differences would soon cease to have political meaning as workers of all colours and cultures found a common interest in a state governed by their own class. They were optimistic that a revolution of a similar type would not be long in coming in South Africa.

The South African communists were tested almost immediately. Less than six months after the Party's establishment, a major strike broke out on the Rand as white miners protested against a series of measures introduced by the Chamber of Mines reducing their wages. This was combined with a proposal by the mine owners to increase the number of black miners in relation to whites, thus effectively using cheaper black labour to undermine the position of white workers. The strike posed a serious dilemma to the fledgling Party. Most Party members supported it in the belief that it would hasten the revolution which they thought to be imminent. Others, including Bunting, appear to have had strong reservations about the tactical wisdom of supporting a strike for which the Party was ill-prepared and whose success was not assured. He nevertheless sided with the majority of Party members in backing it.

In the event, the 1922 strike turned out to be a disaster for the Party. The government of General Jan Smuts, an Afrikaner general who had become a leading proponent of South Africa's role in the British Empire and was hated by extreme Afrikaner nationalists as well as by socialists, declared martial law and used troops to suppress the strike, as an earlier government had done in similar circumstances in 1913–14. An estimated 230 people were killed in the clashes. Thousands were arrested. After the collapse of the strike some of the white leaders of the workers were hanged, and others were driven to suicide.

Since the strikers' main grievance was the threat posed to their wages by cheap black labour, the strike was marked throughout by a clash of interests between black and white workers. One infamous placard displayed the slogan 'Workers of the World Fight and Unite for a White South Africa'.[2] David Ivon Jones, surprisingly, said he saw a picture of this being paraded among a mixed-race crowd. The slogan has, naturally enough, haunted the Communist Party ever since it was paraded on the streets of Johannesburg, although it is fair to say that it was never a Party slogan, and that the Party tried to dissociate itself from it even at that time. The embarrassment stems from the fact that the Party had supported a strike which, in part at least, arose out of competition between rival workforces. The strike left at least one other unfortunate legacy. A government elected two years later, keen to placate the white workers by satisfying one of their fundamental demands, passed into law provisions reserving better-

2. Eddie Roux, *Time Longer than Rope,* p. 148.

paying jobs for whites and proscribing blacks from rising above certain levels of unskilled labour in industry. The term apartheid had not yet been coined, and was to become a systematic philosophy of government only in 1948, but racial separation was known in South Africa well before that. The strikers of 1922 played their part in putting it on the statute books.

The infant Communist Party had to digest the lessons of the 1922 events. Party members realised that the government strategy of agreeing to white workers' demands for racial quotas presented the Party with a difficult task in targetting white workers for political action. Quite simply, the government had demonstrated that it was prepared to cede some of the demands of white workers, at the expense of blacks, thus reducing the attractiveness of radical action along the lines advocated by socialists. Some communists, among whom Bunting was again prominent, argued that the way forward in these circumstances was to develop the Party's role among black workers.

At its 1924 Congress, one wing of the Communist Party, notably consisting of Young Communists like Eddie Roux, argued successfully that the Party should formally recognise the strategic importance of organising black workers, in accordance with Bunting's view. Another school of thought, led by Bill Andrews, continued to believe that white workers offered the greatest potential for revolutionary politics. It was the former faction which won the argument, and the 1924 Congress became a historic milestone in causing the Party to begin recruiting black members. One of the first black South African communists, T.W. Thibedi, set up a night-school in Johannesburg. It attracted a number of blacks who joined the school to learn how to read and write, were attracted to politics, and later played important roles in the Party. By 1928 1,600 of the Party's 1,750 members were black,[3] and the Party was publishing some material in African languages. But most of this impressive number of black members had been recruited very recently, and the core of the Party's leadership remained solidly white. At this early stage none of the black members had any grounding in Marxist theory and hardly any shared any political outlook beyond their Party membership with the white intellectuals and workers who ran the organisation.

The Party's decision to develop work among blacks brought it into closer contact with other trade union and political organisations which had black members, including the African National Congress. The latter, the premier black political organisation, was founded in Bloemfontein in 1912 as the South African Native National Congress, conceived as a group to represent the political interests of black Africans and to override tribal loyalties. Its first national executive included ministers of religion, lawyers and other professionals, mostly

3. *South African Communists Speak. Documents from the History of the South African Communist Party 1915–1980* (Inkululeko Publications, London, 1981), p. 80.

mission-educated men. Five of the first group of elected leaders had studied abroad, a very rare achievement for a black South African in those days. The organisation included a separate house for chiefs, an illustration of its respect for tradition and a source of funds.[4]

The original ANC was a thoroughly moderate and middle-class organisation, like nationalist pressure groups in other countries of the colonial world. The Congress has never completely lost its original flavour of staunch Christianity and respect for age and aristocratic blood, although these have become mixed with many other elements in the modern ANC, which incorporates a broad spread of opinion among its rank-and-file supporters inside South Africa. ANC meetings still open and close with the singing of a hymn, *Nkosi Sikelel'i Afrika* ('God Save Africa'), the anthem of black South Africa.

The ANC in its early years had little sympathy with the white socialists, who were then concentrating their attentions on white workers. It was an organisation of rather modest aims, mainly representing the interests of those black South Africans who, by reason of high birth or advanced education, considered themselves the natural spokesmen of their people. Its formal activity was generally limited to annual conferences and petitions to government. As an organisation it made no consistent attempt to cultivate a militant mass following, although at times of widespread unrest, such as in 1917–18, the ANC leadership was able to connect with a populist constituency, and the nature of the ANC's leadership gave it access to important political networks in black communities. Its lack of systematic political organisation – membership cards and so on – made it more amorphous but also more broadly based and rooted in society than an organisation like the Communist Party, so that it was able to accommodate Africans of widely different social backgrounds. Since the ANC was conceived as a vehicle for the aspirations of Africans, it did not formally admit people from other racial groups, in theory at any rate, until 1969, and in certain respects until 1985, although successive ANC constitutions did not include formal racial qualifications for membership and ANC leaders worked closely at times with white, coloured and Indian South Africans.

When white communists became interested in developing relations

4. The leading histories of the ANC include Peter Walshe, *The Rise of African Nationalism in South Africa. The African National Congress 1912–1952* (Christopher Hurst, London, 1970), the semi-official *South Africa Belongs to Us* (James Currey, London, 1989) by Francis Meli, and *Foundations of the New South Africa* (Zed Books, London, 1991), by John Pampallis. Thomas Karis and Gwendolen M. Carter (eds), *From Protest to Challenge, a Documentary History of African Politics in South Africa 1882–1964* (4 vols, Hoover Institution Press, Stanford, California, 1972–7) contains essential documents and information on the history of the ANC. Others are Mary Benson, *The African Patriots* (Faber & Faber, London, 1963), Heidi Hollander, *The Struggle: A History of the African National Congress* (George Braziller, New York, 1990); Stephen Davis, *Apartheid's Rebels: Inside South Africa's Hidden War* (Yale University Press, New Haven, Conn., 1987).

with the Congress, one of the most prominent ANC leaders was Josiah Gumede, a Natal schoolteacher and political activist. He was also a talented musician, who in 1892 had toured Europe as a member of a Zulu musical ensemble. One of the founding fathers of the ANC in 1912, he had good connections with rural South African chiefs. In 1919 he travelled to Britain as part of an ANC delegation to petition the Westminster government. In the same year, it is worth noting, he gave court testimony against the socialists Jones and Green.

In 1927, responding to the overtures of the Communist Party, Gumede travelled as a delegate from the ANC to the Brussels-based League Against Imperialism. He accompanied James La Guma, the representative of the Communist Party of South Africa to the same conference. From Brussels, La Guma and Gumede travelled to Berlin and Moscow, where Gumede was duly impressed with the achievements of the Bolshevik government. On his return to South Africa, Gumede was elected President-General of the ANC in June 1927. The post of Secretary-General went to one of the first black South African communists, Eddie Khaile. Gumede urged cooperation with the Communist Party, telling the ANC's annual conference that the Communist Party was 'the only one that honestly and sincerely fights for the oppressed people'.[5]

La Guma and Gumede's 1927 visit to Moscow was the occasion for the Soviet-dominated body concerned with fraternal relations with communist parties worldwide, the Comintern, to take extensive soundings on the situation in South Africa. Comintern officials heard at first hand from La Guma of the disaster of the 1922 strike, the subsequent debate within the South African Party on strategy, and the potential for forming a broad alliance with black organisations. These discussions took place at a time when Soviet strategists were beginning to take a longer-term view of the strategy of encouraging socialist revolutions in the industrialised countries of the world. They regarded the British Empire as potentially the leading enemy of the Soviet Union, and considered it logical to support nationalist movements in British dominions such as South Africa with a view to encouraging subject peoples to throw off the British connection. The Comintern officials decided that the best line would be to urge the Communist Party of South Africa to work for the long-term goal of what became known as an 'independent native republic', in other words to work with black nationalists with the goal of establishing majority rule.

After La Guma and Gumede had returned to South Africa, and after Gumede had been elected President-General of the ANC in June 1927, the Comintern invited the two to return to Moscow for the tenth anniversary of the Bolshevik revolution later in the year. Comintern officials began to draw up recommendations to the South African Party, encouraging it to adopt the new line of the independent

5. A. Lerumo, *Fifty Fighting Years*, p. 56.

native republic. Eventually they suggested that the subject should be debated at the Sixth Congress of the Comintern, scheduled for mid-1928, and forwarded a draft resolution from Moscow to South Africa for prior discussion.

During his second trip to Moscow, Gumede was received most handsomely. He met Stalin and travelled in the Soviet provinces. He seems to have been particularly impressed by the observation that the USSR bore more than a passing resemblance to South Africa in the diversity of its nationalities, the comparatively underdeveloped nature of its capitalism before the revolution, and the rural poverty of the majority of people. Gumede saw the USSR as a model of what could be done in South Africa, and he became a keen admirer of communism although he did not join the Party until the last years of his life, when he had ceased to be President-General of the ANC.

Josiah Gumede's son, Archie Gumede, was later to become a president of the United Democratic Front in 1983. It is striking just how many of the early pioneers of the ANC and of the Communist Party established family traditions of political loyalty which remain binding today. Sidney Bunting's son, Brian Bunting, became a long-standing member of the Central Committee of the South African Communist Party, a leading historian of the Party and the editor of its journal *The African Communist*. Albie Sachs, Thabo Mbeki and the brothers Zwelakhe and Max Sisulu are all modern examples of prominent political figures who are the sons of nationalist or communist politicians of an earlier generation.

When the South African delegation consisting of Sidney and Rebecca Bunting and Eddie Roux arrived in Moscow for the Sixth Congress of the Comintern in 1928, they found the atmosphere very hostile and Soviet officials interested only in imposing their point of view on the South African comrades, at least according to Eddie Roux's later testimony.[6] The international body took the South African communists to task especially over the 1922 strike. The Moscow officials had decided that South Africa was not on the verge of a socialist revolution and that the black population especially was unready for it. 'South Africa is a British dominion of a colonial type', the Comintern maintained, suggesting that South Africa was no nearer to socialism than, say, Canada. What was needed was for the CPSA to take a long view. Before it could aim to stage a socialist revolution it should fight to establish an 'independent native republic' in South Africa. The CPSA, to this end, 'should pay particular attention to the ANC. Our aim should be to transform the ANC into a fighting nationalist revolutionary organisation against the white bourgeoisie and the British imperialists, based upon the trade unions, peasants' organisations, etc.'[7]

6. Eddie & Win Roux, *Rebel Pity*, pp. 72–8.
7. *Umsebenzi*, Vol. 2, No. 1, 1986.

The 1928 decision of the Comintern, like all Comintern decisions, was considered to be scientifically correct and therefore more or less infallible. It was based on the belief that socialism could come about only after the development of bourgeois nationalism, and that this was as true for South Africa as for any other country since the basic laws of scientific socialism are held to be universal. The belief that socialism can be established only after South Africa has gone through a phase of bourgeois nationalism has marked the thinking of the Communist Party ever since. It has periodically been contested by other socialists, who see it as a sell-out, stopping short of socialism, or who consider it to be racist, since it can be misinterpreted to mean that true revolution is for whites only. At the time, virtually all South African communists were dismayed by the new line imposed by the Comintern. They were being instructed to forego work with the group still seen as a socialist vanguard, white workers, in favour of working with blacks – not for an immediate socialist transition, their objective, but for a black-governed republic. In the context of South Africa in 1928 it appeared an almost preposterous aim.

It was the unfortunate Bunting, who had himself gone further than many of his comrades in arguing the need to work among black South Africans, but who had then been treated in Moscow as little more than a white supremacist, who had the unenviable task of bringing the new Comintern line back to South Africa. Rebecca and Sidney Bunting came home to find the Party already split into opposed factions. Many comrades didn't like the new policy, which effectively consigned white Party members to a back seat in a struggle led by blacks. But despite the distaste of many white communists for the policy of working for an independent native republic, they faithfully implemented the new line and set about recruiting more black members and placing blacks in the Party leadership. E.J. Khaile, who was at that time the Secretary-General of the ANC, became a member of the Party's Central Committee. In 1929 the Party appointed its first black General Secretary, Albert Nzula, who had joined only two years earlier.

The new line imposed by the Comintern proved extremely divisive. It gave rise to years of in-fighting, fuelled by personality clashes, which crippled the Party and precipitated the worst period in the history of South African communism. Control of the Party passed to an ultra-left group which claimed Moscow's backing, and which succeeded in condemning Bunting and others as right-wing deviationists. Bunting was expelled from the Party in 1931, accused of a heresy known as 'Buntingism'. The leading personalities were Lazar Bach, a young immigrant from Latvia, and a husband-and-wife team, Douglas and Molly Wolton. Bach had the reputation of being able to clinch any argument by quoting by heart chunks from the writings of Marx and Engels and other communist classics. Party meetings turned into debates of a near-theological nature guaranteed to bore, confuse or repel all but the most dedicated. Party literature became so turgid that it soon lost its once-promising black readership.

The new situation also proved divisive in the ANC. Gumede remained impressed by his Soviet experience and convinced that the communists were the only party in South Africa ready to work with blacks, which was true enough. But his enthusiasm for a closer association with the communists – limited, since he refused to work with Bunting's League of African Rights, for example – was not universally shared in the ANC. The considerable number of chiefs in the Congress were not slow to observe that one of the principal acts of the Bolsheviks in the USSR had been to execute that great hereditary chief the Czar, which did not bode well for traditional leaders in a socialist South Africa. In 1930, a conservative faction in the ANC led by a founder-member, Dr Pixley ka Isaka Seme, educated in the United States and at Oxford, unseated Gumede. Seme himself, rather less friendly to the Communists, was elected President-General of the ANC.

One of those who suffered at Bach's hands in the repeated purges of the early 1930s was Moses Kotane, born in Rustenburg in the Transvaal in 1905, who had learned to read and write at the Party's night-school and became a frequent contributor to the Party newspaper. He was one of a handful of black South Africans to have been to Moscow, where he studied from 1931 to 1933. He was also a member of the ANC, so that, as well as enduring personal attacks by Bach and other ultra-leftists, he was handicapped by their general attack on the ANC as a bourgeois organisation.

However, of all the purges and expulsions, the roughest justice was reserved for Lazar Bach himself and two of his colleagues, the brothers Maurice and Paul Richter. In 1935 Bach and the Richters went to Moscow to seek support for their battles in the South African Party. They never came back. The Soviet authorities prevented them from returning to South Africa while they mounted an inquisition into the affairs of the CPSA. The Seventh Congress of the Comintern in 1936 introduced the new line of the Popular Front, advocating that it was now the duty of all communists to ally with liberals and others in the fight against fascism, which had made its appearance in Europe and had rapidly become a leading enemy of communism. Bach and the Richters were hopelessly identified with a strategy which had now been superseded and with officials in Moscow who had become expendable. In 1937 all three men were arrested by Stalin's secret police and charged with counter-revolutionary activity. They were interrogated and made to sign false confessions. On the basis of their confessions of guilt, they were expelled from the CPSA by the Comintern and sentenced to imprisonment in Soviet labour camps.

The Richters were shot on 1 March 1938. Bach died on 10 March 1941 of natural causes in a labour camp. The truth of their fate was not publicly known for 50 years. It was only in June 1989, after Mikhail

Gorbachev had clearly condemned Stalinism in the Soviet Union, that the SACP publicly admitted what had happened to Bach and the Richters and rehabilitated them posthumously, together with Sidney Bunting, who had been spared from death but whose name had been vilified during the purges of the 1930s.

The handful of South African communists who managed to get to Moscow for training, such as Moses Kotane, came home to find the Party riven by personal feuds and by disagreements generated by the question of the independent native republic. For black communists the slogan of the independent native republic was more attractive than to most white communists. Some, such as Edwin Mofutsanyana, who had joined the Party in 1927 and trained at Moscow's prestigious Lenin School, the university of Marxist-Leninist theory, saw the independent native republic slogan primarily as a means of winning blacks over to communism. It meant that the Party was proposing to blacks to fight in the first instance for power in their own country. Others, especially white communists, were rather ambivalent about the concept, and preferred not to work out its implications too far, but to postpone deeper study of it to the future, when the Party would have captured power.

The in-fighting in the Party in the 1930s was so intense that, after Bach's departure for the Soviet Union and subsequent disappearance, the Party almost ceased to exist as an effective unit. Some of the leading Communists decided to make a new start, moving the headquarters from Johannesburg to Cape Town. The revival owed much to Mofutsanyana, Jack Simons, and a Latvian immigrant called Rachel ('Ray') Alexander, a prominent trade unionist. Born in 1913, she had joined the Communist Party in Latvia in 1928 and arrived with her parents in South Africa in 1929, where she immediately became active in Party and trade union work. She and Simons were later married. In Cape Town, communists from the Rand made new contact with Moses Kotane, who had moved there during the period after his suspension from the Party's Politburo at the hands of Lazar Bach. Kotane married in Cape Town and settled there, naming his eldest son Joseph in honour of the General Secretary of the Communist Party of the Soviet Union. Kotane became General Secretary of the CPSA, now based in Cape Town, in 1939, a post which he was to fill for the next 39 years. The generation which breathed new life into the Party in Cape Town, thoroughly steeped in Stalinism, continued to dominate the Party until the 1970s. After his appointment as Party General Secretary, Kotane continued to be a most active member of the ANC, gradually building a new groundwork of trust between the ANC and the Communist Party and repairing the damage done to relations between the two organisations.

Ideological questions often overlapped with racial differences, and not only on the precise meaning given to the slogan of the independent native republic. Kotane, for example, was always rather lukewarm in trade union work, since many unions were led by white socialists. The different spheres in which blacks and whites lived, even before the systematic implementation of apartheid, meant that black and white communists tended to work in different areas, among their own people, to the point that Edwin Mofutsanyana, editor of the Party newspaper, at one stage proposed that the Party should be split into separate European and African sections, a proposal defeated in the Party's executive only by six votes to five. One leading black Communist, J.B. Marks, at one stage argued for the maintenance of separate black trade unions where black members would not be swamped by whites. Kotane held the Party steady throughout all these vicissitudes. His patience and his steady long-term view won him the respect even of those ANC members who were generally suspicious of communism.

The Second World War erupted with the Party hardly recovered from the disasters of the 1930s. South Africa was committed on the side of Britain to the war against Nazi Germany. Faithful to the dictates of Soviet foreign policy, which was then aligned with Germany as a result of the Nazi-Soviet Pact, the CPSA agitated against the war, arguing that it was a carve-up of markets and a search for raw materials by imperialist powers. Only after the Soviet Union's entry into the war on the side of the Allies in 1941 did the Party change tack and pronounce itself in support of the war effort. At this point the government of South Africa, the Soviet Union, and the CPSA all became allies. This meant that there was an effective truce in the government's general harassment of the Party. The government tolerated communist activity in the interests of the war effort and allowed the Party an unprecedented degree of freedom, encouraging it to argue in favour of industrial peace for the duration of the war. The Party refrained from its revolutionary work in the interests of defeating fascism. Bill Andrews was even permitted to broadcast on the air-waves of the South African Broadcasting Corporation. The unusual spectacle of the government and the Communist Party on the same side enabled the Party to recruit and organise freely and openly, and led to a spectacular growth in white membership especially, by comparison with the lean years of the 1930s.

The war years also witnessed the rise of a new generation of black intellectuals who wished to breathe new life into the ANC. Some were also concerned about the Congress's association with the Communist Party, brought about by Kotane and emphasised by the number of black communists who were also ANC members. The ANC Youth League was founded in 1944 by a group of radicals, many still in their twenties, who included Walter Sisulu, Nelson Mandela, Oliver Tambo, Anton Lembede, A.P. Mda and Jordan Ngubane. Mandela and Tambo were among those who, alarmed by the influence of communists in the ANC, at one stage argued for their exclusion from the Congress. Among others who joined the Youth League a little later was Robert Sobukwe, then at Fort Hare University

College, the *alma mater* of Mandela and Tambo.

Meanwhile, the most extreme Afrikaner nationalists sympathised with the Nazi cause, partly on ideological grounds but also because of their hope that the defeat of Britain would lead to the restoration of Afrikaner independence, lost in 1902. Some of the most determined joined fringe political groups like the Ossewa Brandwag. Radical young Afrikaner nationalists like John Vorster, later to be Prime Minister, were interned on account of their Nazi sympathies. Hendrik Verwoerd, also a future prime minister, studied in Nazi Germany. They dreamed of a lost paradise in the shape of the independent Afrikaner republics of the ninteenth century, while building the modern foundations of Afrikanerdom through a range of economic, cultural and labour organisations. It was as a result of this type of ethnic politics that the National Party was able to form a governing coalition in the South African parliament at the general election of 1948.

The 1948 election which brought the Nationalists to power was mostly a white affair, although there were still some coloured people with voting rights. The new National Party government set about disenfranchising remaining black and coloured voters and systematically applying the philosophy of racial separation which it called apartheid. The idea was not new to South Africa, but the thoroughness and fanaticism with which it was applied were. As part of their programme to construct a God-fearing South Africa which would be ruled by Afrikaners for ever, the Nationalists made no secret of their intention to abolish the Communist Party. Communists were well aware of this. As soon as the Nationalists had won the 1948 elections, the Communist Party began preparing for the day when it would be outlawed.

Since shifting its headquarters to Cape Town, the Party had tended to develop fairly distinct regional patterns. The Transvaal communists were increasingly successful in recruiting black members in the townships, campaigning on community issues, and reaching out into the rural areas through cultivating migrant workers. The Cape communists, especially in Port Elizabeth which was developing a modern manufacturing industry organised on different lines from the mines, became more prominent in the trade unions. Close relations developed between Communist activists, trade unionists and ANC members, with people like Raymond Mhlaba (released after 25 years on Robben Island in October 1989), prominent in all three fields at once. The relationship between the ANC and the Party, such as it was, was rooted in the presence of people like these, and particularly of the older generation represented by Kotane and Marks, who had been members of the ANC since the 1920s. There were no formal relations between the ANC and the Party, and in its public pronouncements the Party was often quite disparaging of the ANC which it persisted in regarding as a bourgeois organisation.

At the national level, the view of General Secretary Moses Kotane was that Party members should prepare for the imminent persecution promised by the victorious National Party government by seeking cover inside legal organisations. There they could continue to work once the Party had been suppressed, as Kotane was sure it would be. Finding cover was made easier because most black communists, like Kotane himself, were already members of the ANC. Kotane had been elected a member of the ANC's National Executive Committee in 1946. But perhaps the most dynamic group in the ANC at the time was the Youth League, which contained a number of anti-communists and was seeking to impose its own radical nationalist ideas on the ANC. As a result of the ANC's 1949 elections Kotane and his fellow-communist Dan Tloome – a Party member since 1936 and today chairman of the SACP – were elected to membership of the ANC's National Executive Committee. Another black communist and trade unionist, J.B. Marks, became an *ex officio* member of the National Executive Committee of the ANC after being elected president of the ANC's powerful Transvaal branch in 1950. Marks had been very active in the ANC's Transvaal branch for many years. Tloome had stood for election for the post of ANC Secretary-General but was narrowly defeated by Walter Sisulu, a Youth League member. Communists also secured election to other organisations where they could survive the forthcoming banning. Thus, in 1950, the Indian Communist Yusuf Dadoo was elected president of the South African Indian Congress.

The white Parliament duly voted in 1950 to make the Communist Party illegal. The Party at that time probably had some 2,500 members, of whom some 900 were whites.[8] The ANC, which remained legal, had somewhere over twice as many members,[9] and that number was to expand rapidly in the next decade. But the figures of formal ANC membership were misleading, since it was able to command a much wider and deeper degree of informal support than was suggested by the relatively small size of its formal membership.

The Suppression of Communism Act of 1950, while not unexpected, was nevertheless a severe blow. Shortly before the axe fell, the Party's executive voted to dissolve the Party, since the police Special Branch had captured lists of Party members and would easily detect any attempt by the Party simply to carry on illegally. Only Bill Andrews and Michael Harmel voted for it to continue underground. The majority view was that the Party should set up front organisations which would allow it to continue under legal cover and that Party members should attempt to continue political work, as far as possible, through whatever other organisations were at hand. Only three years later, in 1953, did the comrades secretly revive the Party as an underground organisation now calling itself the South African Communist Party.

8. Henry Pike, *A History of Communism in South Africa*, p. 272.
9. Peter Walshe, *The Rise of African Nationalism*, p. 397.

The leaders of the National Party do not appear to have foreseen that the effect of banning the Communist Party would be to cause Party cadres to seek to work through membership of legal organisations, including the ANC. Until then, the Party and the ANC had at times hardly been on speaking terms, and the main connection betweeen them was the personal friendship and respect between the great majority of ANC leaders who were not communists and Party members such as Kotane and Marks. Otherwise, the Party had maintained a rather distant and at times hostile relationship with the ANC. In fact, the Party had played a rather marginal role in South African politics outside the sphere of the trade unions. Only on the eve of its impending banishment did the Party adopt a full-scale policy of entryism; by this means, and by dint of enormous discipline and determination, it survived.

2
The Spear
of the Nation
1951-68

The ANC was strongly opposed to the banning of the Communist Party. The two organisations had no formal alliance, and relations between them were often cool, but the existence of people with dual membership created a link between them, and above all they shared the same enemy: the National Party government of South Africa.

Nevertheless, the Communist Party's suppression in 1950 was not utterly without benefit to the Congress. The rather small number of ANC members who were also communists were able to dedicate more of their time to ANC work, since the Party had ceased to exist. White, Indian and coloured communists, although they were ineligible for formal membership of the ANC, put their expertise and knowledge of political organisation at the service of the ANC. It increased the ANC's importance as a legal means of political expression for black South Africans, without depriving the Congress of its character as a broad organisation able to accommodate comfortably both communists and non-communists like Albert Luthuli, a chief and a staunch Christian, winner of the 1960 Nobel Peace Prize and ANC President-General from 1952 to 1967. In the wake of the Communist Party's banning, both communists and ANC members began to consider one another in a new light.

On the whole, it was the aim of the communists inside the ANC, and those working with it, to galvanise the Congress into becoming a more radical and populist organisation than before. One other organised strand of opinion in the ANC, the Youth League, had similar ambitions. At the same time the systematic implementation of the policy of apartheid by a zealous National Party government was putting South Africa's black population under intense pressure, provoking protests which in turn caused the ANC to adopt more radical positions than it had done in the past. In 1952 the ANC launched its first-ever mass campaign, dubbed the defiance campaign, the first time that the ANC had encouraged mass defiance of the law as part of a planned and sustained campaign of Gandhian civil disobedience. The Congress increasingly explored a whole range of techniques of extra-parliamentary agitation, including boycotts and demonstrations.

At the same time as black communists took refuge inside the ANC, and Indians inside the existing South African Indian Congress, coloured and white communists developed plans to set up front organisations where they too could continue to operate as members of a legal organisation. In September 1953 the Coloured People's Organisation was launched, later renamed the Coloured People's Congress. A month later came the Congress of Democrats, manned largely by white communists. The South African Congress of Trade Unions was established as a trade union umbrella in March 1955. Together these organisations formed what was known as the Congress Alliance, a rather unwieldy coalition of anti-apartheid organisations in which communists formed the most disciplined single bloc, having an influence out of proportion to their numbers.

During the 1950s the Congress organisations used a range of methods in campaigns of mass mobilisation. The climactic episode originated in an idea put forward by Professor Z.K. Matthews at the 1953 annual meeting of the ANC, to call a national congress of the people which would draw up a Freedom Charter, a basic political manifesto for all the components of the movement. After months of preparation, the Congress of the People was held in Kliptown, Johannesburg, on 26 June 1955. Some 3,000 people assembled in response to a call by the ANC and the various other components of the Congress Alliance. Others who had intended to go to the meeting were prevented from doing so by the police.

Anti-communists have always claimed that the Freedom Charter was drafted by members of the Communist Party, secretly re-established in 1953, before being put to the Kliptown meeting clause by clause for approval. Gerard Ludi, for example, an undercover policeman who infiltrated the Party, claimed that 'the Freedom Charter was, in fact, drafted at a secret meeting of the Central Committee of the CPSA and sent to the Moscow Africa Institute for approval.'[1] Bartholomew Hlapane, a communist who later turned informer against his former comrades, also maintained that it was drafted by Joe Slovo on behalf of the Party.[2] Jordan Ngubane, a founder-member of the Youth League who remained strongly opposed to the Communist Party throughout his life, and later joined Chief Mangosuthu Gatsha Buthelezi's Inkatha organisation, maintained that the ANC President-General Albert Luthuli, who was under a banning order and was therefore unable to attend the Congress of the People in Kliptown, never knew who authored the Charter. Not only did the state fail to prove any of these allegations, however, but at least one person who was active in the Congress of Democrats at the time[3] is adamant that there was no central direction in drawing up the document. Although communists contributed to

1. Quoted in Henry Pike, *A History of Communism in South Africa*, p. 317, note 14.
2. In hearings before the US Senate Sub-Committee on Security and Terrorism in March 1982.
3. Baruch Hirson, in interviews with Stephen Ellis. Hirson, a Trotskyist, was strongly opposed to the Communist Party.

the drafting of the Freedom Charter, its final version seems indeed to have represented the input of many different people and influences. It was not a Communist Party document. After arresting 156 leading members of the ANC and its allied organisations and charging them with high treason, the public prosecutor eventually failed to prove that the launching of the Freedom Charter was part of a campaign inspired by international communism and intended to overthrow the state by violence. The trial dragged on until 1961.

Far from being the product of a single hand or a single coherent group, the Freedom Charter represented most of the disparate strands in the ANC, including, of course, the communists. It is a ringing declaration of principle, not a policy document. Many of the paragraphs could hardly raise objections in any person who was not politically eccentric ('The people shall govern') or not a supporter of apartheid ('All shall be equal before the law'). The idea of the Charter was debated for over a year before the final text was adopted, clause by clause, at the Kliptown public meeting. It was not formally adopted as a policy document of the ANC until 1956.

The Congress Alliance was a cumbersome and ill-organised affair. Five organisations lacking resources, and covering a wide variety of political opinions and social and racial groups, could not be expected to operate as a smooth political machine. But for the Communist Party it was a lifeline, since it was what kept the illegal Party in political existence. Communists were able to operate throughout the five congresses and, by dint of awesome discipline, by holding separate meetings and using caucus tactics, the Party could sometimes see its political line adopted by much larger meetings. It is not surprising that the Party was a staunch supporter of the Alliance, and opposed any suggestion that the individual congresses should disband in order for members to join the ANC. The leadership of the ANC also generally took the same line, and was opposed to suggestions by some whites that the Congress of Democrats be disbanded and whites be allowed to join the ANC. Nevertheless there were ANC activists who believed that their organisation was being manipulated through the Alliance, and that the communists' refusal to countenance the dissolution of the minor congresses reflected their fear of being swamped by majority decisions within the ANC if they were to dissolve the congresses and submit to its direction.

It is worthy of note, in considering these contrary opinions, that although the Communist Party was small in size and highly disciplined, there is evidence that internal Party debates were marked by sharply differing opinions on some matters, and that there may even have been an organised opposition tendency within the Party. Baruch Hirson, a non-communist member of the Congress of Democrats, recalls being shown documents by Party members which appeared to indicate the existence of such a group.

Black nationalism was growing stronger during the late 1950s, not just in South Africa but throughout the continent. Britain and France, the two major colonial powers, were discovering that it was impossible to maintain their colonies in the face of rising pressure for independence locally, as well as hostility from both the USSR and, if to a much lesser degree, from the USA. Although some decision-makers in both Britain and France argued for the retention of their African empires, increasingly the most influential strategists considered that the wisest course was to concede political independence to their African colonies while attempting to create a close relationship between the former colonial power and the emerging state. This would allow the old colonial metropole still to play a privileged role. In 1957 Ghana became the first of the European colonies in Africa to achieve independence. Its first president, Kwame Nkrumah, articulated an appealing brand of black internationalism and held up Ghana, with great panache, as the Black Star of Africa whose example would liberate the whole continent. In 1956 France instituted self-government in its African colonies with a view to rapid independence. The French were preoccupied by the emergence of a full-scale war in Algeria: as the conflict continued to sap French resources, the Paris government determined to decolonise its black African colonies by political means to avoid the possibility of such a nightmare anywhere else. Even the Belgian government, which had not foreseen any need to grant independence to its huge central African colony of the Congo, was in the end obliged to concede in conditions which led to civil war. Black South Africans could not fail to be influenced by what was happening elsewhere.

So intense did the debate become within the ANC about the Congress Alliance, and the allegation that it was causing the ANC to be manipulated by non-blacks, that in November 1958 a group broke away, claiming to be the true heirs of the 1912 ANC and of the Youth League of the 1940s. They formed the Pan Africanist Congress five months later, its first president being the former ANC Youth League member Robert Sobukwe. Operating under slogans such as 'Africa for the Africans', the PAC began to compete for support with the ANC, gaining a real foothold in some parts of the country.

The establishment of the PAC, at just the time when most of black Africa was acceding to independence, was a major challenge to the ANC. A wind of change, as Harold Macmillan told the white Parliament in Cape Town in 1960, was blowing through Africa. The PAC and the ANC were both confident that this wind would fill their sails and propel them to their destination, variously conceived as power in their own country (the goal of most PAC leaders), revolution (the SACP's aim) or simply full political rights for all (the aspiration of the ANC). They would probably have been amazed, in 1959, to learn that 32 years later, South Africa would still be run by an all-white government of the National Party.

The ANC prepared a nationwide campaign of resistance to begin at the end of March 1960. The PAC, seeking to upstage its Congress rival, organised its own campaign against the hated law which obliged every black person to carry a pass, indicating whether he or she was entitled to be in a white-designated area. The PAC campaign was timed to start on 21 March 1960. At Sharpeville, the police fired into a crowd which had gathered in support of the PAC call to action, killing 69 people.

For many people in the world, in what was fast becoming the age of instant communication, the Sharpeville massacre was the first time they became aware what sort of government South Africa had. In the West, many people had only vaguely heard of South Africa. Even in Britain, where there was a comparatively large number of people who had visited South Africa or had relatives there, mention of South Africa did not conjure up an image in the mind of the average newspaper-reader much different from that of, say, Australia. Sharpeville changed all that. The South African government was exposed to international view as a ruthless and brutal administration which shot people who claimed what were being conceded in other parts of the world as their fundamental rights. It also coincided with a time when, in the United States, the particular form of racial segregation which had existed in some of the southern states was being abolished to the applause of liberals nationwide. News from South Africa has always caused Americans to compare its situation with their own. A measure of just how innocent the world was earlier in the century is the fact that General Smuts, the man who ordered martial law to suppress strikes in 1913–14 and 1922, and the enactor of much racial legislation, was, in his day, a respected internationalist and one of the leading lights of the League of Nations.

News of the Sharpeville killings struck a discordant note amid the widespread optimism about the future of independent Africa. Britain and France had both opted for African independence. The Soviet Union and China both represented themselves as champions of the rights of oppressed peoples. John Kennedy was in the White House, and his government too was interested in playing the nationalist card in Africa, to the extent of seeking cordial relations with emergent black governments and Algerian nationalists who aimed to overthrow or supersede French rule in Africa. In 1922, South African troops could shoot into a crowd of strikers without provoking an international incident. When the police fired on African demonstrators at Sharpeville, the result was worldwide condemnation of South Africa, a loss of business confidence as foreign investors became nervous, and the imposition of a state of emergency by the Pretoria government during which 20,000 people were detained.

The government also took the radical step of banning both the PAC and the ANC under the terms of a new law, the Unlawful Organisations Act. They were unable to function legally inside South Africa from that date until 2 February 1990, when the Communist

Party too was unbanned. Two days before the banning order, Oliver Tambo, a former Secretary-General of the ANC, slipped out of the country to set up an external mission, under orders from the National Executive. His task was to canvass international support. Other ANC leaders went underground inside the country.

One of the main aspirations of National Party governments after 1948 was to assert South Africa's total independence in a world which is increasingly interdependent. After the Sharpeville massacre, when there was widespread international condemnation and the Commonwealth debated whether to expel South Africa from membership, many National Party supporters were pleased to regard their international isolation not as a disaster but as the opportunity to assert their independence of the old colonial power. The government, after submitting the question to the white electorate in the form of a referendum, declared South Africa to be a republic outside the Commonwealth. At last, white South African nationalists could bask in the satisfaction of knowing that they had comprehensively defeated the old imperial enemy.

The response of the outlawed ANC, on the other hand, was to organise a general strike in protest against its inability to participate in a referendum submitted to whites only. Many of the ANC leaders who had emerged in the 1950s, when the young firebrands from the Youth League had emerged as figures of national stature and had led the popular campaigns which became a notable feature of ANC activity, were now living underground. Among them was Nelson Mandela, who had left his home in Transkei to work in Johannesburg. There he had become one of the first black lawyers to practise, together with his legal partner Oliver Tambo, another lawyer and a devout Christian. Mandela has been a commanding figure in the nationalist movement since the 1950s. Strikingly handsome and articulate, the offspring of an aristocratic family, he was somewhat autocratic in manner. In most countries other than South Africa he would probably be regarded as a rather conservative leader, steeped in the African history which he learned from the elders of his village in his youth. Although Mandela has never been a communist, and was quite strongly opposed to the Party during his early days in the Youth League, in later years he was a staunch defender of the ANC–SACP alliance. Also prominent in the ANC leadership was the former Secretary-General Walter Sisulu, also from the Transkei and formerly Mandela's political mentor. Sisulu was generally more inclined to socialism than Mandela. Although there have been suggestions that he may have been a member of the Communist Party at some time in his life, young people who joined the Communist Party in the 1980s were informed by Party veterans that Sisulu had never been a Party member. It indeed seems to be the case that he never joined the Party.

Apart from the overwhelming consideration that their organisation was banned in 1960, leaving them no possibility of lawful political action, there were a number of factors compelling both ANC and Communist Party leaders to contemplate the use of violence. The rest of Africa was receiving its freedom, so they could be sure of support in the newly emerging nations to the north. In Algeria, armed nationalists were nearing the climax of their long and bitter war against France in conditions not dissimilar to those of South Africa. And those ANC leaders who, like Mandela, Sisulu, Tambo, Mbeki and many others, came from the Transkei, were deeply affected by the rural rebellion which broke out there in 1960. Peasant leaders were asking the ANC for guns and the ANC was embarrassed by its inability to satisfy them. Some sources[4] also maintain that the turn to violence, on the part of the Communist Party at least, was motivated by the knowledge that another organisation, the National Committee of Liberation, was making preparations to begin sabotage operations. NCL members, including a former member of the Communist Party, Monty Berman, had approached the Party with a suggestion that the two organisations should work together in a sabotage campaign. The Party refused but, conscious of the danger of being outflanked on the left, determined to start its own campaign of violence.

In the end, the decision to launch a campaign of sabotage was taken on a personal basis as a result of consultations between friends and comrades in mid-1961. That is, it was not the result of a resolution by any organised body of either the ANC or the SACP but only of groups of members meeting informally. In fact, a meeting of the ANC's National Executive Committee in June 1961 debated the question of armed struggle but took no position on it. The National Executive nevertheless gave its blessing to those ANC members who wished to join the new guerrilla organisation whose foundation was being discussed in ANC and Communist Party circles. The ANC President, Albert Luthuli, was under house arrest and only heard of the decision to set up a guerrilla army by word of mouth. He had to ask Moses Kotane, the Communist Party General Secretary as well as a trusted ANC colleague, to inform him of the details.

The new organisation was dubbed Umkhonto we Sizwe, 'Spear of the Nation', and was known to insiders as MK. It was autonomous, drawing its membership from both the ANC and the SACP but operationally dependent on neither. This decision to launch the army independently appears to have been motivated partly by the likelihood that it would be opposed by advocates of non-violence in the ANC, including the President-General, Chief Luthuli, but also because it would expose to arrest the many members of the ANC who were known to the police on the grounds of belonging to a violent organisation. It did indeed cause some consternation among ANC members who heard of its formation and reasoned that they could expect a visit from the police Special Branch in a quest for information

4. Such as Baruch Hirson, in his unpublished autobiography.

about the new organisation. Only later did Umkhonto we Sizwe develop into the ANC's armed wing and the ANC formally adopt positions in support of the armed struggle. According to the police spy Gerard Ludi,[5] at the time of Umkhonto we Sizwe's foundation the Communist Party Central Committee formally adopted a policy of violence and fully endorsed the establishment of the new army. J.B. Marks and Joe Slovo were sent by the Party to Moscow to organise supplies for the new army, he claimed. The former Communist Party Central Committee member Bartholomew Hlapane maintained, after turning state witness, that Umkhonto we Sizwe operated under orders from the Party,[6] although this seems unlikely in view of the general agreement that the most prominent figure in the new organisation was Mandela, who was not a Party member and did not take orders from the Party. Simply, it was the communist members of Umkhonto we Sizwe who had the best international connections and were best placed to win major outside support for the organisation which Mandela headed.

From June 1961, the Umkhonto we Sizwe High Command, led by Mandela, issued a call for volunteers. ANC and Communist Party members responded in large numbers. The national High Command was responsible for finance, strategy and other general matters. It appointed regional commands which had responsibility for local actions. Umkhonto we Sizwe policy was to target buildings and strategic targets for sabotage and to avoid casualties as far as possible. But this was an army of amateurs, hardly any of whom had knowledge of weapons. Some caused civilian casualties and even blew themselves up with their homemade bombs. Umkhonto we Sizwe specifically avoided attacking whites at a time when the PAC was encouraging attacks on whites by Poqo, a populist insurrectionary and anti-white movement which spread in the Eastern Cape.

Umkhonto we Sizwe was supposed to be unveiled to the public on 16 December 1961, variously known as the Day of the Covenant and Dingane's Day. It has been a key date in South African mythologies, white and black, ever since the day in 1838 when Afrikaner trekkers defeated the army of the Zulu king Dingane in battle. In fact, the Durban command acted prematurely, setting off an explosion the day before the general offensive was due to begin. Nevertheless the organisation achieved its desired effect with a spate of explosions in Johannesburg, Port Elizabeth and Durban on 16 December, at the same time as the new organisation issued a manifesto. It declared:

> The time comes in the life of any nation when there remain only two choices: submit or fight. That time has now come to South Africa. We shall not submit and we have no choice but to hit back by all means within our power in defence of our people, our future and our freedom.

5. Quoted in Henry Pike, *A History of Communism*, p. 350.
6. *Ibid.*, p. 351.

According to Afrikaner mythology, the victors of the 1838 battle of Blood River had pledged to keep the date of 16 December sacred as a memorial of the covenant between God and his chosen people, the Afrikaners, looking for a new home in the African hinterland as the Jews of the Old Testament had found a homeland in Israel. Setting a series of explosions at government offices on such a date damaged more than just property. It was a calculated challenge to the self-image of the National Party government and its voters. Among the targets successfully attacked on 16 December 1961 were a post office, a Bantu Affairs Commissioner's office, other government offices and electricity installations. Over the next 18 months, Umkhonto we Sizwe carried out some 200 attacks and began to make preparations to build a major arsenal. Many attacks, though, remained unpublicised in the press, which limited their psychological impact upon the South African public.

The Umkhonto we Sizwe High Command developed sufficiently good international connections, in part thanks to the influence of Communist Party members in the organisation, to arrange for volunteeers to travel to Eastern Europe, China and Africa for training and to procure equipment. Early in 1962, Mandela embarked on a long trip through Africa and Europe to seek further international support. He came back to South Africa in the middle of the year and lived underground. Both the press and the police Special Branch knew he was back in the country but could not locate him. Inventive journalists had a field day, representing him as the black pimpernel, a master of disguise. The police, more prosaically, regarded him as public enemy number one, a dangerous terrorist and a tool of communists.

Mandela was travelling on a country road in Natal when his luck ran out, on 5 August 1962. His car encountered a police roadblock which had been set up with such precision that most people who heard of the arrest, as the whole of South Africa did within hours, concluded that the police must have been tipped off by an informer. There is strong evidence to suggest that an agent of the US Central Intelligence Agency, the CIA, had learned of his whereabouts and informed the South African police.[7] Three months later, he was convicted of incitement and of leaving South Africa without a passport, which earned him a three-year sentence. The police were well aware that he was the commander of Umkhonto we Sizwe but at that time they still had insufficient evidence to convict Mandela of a crime of violence.

At almost the same moment as Mandela was arrested, the ANC held its first consultative conference in exile. The venue was Lobatse in Botswana, then still the British protectorate of Bechuanaland. The plan was that the internal leaders of the organisation would come out of the country and consult with those who had already gone abroad to set up an External Mission under Oliver Tambo on the orders of

---

7. *The Atlanta Journal and Constitution*, 10 June 1990; *The Star*, 14 July 1986.

the National Executive. A top priority of the Lobatse Conference was to tackle some of the confusion which had arisen from the circumstances in which the armed struggle had been declared. The ANC had still not formally adopted a policy of armed struggle and yet some ANC members had been recruited into the ranks of Umkhonto we Sizwe. Some local ANC leaders inside South Africa were frustrated by the fact that their people were following orders from another organisation while they themselves were trying to maintain the ANC's existence underground. In short, there was a lack of coordination between the armed struggle and the political one.

Oliver Tambo attended the Lobatse Conference as leader of the External Mission. He had been working closely with Tennyson Maki-wane, another intellectual, who had been expelled from Fort Hare University for organising a strike and had left South Africa in 1959. Makiwane had worked with the Communist Party member and journalist Ruth First, and it was probably she who had recruited him to the Party. Also present at Lobatse was Makiwane's cousin Mzwai Piliso, who had joined the ANC with Walter Sisulu and who had left South Africa as long ago as 1950 to study in London. They were joined by others, including Govan Mbeki, from inside the country. The total number of people in attendance was probably little more than fifty. The ANC President-General, Chief Luthuli, was under a banning order and was not allowed to leave South Africa. Mandela was in gaol.

Some of the leading figures in attendance at Lobatse as members of the ANC were also members of the Party. Govan Mbeki presided over the conference, and the steering committee consisted of Moses Kotane, Dan Tloome and Oliver Tambo, all but the last-named being SACP members, as were Makiwane and Piliso. The Party itself was in considerable disarray but was still able to organise secretly inside the country. Among structures set up in the early 1960s, while the Umkhonto we Sizwe High Command was still broadly intact, was said to be an exclusively communist Regional Command in Durban designed to promote the sabotage campaign, which included Ronnie Kasrils, Curnick Ndhlovu and Billy Nair, a founder-member of SACTU in 1955.[8]

The decision to build a guerrilla organisation and to declare war on the government greatly increased the Party's weight in its alliance with the ANC. The communists had a number of valuable assets. They had already developed experience of working in underground conditions during a decade of illegality. Moreover, South African communists could draw on an international experience of underground struggle dating back to the first years of the century, and they could secure the backing of a superpower which was developing a keen interest in the future of independent Africa and which was intent

8. Henry Pike, *A History of Communism*, p. 349.

on fighting Western imperialism worldwide. In fact, from the point of view of Soviet strategists, the conditions of the Cold War were such that it was better to confront the arch-imperialist power, the USA, by backing nationalist or incipient socialist movements in Africa and Asia than by direct confrontation, which carried the awful risk of nuclear war.

We do not know to what degree, or if at all, the South African Communist Party sought advice from Moscow before taking the decision to launch the armed struggle in mid-1961. It is clear, though, that the decision met with Moscow's approval. And indeed, it seemed logical enough in the context of 'emergent' Africa, where nationalist movements in the remaining European colonies or settler-governed states throughout the continent were resorting to arms to win their independence. What few people could foresee was that, over the years, the armed struggle would have a profound effect on the nature of the ANC–SACP alliance. During its years underground, the ANC came to lose the character of a mass movement which it had developed in the 1950s and became more of an elite organisation. This was hardly surprising since it was now deprived of the possibility of working legally to cultivate support at the local level. The Party, which in any case had never aspired to be a mass organisation but always regarded itself as the vanguard of the revolutionary struggle, also had few possibilities for grassroots work. The Party came to devote a large part of its energies to cultivating an elite force of saboteurs, highly trained in political theory as well as in military matters. It was not that Party strategists believed they would bring down the government with bombs alone, but, rather, that the armed struggle would itself alter the political context, making the ground more fertile for political action in the future. It would also be useful in testing the mettle of Party members, producing cadres hardened for the revolutionary task ahead.

Just as the ANC in 1962 felt the need for a conference to take stock and coordinate its activities better, so too did the Party. Recognising the need to adapt to the new circumstances, the SACP held the second congress of its history, in secret, inside South Africa. Several leading communists were still living inside the country, many of them known to the police, who were unable to prove any sort of criminal offence against them and were obliged to adopt tactics of surveillance and harassment. Again according to police agent Ludi, who managed to infiltrate the Party at this time, the Central Committee was able to meet in the form of very small numbers of people meeting in private houses. In November 1962 the Party succeeded in holding its second underground congress in Johannesburg. In the chair was J.B. Marks.[9] The congress elected a new Central Committee which, again according to Ludi, included ANC members Marks, Duma Nokwe, Party General Secretary Moses Kotane, Govan Mbeki, Bartholomew

9.   Ludi, quoted in Henry Pike, *A History of Communism*, pp. 370–1.

Hlapane and Walter Sisulu. However, Ludi's evidence on the last-named in particular seems doubtful. Apart from the fact that Ludi was a police informer, and therefore not a source of evidence of high quality, people joining the Party in the 1980s were told by older members that Sisulu had never been a Party member, although he certainly worked closely with some communists at various stages of his ANC career.

The 1962 SACP National Conference – a somewhat pretentious title for what was by now a handful of men and women obliged to meet only in the greatest secrecy – adopted a new programme called *The Road to South African Freedom*. It characterised the South African situation as 'colonialism of a special type' and declared that the first aim of struggle was a 'national democratic revolution', the latest incarnation of the 'independent native republic' identified by the Comintern in 1928 as the aim of the struggle in the first instance. The SACP reaffirmed its belief that nationalism can be a progressive force only when it is under the Party's leadership, reiterating its long-standing strategy of seeking to work with a broad front of political groups for the attainment of a national revolution in South Africa as the necessary first stage leading to the eventual triumph of socialism. It reaffirmed its commitment to the armed struggle.

Scientific socialism maintains that a given political situation, if identified and analysed correctly, may be situated in a more general scheme of political economy. The Party's persistent identification of the South African condition as being basically a colonial one, albeit of a special type not found elsewhere, had important implications in Marxist theory and therefore in determining the strategy to be adopted by the Party. The nub of the Party's analysis was that when Britain, the colonial power, had accorded South Africa self-government in 1910 it had simply transferred power to a local elite, the whites, who not only continued to serve the colonial interest but were themselves colonisers. In this view, the whites of South Africa continued to oppress the country's African inhabitants just as in colonial times, on the basis of colour. The only significant political difference between South Africa and Kenya, Congo, Algeria or any of the other former colonies of settlement was that black South Africa had become a colony of white South Africa rather than of Great Britain, France or Belgium.

By the end of 1962, then, both the ANC and the Party had formally taken stock of the new situation which had arisen as a result of the suppression of the ANC and the resort to violence. The Party in particular, with its characteristic clarity and espousal of the long view, had incorporated these changes into a coherent political manifesto which was to remain its guide for the next 27 years. But, in the event, the next phase of political life started about as badly as it possibly could. This was largely because of first-class detective work by the South African police, especially by a detective named Donald Card, who devoted himself to painstaking analysis of clues and forensic evidence left by Umkhonto we Sizwe bombers, building up a prosecution case against dozens of Umkhonto we Sizwe personnel. Another policeman, Lieutenant Willem van Wyk, also figured prominently in the campaign against Umkhonto we Sizwe by cultivating a thorough network of informers. In due course, one of van Wyk's agents told him of a house near Johannesburg where the Umkhonto we Sizwe High Command met. Van Wyk eventually identified the place as Lilliesleaf farm, at Rivonia near Johannesburg.

The police returned in force and raided the farmhouse on 11 July 1963, capturing seven leaders of the underground army and a large quantity of documents and other material, including explosives. The seven arrested on the spot were Walter Sisulu, Govan Mbeki, Ahmed Kathrada, Lionel Bernstein, Bob Hepple, Raymond Mhlaba and Dennis Goldberg. Among captured documents was the six-page blueprint of Operation Mayibuye, the main Umkhonto we Sizwe battle-plan. Others arrested as a result of information found at the farm included Elias Motsoaledi and Andrew Mlangeni. The farm had been rented by Arthur Goldreich, who had experience of urban guerrilla warfare from his days with the Jewish nationalist underground in Palestine.

The police maintained that Lilliesleaf farm, as well as serving as the headquarters of Umkhonto we Sizwe, was also the headquarters of the Communist Party. Among the guerrilla leaders detained were leading communists including Goldreich, Goldberg, Kathrada and Mbeki. The evidence the police found at Rivonia was sufficient to convict seven of those captured and also to lay new charges, this time of treason, against Mandela. Mandela and seven comrades were sentenced to life imprisonment the following year. All but Mandela were released by October 1989 and Mandela himself only in February 1990.

It would be hard to overestimate the severity of the blow which the Rivonia arrests and their aftermath dealt to the Communist Party, the ANC and Umkhonto we Sizwe. As far as the police and the white public were concerned, they had eliminated the active opposition and put an end to the period of doubt which had set in among white South Africans and foreign investors at the time of the Sharpeville killings in 1960. In the next few years the police proceeded to arrest or otherwise neutralise virtually all the remaining ANC activists in South Africa, even those who were not active members of Umkhonto we Sizwe. The Communist Party inside the country was also shattered. Joe Slovo and his wife Ruth First went into exile to escape arrest, leaving Party Chairman Bram Fischer to run the Central Committee singlehanded. He remained in contact with other Party members inside the country, including Ray Alexander, Mac Maharaj, active in the Congress movement since 1951, Bartholomew Hlapane and Gerard Ludi, not yet revealed as an infiltrator. Later in 1964, members of a small group who had tried to re-establish the Umkhonto we Sizwe High Command, including Wilton Mkwayi and Mac Maharaj, were arrested. Fischer, too, the last member of the Central Committee surviving inside the country, was arrested that same year, and later sentenced to life imprisonment.

With hindsight, Party members later realised that they had paid insufficient attention to the question of security. Both Umkhonto we Sizwe and the Communist Party itself seriously underestimated the sophistication of the South African security apparatus, now strengthened by the reorganisation of the Special Branch of the police as the Security Police and the establishment of the Bureau of State Security, an intelligence organisation designed to complement the work of political surveillance and repression. BOSS, as it was known, was to work abroad as well as at home and developed a reputation sordid even by the standards of secret services.[10] Parliament introduced new laws to facilitate detention without trial, guided by Justice Minister John Vorster, himself interned on account of his pro-Nazi sympathies during the Second World War. It was around this time that reports of detainees being tortured became more frequent. South Africa's secret servants became adept at using a whole range of techniques to acquire information and to plant spies in the ranks of enemy organisations, according pride of place to the Communist Party. By 1965, most of the Party's secret network inside South Africa had been rolled up by the Security Police, and the Party had taken such a series of blows as hardly to exist as a coherent organisation. Numbers of individual communists lived and met abroad, but the Party's existence as a South African organisation was in peril.

Not the least demoralising aspect of the 1964 Rivonia trial, as well as of the later trial of Bram Fischer, was that the prosecution made use of several witnesses who were persuaded, terrorised or otherwise pressured to testify against their former comrades. These included a former communist, Bruno Mtolo, who testified against Mandela and others, the police spy Gerard Ludi, and a former member of the SACP Central Committee, Bartholomew Hlapane, who testified against Fischer. Umkhonto we Sizwe was eventually to take its revenge by murdering Hlapane on 16 December 1982, the twenty-first anniversary of the armed struggle and the one hundred and forty-fourth anniversary of the Battle of Blood River.

The Rivonia trial, and the subsequent trials of Wilton Mkwayi and others, and of Bram Fischer, were in effect mopping-up operations against the guerrilla underground. The Pretoria government, which had already built the legal and psychological edifice of apartheid, could now contemplate completing the historic task of the National Party by diverting black politics into channels entirely of its own choice and making South Africa a white-ruled state for ever. International

10. Gordon Winter, *Inside Boss* (Penguin, Harmondsworth, 1981).

confidence in the South African economy had been restored, and the country was developing at an impressive speed from being a mining-based economy providing the Western world with vital minerals to one manufacturing for a wider market in the developing countries of southern and central Africa. Few white South Africans, other than those with a professional interest, such as security policemen and a handful of journalists, gave much thought to the possibility of an organised black or socialist opposition. Few opponents of the system, at first, had the heart to pick up the pieces and start building again. All that was left of the nationalist organisations, it seemed, was a few sad exiles out of touch with home.

Matters were indeed serious for the exiles. For the ANC, Albert Luthuli remained the organisation's President-General until his death in 1967, but he was under house arrest in Natal and could play no active role. The organisation was effectively leaderless, although Oliver Tambo, as the head of the External Mission, was the most senior official outside the country and gradually emerged as the effective chairman of the ANC in exile. Moses Kotane, the veteran Communist Party General Secretary, became ANC Treasurer-General and also wielded influence among the exiles, helping to re-establish the Party's structures in exile while retaining the confidence of Tambo. The leadership of Umkhonto we Sizwe passed from Wilton Mkwayi, now on Robben Island, to Joe Modise, a tough street-fighter from Alexandra who had been recruited to the ANC in the early 1950s on account of his strong-arm skills but who was never recruited to the Party. For a brief period, a contender for the post of acting commander of the army was Ambrose Makiwane, a former president of the Student Representative Council at Fort Hare University, and cousin of the influential ANC member and communist Tennyson Makiwane.

In the difficult and even confused circumstances which obtained in the mid-1960s, many of the patterns and habits which were to govern the ANC and the Communist Party throughout their years of underground struggle were established. Membership of the Communist Party had traditionally been secret; now that the Party was also waging a war it became more secretive than ever. And the Party as an institution maintained a high degree of discretion, restricting its publications to occasional public statements signed either collectively or by the Party's general secretary or chairman, normally the only two Party functionaries who were permitted to identify themselves. The Party's journals, and especially its flagship, *The African Communist*, generally carried articles signed with pen-names. Probably the main concentration of Party members was to be found in London, where they enjoyed good relations with members of the Communist Party of Great Britain. But the Party received little public attention. In as much as the Party-ANC alliance received the attention of the press or the public, the spotlight generally fell on the ANC alone. Most of the ANC's membership in exile was in southern Africa, notably in

Tanzania, which provided a home after the organisation had been obliged to leave South Africa. Tambo was the nearest thing the alliance had to a figurehead, but he was no more than the first among equals in the ANC's collective leadership for some time. He had no authority whatever over the Communist Party, of which he was not a member, other than by virtue of his friendship with Kotane. Mild-mannered and unassertive in character. Tambo was not appointed acting President-General of the ANC until Luthuli's death in South Africa in 1967, and even then he continued to adopt the same low-key style.

All things considered, the mid-1960s was the most depressing period in the history of the ANC, and were very difficult for the Communist Party too. Internal supporters were neutralised or imprisoned, senior leaders were sentenced to life imprisonment, and many exiled members were demoralised. The Communist Party showed itself more resilient than the ANC, perhaps because of its greater discipline and longer history of underground existence, or perhaps because of the greater ideological commitment required of its members, which guided them through hardships unacceptable to others.

In the ANC, some exiles left the organisation altogether. According to modern recollection the government of Tanzania, where the ANC in exile was based, even offered Oliver Tambo a job as Attorney-General of Tanzania. If this offer was indeed made, Tambo rejected it. He preferred to soldier on, and this patient and self-effacing determination was to be the hallmark of his years as the leader of the ANC. The main criticism levelled at Tambo over the years by critics within the ANC has been that his relaxed and unassertive style, considered by some to be weakness, allowed the ANC to be hijacked by communists, who gradually took over the dominant role in the triple alliance of the ANC, the Party and SACTU, and the effective leadership of Umkhonto we Sizwe. It is true that Tambo's leadership of the ANC coincided with a period when members of the Communist Party gradually took over the central role in ANC policy-making. Such criticism must take account of the primacy of the need to hold the ANC together through years in the wilderness, when it could so easily have split apart. Tambo's great achievement has always been to maintain unity in the organisation, and this he could not easily have done if he had taken an anti-communist stand, even had it been his inclination to do so. Tambo repeatedly responded to internal crises by seeking conciliation rather than confrontation with the risk of provoking a split. He was most sensitive to the danger, in the circumstances of exile, of ethnic rivalries. Himself a Xhosa, he took particular care to carry with him ANC members from other South African language groups whenever there could conceivably be an accusation of ethnic favouritism. Tambo, for example, consistently defended Joe Modise, enabling him to remain as Umkhonto we Sizwe commander from 1964 until 1991 in spite of the frequent criticisms made against him.

Tambo's greatest personal quality has probably been his simple Christian morality which has served the organisation well, preventing it from collapsing into the mass of corruption which afflicted the PAC's exiled leadership. Some insiders attribute Tambo's low profile to the fact that he is a Pondo, a branch of the Xhosa-speaking family who have a distinct dialect and archaic tribal customs such as *ukungena*. Owing to this, Pondos are generally looked down upon by other Xhosa-speakers, and this is accentuated by their distinct manner of speech and the fact that, like Tambo himself, many carry ritual scars on their faces. Commenting on Tambo, a woman from a leading ANC family once remarked, in the hearing of one of the authors,[11] that 'O.R. strangely has never overcome the fact that *ulimpondo* [he is Pondo].' Although we do not necessarily share this view, there are those in the ANC who consider that Tambo's style of leadership was influenced by this background.

While Tambo has his critics in the ANC, there is nobody who is more respected by all shades of opinion. This was the man who, to the world at large, for almost thirty years represented the face of the ANC-Communist Party alliance. In fact, he was never a president with a really strong position, being in effect the chairman of a cumbersome apparatus in which Communist Party members constituted an inner core, able on occasion to push their own line through the ANC's governing body by virtue of the discipline and cohesiveness which was often lacking in other elements constituting the ANC leadership.

The move into exile had other effects on the leadership of the alliance which became apparent over the passage of time. The ANC was cut off from its base of support inside South Africa and inevitably became more oriented towards international opinion. Without diplomatic and financial support from abroad, it would have ceased to exist at all other than as a fading memory. This internationalisation of the ANC ran somewhat counter to its nature and tradition. It had always been an organisation little concerned with events outside South Africa and without any ideology or political programme beyond a broad African nationalism. The Communist Party, on the other hand, was better adapted to life in exile. From its inception it had been shaped by a strong internationalism and an ideology which transcended national and racial classifications. The ANC looked to its communist allies for guidance and support in exile. It became embroiled in the quarrels and debates of international socialism, notably after the mid-1960s rift between the Soviet Union and China had split the communist world into two armed camps.

One of the most valuable assets which the Communist Party brought to the alliance at this time was its certainty. Communists looked at their problems in the long term, certain of the eventual

11. Tsepo Sechaba.

triumph of socialism and the ultimate downfall of the apartheid state. They also looked at the problem in its broadest international scope, comparing the South African condition with those of other anti-colonial struggles, in Africa or further afield. These wider perspectives were transmitted to the ANC and to Umkhonto we Sizwe, now acknowledged as the armed wing of the ANC-Communist Party alliance. Looking at the map of southern Africa in 1964, the year of the Rivonia trial, it was immediately striking that South Africa was insulated from externally inspired revolution by the colonial territories of Angola and Mozambique, still under Portuguese rule, and Rhodesia, technically a British colony even after white settlers under Ian Smith had unilaterally and illegally declared independence in 1965. Other than that there were the British-ruled protectorates of Bechuanaland and Swaziland and the crown colony of Basutoland. Even after they had become independent (by 1968), their governments were dominated by the giant in Pretoria. They were in no position to give major help to Umkhonto we Sizwe, whatever opinions their rulers may have held privately about apartheid.

Conventional wisdom has it that for any guerrilla army to succeed, it needs a reliable rear base close to the territory under attack. The Algerian nationalists, for example, could work out of Tunisia. South Vietnam had North Vietnam. South Africa is no exception to this general principle, and Umkhonto we Sizwe's High Command knew that their army could be effective only if they could infiltrate trained fighters into the country and funnel in material from a friendly neighbouring country. But this was impossible because hostile colonial regimes ruled all of South Africa's neighbours. The best course for the exiled South African revolutionaries, as they contemplated the future in the wake of the Rivonia disaster, seemed to be to assist in the liberation of Rhodesia, Angola and Mozambique as a prelude to attacking South Africa at close quarters.

All three superpowers in the world at that time, the Soviet Union, the United States and China, broadly shared this analysis of the southern African situation. In many ways the USA was in the least comfortable position of the three. Successive US governments had shown a faint degree of antipathy to colonialism and were not displeased to see Britain and France abandoning their colonial empires providing that the successor states were allied with the West rather than with the communist powers. But US anti-colonialism was shallow. When Washington tried to put pressure on Portugal to decolonise also, it rapidly ran into a maze of contradictions. Portugal was a member of the North Atlantic Treaty Organisation (NATO) and controlled important strategic facilities in the Atlantic Ocean. It came to seem less important for the USA to be on the side of African nationalism in Mozambique or Angola than to maintain a working relationship with Lisbon. In regard to South Africa itself, the US government did not regard the situation as a colonial one and therefore need have no qualms on that score. Nevertheless it was obviously embarrassing for Washington to support an apartheid government, when the USA itself was becoming acutely aware of its own racial problem and when US politicians were beginning to respond to the fact that there were millions of black votes to be won in their own electorate. These were among the considerations that contributed to forming US policy on South and southern Africa.

The Soviet Union in particular enjoyed a far clearer and more consistent position, although it was not without conflicts of interest, notably in the sensitive matter of marketing gold and diamonds, where both the Soviet Union and South Africa had a mutual interest in cooperation to keep prices high. Nevertheless the Soviet government could maintain a consistent anti-colonialist line on all the settler-governed countries of the region. In its search for local allies, naturally enough it accorded pride of place to the South African Communist Party, by far the most disciplined and respectable socialist party in sub-Saharan Africa in Soviet eyes. The Chinese government was left to cultivate the alternative force in South African revolutionary politics, the Pan Africanist Congress, at least until the Chinese lost interest in Africa after the death of Mao Ze-Dong in 1976. Independent African states were divided in their loyalties but many preferred the PAC, whose Africanist philosophy was closer to the hearts of leaders like Kwame Nkrumah and Julius Nyerere than were the ponderous dialectics of the communists.

Overall, the superpower governments generally viewed developments in southern Africa primarily in terms of the Cold War. Whatever slight reservation the Americans may have had about the existence of colonial governments in Mozambique and Angola, whatever their finer feelings about the illegal Ian Smith government in Rhodesia, whatever dislike they had for apartheid, paled into insignificance beside the fact that the main opposition movements in all these countries were armed and supported by the Soviet Union or China, the communist enemies. And of all the revolutionary movements of the region, none was viewed with such hostility in Washington as the South African Communist Party. American policy-makers could reason that FRELIMO, the Mozambican Liberation Front, was primarily a nationalist movement, and therefore, in spite of its communist connections, it was not beyond American influence. Indeed Frelimo's founder, Eduardo Mondlane, had lived for years in the USA, had married an American woman, and had a strong admiration for the country. Similarly, in the course of time, it was not difficult for the US government to forge an alliance with the UNITA nationalist movement in Angola, in spite of UNITA's historical entanglements with socialist countries and the Maoist influence imbibed by Jonas Savimbi, the UNITA leader.

The one exception to the cynical American view that any nationalist or revolutionary movement could be co-opted, no matter what its previous allegiances or present rhetoric, was the South African Communist Party. Its whole history, its early devotion to the Comintern line, its fundamentalist Marxist-Leninist beliefs, and the fact that many of its leaders were white socialist intellectuals who would be unlikely to be seduced by the creed of black nationalism, all these factors made it the surest point of reference on the revolutionary map of southern Africa. It could never be co-opted by the USA. It was Moscow's surest ally in the region.

As long as world communism looked to Moscow for its inspiration, the exiled opposition forces of South Africa, Rhodesia, Angola and Mozambique could be united on one thing at least. But by 1965 they were being forced to choose. Growing differences between Soviet and Chinese communism came to a head, posing a dilemma for communists worldwide. Both Soviet and Chinese diplomats put pressure on their Third World allies. The South African Communist Party, still led by Kotane, its General Secretary, and dominated by the generation of members who, like him, had been trained in Moscow in the 1930s, strongly supported the Soviet line, although the Natal communists Rowley Arenstein and Harry Gwala sympathised with Beijing. In the early days, Umkhonto we Sizwe had sent cadres for training to any country willing to take them, including China. One of the earliest guerrillas, the Communist Joe Gqabi, was trained for 18 months in the Chinese city of Nanking before he was arrested by Rhodesian police in 1963 while helping to spirit volunteers out of South Africa and into exile. Gqabi was probably the most thoroughly trained fighter in Umkhonto we Sizwe at the time of his arrest. Wilton Mkwayi, briefly the commander of Umkhonto we Sizwe, was also Chinese-trained.

As soon as the Sino-Soviet split became irrevocable, the South African Communist Party used all its influence to persuade its allies to side with Moscow. So, in spite of the importance of its Chinese connection, the ANC broke all contacts with the Chinese, even withdrawing its people from training camps in China. In the fullness of time the Sino-Soviet question was to cause sharp divisions within the southern African liberation movements and was to play a significant role in determining the ANC's regional alliances. Some respected nationalist and socialist leaders, particularly Samora Machel in Mozambique, had absorbed Mao Ze-Dong's widely acclaimed teachings on guerrilla warfare which emphasised, more than did Soviet doctrine, the importance of working in the rural areas. Mao's famous dictum was that guerrillas must move among peasants as fish live in the sea, living off the land and learning from the people. While Machel was attempting to implement these ideas in Mozambique the same literature was being cleared from bookshelves in Umkhonto we Sizwe camps.

The Sino-Soviet dispute even made itself felt on Robben Island, the island prison of Cape Town. So many black prisoners were sent

45

to Robben Island from the 1960s onwards that it became a finishing-school for advanced guerrilla fighters and political activists, where there was time and opportunity to contemplate the struggle and to hone theoretical knowledge by discussion with other convicts. For over 25 years young political prisoners who were sent there had the opportunity to study at the feet of the older generation of radicals led by Mandela, Sisulu and Mbeki. Here too the Sino-Soviet dispute gave rise to arguments, with the prominent Natal communist Harry Gwala, who had joined the Party in 1942 and the ANC two years later, espousing the Maoist cause briefly before reverting to an orthodox pro-Soviet position. The Moscow camp was led by Govan Mbeki. The considerable number of PAC prisoners on the Island remained staunchly pro-Chinese.

In pursuit of its long-term military policy of 'hacking its way home', by fighting for the liberation of colonial Angola, Mozambique and Rhodesia as a prelude to concentrating on South Africa itself, the Umkhonto we Sizwe High Command not only had to ensure the military training of its personnel but also the integration of political and military strategy. It was in order to wage war more effectively that the Communist Party and the ANC became more closely integrated. In theory they were separate but equal allies. The governing body of the ANC was the National Executive Committee. The governing body of the Party was the Politburo. Some people, notably Moses Kotane, were members of both bodies. The ANC did not permit whites, coloureds or Indians to become formal members of the organisation, although in practice white, Indian and coloured communists occasionally observed meetings of the ANC's National Executive Committee and represented the ANC at international gatherings. In spite of these differences, there was a need for the closest possible coordination between the two organisations for the purposes of the armed struggle. Quite apart from considerations of military efficiency, Umkhonto we Sizwe was the armed wing of both the ANC and the Communist Party, and therefore both needed to have an input into its direction. To coordinate political and military policy, it was agreed to establish a Revolutionary Council which would be composed of members of both organisations and which would have day-to-day control of policy. In the mid-1960s the secretary and effective leader of the Revolutionary Council was the communist lawyer Joe Matthews. Like so many in the ANC, he was the son of a famous nationalist father. Matthews, born in 1929, was the son of Professor Z.K. Matthews, a prominent ANC leader of the 1950s who is credited with having conceived the idea of the Freedom Charter. Joe Matthews had joined the ANC Youth League under the influence of Oliver Tambo and had attended Fort Hare, the *alma mater* of so many Youth Leaguers. During the 1950s he had moved away from the Youth League's strongly nationalist line and had joined the Communist Party.

Umkhonto we Sizwe itself was, after Wilton Mkwayi's arrest in 1964, under the command of Joe Modise. He commanded up to two thousand South African exiles based in camps in Tanzania, at Kongwa, Mbeya, Bagamoyo and Morogoro. In the months after the Rivonia arrests, these fighters were badly affected by demoralisation, boredom, personal disputes and ideological differences, as well as poor food and living-conditions. These combined to produce a dangerous atmosphere in the camps, verging on mutiny.

One of the people who emerged as a leader of the rank and file in Umkhonto we Sizwe in the period after the Rivonia trials was a young man called Chris Hani. Born in 1942, he was the son of a migrant labourer from the Transkei but had managed to receive an education thanks to the efforts of an aunt. He studied at Lovedale High School, almost as prominent as Fort Hare in producing South African revolutionaries, and there he was recruited into the ANC by Simon Makana, later to become the ANC ambassador in Moscow. Hani graduated from Fort Hare University at the age of only 19, thanks to his academic brilliance, with a degree in English and Classics. Moving to Cape Town, he met the veteran communists Ray Alexander and her husband Jack Simons, Professor of African Law and Administration at the University of Cape Town. He was also much influenced by his uncle, a veteran activist. Hani was arrested in 1962 but jumped bail the following year and, together with his father, went into exile. Once in exile Hani volunteered to work with Umkhonto we Sizwe and was assigned to administrative tasks. Already conspicuous by the quality of his education as well as his natural ability, he soon become popular among the rank and file, especially with those recruits who, like him, were from the Transkei or the Eastern Cape.

In the troubled circumstances in the camps in 1966–7, Hani was a natural sounding-board for the grievances of the Umkhonto we Sizwe soldiers. Eventually he took the leading role in writing a memorandum on their behalf, addressed to the leadership of the organization. The document was critical of their perks and privileges, their lack of vigour in pursuing the war, and the squalid conditions which the guerrillas had to endure in their camps. It singled out for criticism Joe Matthews, the secretary of the Revolutionary Council, and, it is said, attacked by name Umkhonto we Sizwe's commander Joe Modise.

It is not possible, in the light of our present knowledge, to reconstruct the precise course of events after Hani and others had written their memorandum of grievances against the army leadership. Some veterans of the period maintain that Hani and some others were sentenced to death for mutiny, and that the sentences were not carried out thanks only to the intervention of other members of the ANC's political leadership. Hani himself is not known ever to have commented on the episode or given his version of it.

The agitation in the ranks, which appears to have occurred in 1966, was only one sign of the dangers of keeping a guerrilla force in poor conditions and without military activity. Armies, especially those motivated by revolutionary idealism, exist to fight. It was in these circumstances that the army command under Joe Modise and the Revolutionary Council under Joe Matthews determined to launch Umkhonto we Sizwe's first campaign from exile. Their plan was to assemble two fighting units, one of them led by Hani and including some of the former mutineers. It was to be under the overall command of Lennox Zuma, the Umkhonto we Sizwe Chief of Staff. The action was to be carried out as a joint operation with the guerrillas of Joshua Nkomo's Zimbabwe African People's Union (ZAPU), then the leading Zimbabwean liberation movement, whose own pro-Moscow stance made it a natural ally of the ANC and the South African Communist Party. The mutineers were to participate in the campaign, which seems to have been conceived as a way of allowing them to prove themselves, but was seen by some dissidents as an attempt to eliminate dissenters by sending them on a suicide mission.[12] The ANC guerrillas would move into Zambia, where ZAPU already had bases. The first wave of Zimbabwean and South African guerrillas would then slip across the Zambezi river and infiltrate Rhodesia, clearing the path for a second wave of ANC fighters under Hani to penetrate through to South Africa itself.

There remains a puzzle about the exact conception of what became known, by reference to the north-western area of Zimbabwe, as the Wankie campaign. There is little doubt that it was planned and implemented hastily, apparently because of the wish to move the disaffected guerrillas into action, and that the lack of detailed advance planning hampered the campaign throughout. The South African Communist Party was later to claim that its Central Committee 'was totally unaware of the Zimbabwe events of 1967 until they hit the world's press'.[13] The Party's Central Committee by this time was in London, and was not close to events in southern Africa, so it is quite possible that it had not been formally informed of the campaign. But even if this is so, it is inconceivable that the campaign could have been prepared without senior Party officials knowing, starting with Joe Matthews, the secretary of the Revolutionary Council. Recruits began to slip from Tanzania into Zambia in early 1967 in preparation for the offensive. Oliver Tambo accompanied the fighters right down to the Zambian bank of the Zambezi River; with him was Thomas Nkobi, then the ANC representative in Zambia, later to be elected ANC Treasurer-General. In August 1967, a mixed force of about 80 ZAPU and ANC guerrillas waded across the Zambezi River upstream from the Victoria Falls and headed south through the Wankie game reserve.

Within a few days, the presence of the mixed South African-

---

12. Tom Lodge, *Black Politics in South Africa*, p. 300.
13. Quoted in *ibid.*, p. 299.

Zimbabwean guerrilla force had been reported to the Rhodesian security forces who were airlifted in to confront the invaders. There was a series of hard-fought engagements. According to official Rhodesian statistics, which are probably substantially correct in this case, the Rhodesians lost seven dead in the first clashes between the two sides while the guerrillas lost 50 men, of whom 30 were killed and 20 captured. The security forces noted with some consternation, though, that the guerrillas' performance and training were far superior to anything yet seen in Rhodesia. The ANC and ZAPU soldiers fought at least one pitched battle against the Rhodesian security forces and were defeated only by the Rhodesians' vastly superior logistics which enabled them to evacuate their casualties rapidly and bring in reinforcements by air or vehicle.[14]

News of the infiltration reached Pretoria within minutes of its being discovered by the Rhodesians. As soon as he heard the news, the head of the Bureau of State Security, Hendrik van den Bergh, contacted Prime Minister John Vorster and urged him to despatch South African assistance. Vorster agreed and secured Rhodesian approval. Within hours a detachment of riot police and helicopters were on their way to help in the defence of the Rhodesian border. The Rhodesian intelligence chief, Ken Flower, later claimed that the South Africans, unused to this type of counter-insurgency operation, were rather ineffective. There may have been an element of professional jealousy in this put-down remark. If it was true that the South Africans were unskilled in this type of warfare, they certainly lost no opportunity to use the Rhodesian front for training purposes. A whole generation of South African security chiefs gained vital practical experience in the late 1960s on detachment to Rhodesia. They included in particular the men who later founded the Namibian counter-insurgency unit Koevoet and many of those who later commanded Security Police or army death squads operating against the ANC inside South Africa and abroad, such as the so-called Civil Cooperation Bureau.

For the Zimbabwean and South African guerrillas of ZAPU and the ANC, their first battle with the Rhodesians in August 1967 taught them the folly of engaging a better-equipped enemy head-on in the conventional manner then favoured by Soviet instructors. They realised that they had to adapt their tactics to avoiding confrontations where the Rhodesians could concentrate their superior firepower. A second wave went in and tried to avoid contact. But once the infiltrators' tracks had been spotted, they were again hugely out-numbered by the Rhodesian forces. In March and April 1968 the Rhodesians killed 69 guerrillas, according to their own figures, for the loss of six men in a series of skirmishes. The Rhodesians were already one step ahead in the technique of guerrilla warfare which they had

14. The following is based largely on Ken Flower, *Serving Secretly. Rhodesia into Zimbabwe, 1964–1981* (John Murray, London, 1987).

learned partly from the British army, whereas the guerrillas were relative novices at this early stage of their campaign.[15]

From the ANC point of view, the Wankie campaign was a military defeat, but it did have a positive symbolic value. It became part of the Umkhonto we Sizwe mythology as the opening round in a new phase of the struggle. The campaign created heroes whose stories inspired unblooded recruits. Among these was Paul Petersen, a coloured intellectual who was also known as Basil February. A former medical student from the University of Cape Town, he had published a number of articles on political theory. Legend has it that, after he had been seriously wounded, he asked his colleagues to leave him with a She machine-gun so that he could fight to the death. That particular type of Czechoslovakian-manufactured machine-gun has been named after Petersen in ANC circles ever since, and is known as the 'She Petersen'.

Another prominent victim of the campaign was Patrick Molaoa. Born in Johannesburg in 1925, he was one of the first volunteers from the Transvaal in the ANC's 1952 defiance campaign and was elected national president of the ANC's Youth League in July 1959, the last person to hold that office before the banning of the ANC. By the time of the Wankie campaign, he was a member of the ANC's National Executive Committee and could easily have avoided front-line combat. Instead, he volunteered for active service and was killed in battle in 1968.

Many others were captured by the Rhodesians and sentenced to death, although these sentences were never carried out. Hani managed to escape to Botswana with other remnants of his party, where they were arrested and convicted of illegal possession of firearms. They were not detained for long in Botswana and filtered slowly back to the Umkhonto we Sizwe camps. Lennox Zuma survived unscathed and went on to fight with FRELIMO in Mozambique, where he served under a variety of assumed names.

Amazingly, some of the Wankie contingent actually succeeded in making their way to South Africa. One ANC guerrilla who got through, Daluxolo Luthuli, known as 'Kenken', was sent to Robben Island and later joined Chief Mangosuthu Gatsha Buthelezi's Inkatha organisation. Another, Leonard Nkosi, was betrayed to the authorities by one of his family while living underground. He was recruited into the Security Police and became one of their leading officers, specialising in working against his former comrades. He was shot dead in the late 1970s by an Umkhonto we Sizwe unit which surprised him while he was in bed with his wife. It was not to be the last time that the Security Police succeeded in 'turning' a captured guerrilla.

The survivors of the Wankie campaign were bitter about its failure. They blamed their High Command in particular for having launched

---

15. Ken Flower, *Serving Secretly*, pp. 108–10.

them into enemy territory and then having failed to resupply them once they were inside Rhodesia. One group of survivors who criticised the operation were detained in an ANC camp in Tanzania in an attempt to suppress their dissenting views. Those captured by the Rhodesians, whose death sentences were later reprieved, stayed in gaol until Zimbabwean independence in 1980, when the ANC persuaded them to rejoin the organisation. Even after all those years many of the prisoners were so bitter about the way that the leadership had let them down that they refused to rejoin Umkhonto we Sizwe as long as the army command remained unchanged. Some of the Wankie veterans gaoled in Rhodesia until 1980 were eventually persuaded to rejoin Umkhonto we Sizwe by Chris Hani, one of the few who survived the Wankie campaign with his reputation enhanced. He established a following in the army in these years which was to be a vitally important power base in his rise to prominence.

3
The Party Triumphant
1969-75

In the aftermath of the Wankie campaign, the ANC and the Party were beset by problems so daunting as to call into question the whole nature of their alliance and its future strategy. Changes of this magnitude could not be debated or effected without a general congress of the ANC. In any case, the membership of the ANC in exile, most of them living in Umkhonto we Sizwe camps in Tanzania, had so clearly lost confidence in their leaders that there would have to be an election. Moreover the alliance lacked a proper leader. After Albert Luthuli's death in South Africa in 1967, Oliver Tambo had been appointed only as acting President-General of the ANC. The provisional nature of the appointment, combined with his own understated style, meant that his authority was somewhat less than unquestioned. It was clearly a matter of the greatest urgency to examine the leadership of the ANC, to try and instil a greater sense of purpose, and to work out a comprehensive military and political strategy.

The leaders of the Party, itself hardly recovered from the setbacks it had encountered and with its membership scattered across two continents, believed that the way forward was to draw the ANC and the Party into a closer alliance as the basis for greater cohesion and unity than was the case at present. This would then permit them to hammer out a clear medium-term political and military strategy. White, coloured and Indian Party members especially wanted the ANC to state formally its commitment to non-racial membership so that they themselves could be formally admitted. After all, they argued, whites, coloureds and Indians were conspicuous in the ranks of Umkhonto we Sizwe, the armed wing of the ANC, so it was right that they should have a voice in choosing their own leaders. Moreover, according to the Freedom Charter, the basic manifesto of the ANC, the organisation aimed to construct a non-racial South Africa. It would be logical for the ANC to emphasise its nature as a movement open to all South Africans, irrespective of race, by admitting people of any race. Once the ANC was open to all, the lines of management and decision-making would be much clearer since they would be contained within one body rather than being spread across separate organisations. Nevertheless, there were some in the ANC, as was to become clear in the course of the next few years, who regarded the Party as having a disproportionate number of whites and Indians in its senior ranks, and who feared that a closer association with the ANC, and especially the formal provision of non-racial membership, would tip the balance of forces inside the ANC in favour of the Party and of whites and Indians especially.

The Wankie campaign also underlined the need for an overhaul of the army. Again, this led to pressure for the ANC to hold a conference where questions of strategy and purpose could be debated. Umkhonto we Sizwe was in poor condition. Apart from those it had lost in Rhodesia, and those who had been imprisoned in Botswana, it had suffered desertions by disillusioned fighters drifting off to Europe or even back to South Africa. One group of Umkhonto we Sizwe defectors who sought asylum in Kenya in 1968 publicly justified their desertion by accusing their commanders of extravagant living and favouritism. Some from Hani's group who had been detained in Botswana after the Wankie fiasco also complained about the army command.[1] As in the earlier criticisms by the rank and file which had preceded the Wankie campaign, the position of Joe Modise was called into question. As the army commander, it was inevitable that he would bear responsibility for problems in the army generally. Not for the last time, Tambo used all his influence to deflect criticism away from Modise, probably because of his fear that, if Modise went, he would be replaced by a Xhosa. This would have risked accusations of favouritism, directed against the many ANC leaders who, like Tambo, were from the Transkei.

The Wankie campaign had resulted in feelings of bitterness and accusations of incompetence or betrayal by the rank and file against almost the whole leadership of the ANC. Joe Matthews especially was the butt of severe criticism, which again was to be expected since he was head of the Revolutionary Council in charge of military and political strategy. Although no one doubted his ability or his capacity for hard work, he was accused of increasingly erratic behaviour. Tambo defended him too, perhaps for the same reason, perhaps out of regard for Matthews' undoubted ability, or perhaps out of deference to his family's prominence in the ANC over two generations.

To make matters worse, the ANC developed very bad relations with its host, the government of Tanzania. In the early 1960s Tanzania had acquired a reputation as a champion of African liberation, partly due to the efforts of Julius Nyerere, the Tanzanian President who was a leading voice in African diplomacy, but thanks also to his number two Oscar Kambona, Minister of Foreign Affairs from 1963 to 1965 and Chairman of the African Liberation Committee of the Organisation of African Unity, based in Dar es Salaam. Kambona's chairmanship of the African Liberation Committee gave him power to channel funds and international support to liberation movements

---

1. Tom Lodge, *Black Politics in South Africa*, p. 300.

which he favoured. Tanzania was the headquarters of both South African liberation movements, the ANC and the PAC.

Kambona, once tipped as Nyerere's heir, had fallen out with his President and had been gradually sidelined. In 1967 relations between the two men became so tense that Kambona went to Britain for an indefinite stay, but continued to plot his return to power from his new base in Europe. This much was later demonstrated by court proceedings in Tanzania, although in a private interview Kambona has denied any such intention. Towards the end of 1968 he entered into secret communication with the Tanzania-based leaders of both the PAC and the ANC to see if they would use their armed forces to help him launch a coup against Nyerere. PAC leader Potlako Leballo agreed to help. The ever-cautious Tambo refused but neglected to report the approach to the Tanzanian authorities. Tambo was in a difficult position, since if the Kambona coup plot had succeeded, expulsion of the ANC from the country by a hostile new government was a likely consequence. Failure to report the plot, on the other hand, carried the risk of being accused of disloyalty to Nyerere. Leballo, in fact, later informed President Nyerere about the plot and was enlisted by the Tanzanian government as a double agent. He then testified as the most important state witness in the trial on treason charges of seven pro-Kambona plotters, and Kambona himself in his absence, in 1970.

Although these intrigues were not widely known at the time, there were enough rumours in the air to poison the atmosphere in Tanzania. Moreover the Kambona affair was not the only bone of contention between the ANC and its Tanzanian host. Ever since the Sino-Soviet split of the mid-1960s, the ANC's staunchly pro-Soviet line, followed at the urging of its Communist Party ally, had increasingly estranged it from Nyerere, who was much closer to the Chinese than he was to the Soviets. He considered Maoism more sympathetic to the plight of the peasantry who make up the majority of the population in Africa. Nyerere had articulated his own brand of agrarian socialism which was anathema to the Stalinists of the SACP. It naturally brought him closer to the PAC, which was also pro-Chinese.

It was in these rather inauspicious circumstances that the ANC called a consultative conference, the first since 1962, to be held at its Tanzanian headquarters at Morogoro. Even before the meeting was convened there was intense manoeuvring between different groups. The Party hierarchy, led by Kotane and the Party chairman, J.B. Marks, and including Joe Slovo and Joe Matthews, put its weight behind critics of the ANC leadership, canvassing for a clean sweep of the National Executive Committee. They were also in favour of a radical restructuring of the ANC-Party alliance, giving it more cohesion and a clearer strategy. In their view it was desirable to abolish racial restrictions on ANC membership. This view was not shared by all in the Party or in the ANC. Opponents, including some African communists, warned of the danger of the ANC coming under the influence of white and Indian communists. Open membership was a controversial proposal in itself for a body which had existed for 57 years as an exclusively African organisation. Moreover, it was clear to any experienced political in-fighter that serving members of the National Executive Committee who were voted out of office as a result of conference decisions might be inclined to represent themselves as the victims of a conspiracy by members of other ethnic groups, virtually all of them communists, echoing some of the criticisms which had been made against the Congress Alliance in the 1950s and which had resulted in the formation of the PAC.[2]

The meeting began on 25 April 1969 and lasted for seven days. It was attended by some 70 delegates from the ANC and its allied organisations, many of them members of Umkhonto we Sizwe. Those present included 11 who were not, technically speaking, members of the ANC – three whites, five Indians and three coloureds, invited in their capacity as members of allied organisations, in conformity with the established tradition whereby people who were not members of the ANC could attend meetings as observers on occasion, and in recognition of the fact that there were matters on the agenda relevant to the whole of the alliance. The conference was chaired by J.B. Marks, known to all and sundry as 'Uncle J.B.', a veteran of both the Communist Party and the ANC. After studying in Moscow and being elected to the Politburo, Marks had been purged from the Party briefly in 1937, after which he had thrown himself into work for the ANC. After rejoining the Party, he had gone on to become an ANC executive member. He left South Africa with Joe Slovo in 1963 and was elected to the post of Party Chairman in 1969, the same year that he was given the honour of presiding over the Morogoro Conference.

It was widely expected that the meeting would be stormy. In deference to the criticisms of the ANC's leadership, the entire National Executive Committee was required to resign before the meeting so as to start with a clean sheet. Two NEC members, Temba Mqota and Ambrose Makiwane, were also suspended for allegedly attempting to organise a faction in advance of the conference.

The debate on the membership question was the key issue of the conference. Perhaps the most telling interventions were made by Flag Boshielo, a communist and ANC member since the 1940s, who had the prestige of having been the leader of the Transvaal volunteers in the 1952 defiance campaign. As the Commissar of Umkhonto we Sizwe he had particular influence with the rank-and-file guerrillas who formed the main block of conference delegates. Boshielo stated the case of the Party's mainstream for the instalment of open membership with a hard-hitting speech ridiculing those who argued

2. A full account of the conference manoeuvres, as seen from the Communist Party point of view, is in *South African Communists Speak*, pp. 408–17.

that opening the ANC to non-black members would fatally alter its character. This view won the day, not least because the Party leadership was known to favour it. The conference approved a motion opening to all ordinary membership of the ANC and its organs in exile, but not in South Africa, which was to be decided upon later. The Morogoro Conference did not alter the requirement for election to the organisation's governing body, which remained open to Africans only. Three non-Africans (in the ethnic sense), all communists, were promptly elected to serve on the Revolutionary Council, now given a formal and constitutional existence for the first time as the organ responsible for implementing policy. The three were Yusuf Dadoo, an Indian; Reg September, a coloured trade unionist; and Joe Slovo, a white. September and Dadoo had both represented the ANC at various international functions although neither was technically a member. They and Slovo had all been permitted to attend some meetings of the ANC's National Executive in the past,[3] and were already members of the ANC in all but name.

All three were leading figures in the history of the Party. Dadoo was born in South Africa but had studied in India and Britain, returning to a professional career as a doctor and immersing himself in political activity. He joined the Party in 1939 and was soon elevated to the Central Committee. He was also active in the Indian Congress, becoming President of the Transvaal Indian Congress in 1945. After Morogoro he became Vice-President of the Revolutionary Council and eventually Chairman of the Communist Party after Marks's death in Moscow in 1972, serving in that capacity until his own death in 1983.

Reg September was also a veteran of the Congress Alliance. He had joined the Party in the Western Cape early in the 1950s and served as General Secretary of the Coloured People's Congress, one of the front organisations developed by the Party after its suppression. September later became the ANC's representative in Britain and was appointed to the organisation's National Executive Committee in 1985. Trained as a political analyst, he was treasurer of the important Political-Military Council until 1986 when he had to move to London due to ill health. He later worked in the field of political education.

Joe Slovo, the third of the 'non-Africans' appointed to the Revolutionary Council, is one of the key figures in the history of both the ANC and the Communist Party. Over the years he has achieved the status of the person most feared by the legion of white South African anti-communists. But, more remarkably, he has also achieved the standing of a hero revered alike by township youth and by the most hardened exiled revolutionaries.

Slovo was born in 1926 in Lithuania, not then a part of the Soviet Union, and moved with his parents to South Africa at the age of nine;

3. *South African Communists Speak*, p. 412.

there Slovo senior settled and found work as a van driver. Joe Slovo joined the Communist Party as early as 1942, at the age of 16, and served[4] with the Allied forces during the Second World War. Ironically, while the youthful Slovo went to war some of those who were later to become his most dedicated opponents, like Prime Minister John Vorster and intelligence chief Hendrik van den Bergh, were interned on account of their pro-Nazi sympathies.

After the war Slovo took a law degree at Witwatersrand University and threw himself into politics; among other things, he was an active member of a radical ex-servicemen's organisation, the Springbok Legion. After he had been called to the Johannesburg bar he built a practice as a defence lawyer in political trials. In 1949 he married the journalist Ruth First, the daughter of Communist Party Treasurer Julius First. The following year the couple were among 600 people named in terms of the Suppression of Communism Act. Slovo became a legal adviser to the ANC, and is credited with having contributed to the drafting of the 1955 Freedom Charter. In 1956 he was already sufficiently important in the Congress Alliance to be charged in the marathon treason trial, although the charges were later dropped. He was one of the most important founders of Umkhonto we Sizwe in 1961 and for almost 30 years was the key strategic thinker in the underground army, finishing with the title of Chief of Staff, a post which he resigned in 1987 to concentrate on Party work. He left South Africa in 1963 in company with J.B. Marks and is not known to have set foot in the country again until 1990. He was elected Chairman of the SACP at its Sixth Congress, held in Moscow in 1984, and in 1986 became General Secretary, a post which he still holds. It would be fair to say that he is the leading South African communist today, and has been one of the most influential Party leaders over the past 40 years.

Slovo is a model of what a South African communist is expected to be. Brave and possessed of the rigorous intellect of a lawyer, he has been utterly dedicated to Party work since his youth and he has been the victim of numerous assassination attempts. His wife was killed in 1982 by a parcel-bomb prepared by a Security Police assassination team and delivered to her office at Eduardo Mondlane University in Maputo. He is portrayed by some of his colleagues as a man cool and rational almost to the point of coldness, but others recall him as a charming companion, lacking the streak of puritanism which some of the older generation of Stalinists still display. In public interviews he is always thoughtful and courteous, often appearing so avuncular as to disarm the image created by South African government propagandists of a devil in human form. His favourite relaxations include playing bridge, to which he is addicted. His favourite bridge partner for some years was the Indian communist, known as Rashid, who

4. Karis and Carter, Vol. iv, p. 147.

served as the head of Umkhonto we Sizwe's ordnance department. South African government propaganda alleged that Slovo was a colonel of the Soviet KGB, but that seems rather unlikely in view of Slovo's South African nationality. Throughout his career he has been so staunchly pro-Soviet that it would seem pointless for the KGB to make such an appointment. He is a fundamentalist believer in classical Marxism-Leninism of the Soviet school.

By the time of the Morogoro Conference, Slovo was already established as Umkhonto we Sizwe's leading strategist and he was respected by militants of all races. He and Joe Matthews were probably the key authors of a document which was debated at the Morogoro Conference and duly adopted as the ANC policy programme, known as the Strategy and Tactics document. Written in a precise and legal prose, it set out the political and military means which the ANC should follow to achieve revolution, laying great stress on the need to involve the African masses. It was a document in the tradition of the Comintern decision of 1928 calling for the establishment of an independent black republic as the first step towards building a socialist South Africa. Based on the observation that South Africa's borders lack the sort of mountainous or jungle terrain which is the classic refuge for guerrilla fighters, and that there is no black peasantry to provide a natural haven for guerrillas as was the case in Zimbabwe, the Strategy and Tactics document concluded that the correct course was to launch a campaign based upon the urban working class in which the people of the townships would take the place of the jungles and mountains which had hidden guerrilla fighters in other countries. Part of the significance of this document was that, for the first time in ANC policy, it characterised the urban working class as the leading force in the struggle. There was still a residual belief in the ANC that the rural areas appeared to offer better prospects for the intensification of guerrilla warfare, as these areas were generally free of government forces and local government was in the hands of black people whose loyalty to the Pretoria government was relatively weak. The military logic of the new approach also concorded with the classical Marxist-Leninist perception that the urban working class is the section of the population most ripe for socialism which, in the view of some critics, has caused the Party and Umkhonto we Sizwe to neglect work in the rural areas, although Slovo, writing under the pen name Sol Dubula on the tenth anniversary of Umkhonto we Sizwe, still advocated the use of rural warfare as late as 1971. Altogether, the Strategy and Tactics document was the single most authoritative statement of ANC strategy in the war fought over the next two decades with the South African state.

The two most far-reaching decisions of the Morogoro Conference, to allow open membership of the ANC in exile and to adopt the Strategy and Tactics document, marked a sea-change in the history of the Congress alliance. It was the first time that the ANC had had a written programme other than the Freedom Charter of 1955. Adoption of the Strategy and Tactics document undoubtedly sharpened the organisation's focus by giving it a policy document of some description, but it also set the ANC upon a course originally charted by another organisation, the South African Communist Party, and greatly increased the Party's influence over the alliance as a whole by establishing the Party's leading intellectual role. That, combined with the overhaul of ANC structures and the infusion of new blood into the National Executive Committee (NEC) and the Revolutionary Council, was a landmark in ANC history and a triumph for the Party.

Some senior members of the ANC argued hard against these innovations at Morogoro, but were out-voted. On the leadership question, the conference voted merely to confirm Tambo as acting President-General of the ANC without making his position permanent. He was not in fact confirmed in this post until 1977. It is appropriate to observe that it suited the Party to have a relatively weak non-communist president of the ANC serving as the symbolic leader of the triple alliance of the ANC, the Party and SACTU.

It was immediately clear that some of those who were on the losing side of the key arguments at Morogoro, especially the open membership issue, were not going to take things lying down. The ethos of democratic centralism required those who had lost the conference debate to accept the majority verdict, but the internal feuding continued, at a time when there were numerous setbacks to overcome. The following year, the Umkhonto we Sizwe Commissar Flag Boshielo 'disappeared' on a military operation while he was crossing from Zambia into Rhodesia – or possibly into Namibia, in company with a unit from the People's Liberation Army of Namibia.[5] He is presumed to have been shot by Rhodesian security forces. And the Kambona affair returned to haunt the organisation. In May 1970 the Tanzanian government began court proceedings against Kambona, in his absence, on charges of treason. Tambo refused to testify on the grounds that the ANC should be neutral in the internal affairs of Tanzania. A furious Nyerere promptly ordered the ANC out of his country. The leadership decamped to Moscow, from where, after a brief sojourn, the ANC moved its headquarters to Lusaka in Zambia. Nyerere, impressed by the warmth with which the ANC was received in Moscow, then allowed the Algerian government to negotiate a restoration of relations so that the ANC could base some of its personnel in Tanzania once more. Nyerere's suspicion of the ANC, and of its pro-Soviet sympathies, was to linger for many years, and Tanzanian diplomacy continued to favour the PAC over its ANC rival until the mid-1980s.

There were constant rumours, some reaching the South African

5. The latter version was affirmed in an interview with Mishake Muyongo, then a SWAPO official.

press, of arguments between different factions in the ANC leadership during these difficult times. In June 1971 Alfred Nzo, Secretary-General of the ANC since the 1969 Morogoro Conference and a Party member who at one time served on the Party's Central Committee, chaired a commission of inquiry into disagreements in the leadership. He concluded that the trouble stemmed from the fact that some members of the Revolutionary Council and of the ANC's NEC were not being kept fully informed of developments. This led the dissident faction to wonder where power really lay in the organisation. According to the dissidents, a subsequent investigation into the ANC's internal politics was sabotaged by communists.[6] Whether this was indeed so, however, remains unclear.

In theory, it was perfectly clear where power should lie in the ANC: with the governing body, the NEC. This did not preclude communists within the NEC (or, for that matter, any group of members with a common agenda) from coordinating positions before committee meetings. The discipline of the communists made them very effective in tactics of this sort. Over decades of operating inside larger organisations, the Party had evolved the technique of forming a caucus with agreed positions which it could then push through in meetings of the ANC. The ANC's collective style of leadership made this easier. It was certainly true that power did not lie with Tambo, whose authority was stymied by his appointment as acting president only, and who in any case was of a temperament which abhorred confrontation.

The ANC's long tradition of collective leadership, in which the President-General presided with the consent of the NEC, the governing body of the organisation, became subtly altered into a system resembling the Leninist technique of democratic centralism: the governing body decided, and every other organ and individual then had to accept the decision without dissent. Under the circumstances of a guerrilla struggle launched from exile, which in any case is never conducive to political harmony or open decision-making, the ANC's collective leadership itself became prey to the caucus tactics of the Communist Party, whose members were subject to another authority.

The identity of other senior office-holders in the ANC alliance was also important in understanding how the Party was able to win its case in meetings of the various ANC committees. Perhaps the most important position in the ANC after the President was that of Secretary-General, the person with a hand on day-to-day administration and the servicing of committees. From 1958 to 1969 this post had been filled by Duma Nokwe, an accomplished legal draftsman whom Moses Mabhida used to describe as having 'a golden pen', in spite of the alcoholism which was eventually to kill him. Although he was a loyal Party member, Nokwe was personally close to some of

6. Tom Lodge, *Black Politics in South Africa*, pp. 302–3.

those who argued against the changes introduced at Morogoro, which underlines the fact that the argument for and against open membership of the ANC did not fall exclusively along communist versus non-communist lines, and that within the Party there were black communists who were wary of allowing the ANC to fall under the domination of non-blacks. The Morogoro Conference voted to replace Nokwe as Secretary-General with Alfred Nzo, also a communist, but regarded as rather lacklustre. Another senior position in the ANC, that of Treasurer-General, was held by Communist Party General Secretary Moses Kotane until 1973, when he was replaced by Thomas Nkobi, a non-communist. Army commander Joe Modise was also a non-communist. Perhaps what was most important was that Tambo and Nzo both had a low-key style. Nkobi has never been regarded as a political heavyweight, while Modise has been persistently unpopular with the rank-and-file of the army.

Since by 1973 only one of the top four office-holders in the ANC was a Communist Party member, it would be inaccurate to say that the Party took over the top positions in the ANC as a result of the Morogoro Conference. The Party's achievement was not to pack the ANC leadership with sympathisers or members but to buttress its influence by more subtle and, perhaps, more legitimate means. Indeed, it seems to have been the lack of assertiveness of the top office-holders in the ANC which was partly responsible for the shift in the balance of power in the ANC.

Perhaps as important as the NEC, in the machinery of the ANC alliance, was the Revolutionary Council, the organ charged with implementing decisions made by the NEC in both the political and military domains. It was here that there was the most notable influx of Communists. Moses Mabhida took over the Secretary's post, and effective leadership of the Council, from Joe Matthews, who faded entirely from his former prominence after Morogoro and retired to Botswana. He was expelled from the Party after making a statement critical of the ANC's attitude towards the homelands and later worked for the government of Botswana and in private business before fading into obscurity. Today, he lives overseas. Mabhida was an outstanding communist and an assertive leader, who went on to become Party General Secretary from 1978 until his death in 1986. Mabhida was joined, as we have seen, by three other communists, September, Slovo and Dadoo, the last two especially being considered Party heavyweights. Dadoo became Deputy Chairman of the Revolutionary Council and Slovo its leading strategist, representing a Party takeover of this key committee. Cassius Make, also a Party member, became Deputy Secretary of the Revolutionary Council. From 1978, as Mabhida concentrated increasingly on Party affairs after the death of Moses Kotane, Make in fact became the dominant figure in the Council. If there was an official body which can be said to have been packed with Party members as a result of the Morogoro Conference, it was not the NEC but the Revolutionary Council. This was the seat of the Party's power in the alliance.

Although there can be no doubt that the Morogoro Conference and its aftermath were instrumental in putting the Party at the helm of affairs, the process was not a simple one. It was not really true, for example, as some ANC nationalists alleged, echoing the criticisms heard from the PAC breakaway group in the 1950s, that the Party was under the control of whites and Indians, although a disproportionate number of whites and Indians were included in the Party leadership. Moses Mabhida, for example, who held the crucial post of Secretary of the Revolutionary Council, was also noted for his strong attachment to Zulu culture and his Africanist tinge.

The person who emerged as the leader of those opposed to the changes introduced at Morogoro was himself a former communist. This was Tennyson Makiwane, born into a leading family of the Transkei, a former student at Fort Hare who had been expelled after leading a strike there, a former member of the ANC Youth League, a former protégé of Ruth First and once the right-hand man of Oliver Tambo. Makiwane was one of the NEC members who had to accept responsibility for the misfortunes which had befallen the ANC during the 1960s and who was dropped from the leadership at Morogoro. After the conference he continued to fight a rearguard action against the changes taking place in the ANC, and in time came to be regarded as the leader of a dissident faction which included several former members of the NEC whose stars had waned as a result of the Morogoro Conference. Among others associated with Makiwane's group was his cousin Ambrose Makiwane, a former acting commander of Umkhonto we Sizwe, often wrongly described as Tennyson's brother. Other dissidents included Temba Mqota, a communist from the Eastern Cape who had once been a protégé of Govan Mbeki. Elected to the ANC's NEC in 1958, he was regarded as highly able and was at one stage considered potential leadership material in the Communist Party. Pascal Ngakane had been important in the ANC underground in Natal and was Albert Luthuli's son-in-law. Others included Joe Matlou, O.K. Setlapelo, Tami Bonga and George Mbele, the latter particularly popular in Natal. Tennyson Makiwane himself remained close for some time to Duma Nokwe, now relegated to the head of the International Department but still a man whose opinions carried weight in the ANC and the Party. In the end, though, Nokwe became infuriated by the conduct of the dissidents and was to take the lead in causing the NEC to vote on the expulsion of Makiwane and others.

In short, the dissidents included men of real standing in the ANC and even in the Party. Some were regarded as people of high calibre. Some were relatives of senior ANC officials. Four had been members of the ANC's National Executive until 1969. The dissidents claimed to be inspired by Robert Resha, a tough former miner and journalist who had once been acting president of the ANC Youth League and had recruited township street-fighters into the ANC in the 1950s and served on the NEC for many years. In fact, Resha died before the dissidents had split publicly with the ANC. He was known to sympathise with the group, and he may conceivably have joined forces with them if he had lived longer, but he retained a high standing in the NEC and was never considered a member of the dissident faction. In later days, Resha continued to be remembered as a hero of the ANC. Oliver Tambo has always been proud to recount stories of his travels with Resha.

There was undoubtedly a good deal of personal animosity in the grievances of the dissidents. All of them had been held responsible, as NEC members or other senior officials, for failures of the past, or had otherwise suffered a personal loss of power as a result of the changes made at the Morogoro Conference. Tennyson Makiwane and Temba Mqota had both been prominent communists in their time, which rather blunted the force of their protestations that the Party had hijacked the ANC. It was not difficult for the Party to represent them as disgruntled people attacking the Party out of opportunism and self-interest rather than from principle and conviction. Nonetheless, the dissidents certainly had a point, namely that the nature of the ANC had been fundamentally changed by the decisions reached at the Morogoro Conference. Whereas the ANC had been in alliance with the Communist Party for some years, and the two had fought together in Umkhonto we Sizwe, the ANC had now adopted a strategy which was virtually identical to that of the Party, at least in the medium term. And the decision on open membership had opened the organisation to whites, coloureds and Indians who, by reason of their generally superior education, could be expected to rise faster than blacks. Once the Party, with its formidable technique of democratic centralism and its Stalinist methods, had got a grip, it would surely proceed to dominate all other tendencies in the ANC. All this was really the consequence of going underground and fighting a guerrilla war, in which the communists' experience and international connections were bound to give the Party added weight. The Party's concentration on developing its strength within Umkhonto we Sizwe, in the belief that this would become the most important department of the ANC, was vindicated. The dissidents were on the receiving end of the classic Marxist-Leninist manipulation of collective decision-making: the packed meeting, the Party caucus, the resolution by acclamation, the technique of democratic centralism whereby a decision, once made by the appropriate body, may no longer be questioned.

In the months after Morogoro relations between the new leadership and the dissidents degenerated. At one stage Mqota wrote a letter to Wilton Mkwayi, the Umkhonto we Sizwe commander until 1964, who was then imprisoned on Robben Island. He told him that the organisation had been taken over by what Mqota termed boys and *tsotsis*. The former was a reference to Moses Mabhida. It is not in the Zulu tradition to require young men, as many other South African peoples do, to undergo a manhood circumcision ritual: the description of Mabhida as an uncircumcised 'boy' was clearly an insult, and a tribal one at that. The mention of *tsotsis*, the township gangsters, was a disparaging reference to Modise who, in his younger days, had a reputation as one of the toughest street-fighters in Alexandra and was even accused by his enemies of having been a member of the notorious Msomi gang. The prison authorities on Robben Island allowed the letter of complaint to reach Mkwayi uncensored, hoping no doubt that his reply might exacerbate the differences in the ANC. But Mkwayi replied with a blanket condemnation of the dissidents.

For six years the feuding between the dissidents and the alliance leadership continued behind closed doors, occasionally surfacing in the form of rumours reported in the press. The length of the dispute is a measure of the degree to which Stalinist principles were still in dispute, and the existence of an organised opposition still possible within the ANC. Eventually the dissidents decided to make a break in public, and they chose the occasion of Robert Resha's funeral in London in 1975 to do so, since Resha had been renowned as a nationalist rather than a communist. Eight ANC members led by Tennyson Makiwane publicly criticised the ANC and attacked the role of communists within it, accusing Tambo of being manipulated by the Party. The thrust of their argument was that non-Africans, organised in the Communist Party, had 'hijacked' the ANC and had changed the nature of the alliance, transforming the struggle from a nationalist into a class one. In the course of carrying out this manoeuvre, they alleged, the communists had suppressed freedom of speech: 'Criticism of official ANC policy and practice has come to be regarded within the leadership circles as nothing less than treason.'[7]

Derided by their critics as the 'Gang of Eight' they were expelled from the ANC in October 1975 for their 'destabilising activities'. In December, the Eight launched a rival organisation which they called ANC (African Nationalists), claiming to represent the true and unadulterated spirit of the ANC, rather as Robert Sobukwe had done in 1959. The Communist Party produced a pamphlet[8] pointing out that, of the eight, two were former Party members, and two had acted as state witnesses in South African trials, portraying them as opportunists motivated only by their own removal from senior office. The breakaway group attracted little support and soon collapsed.

It is impossible to say with certainty whether, if the dissidents had taken their stand at another moment, or in different circumstances, things would have been different. But it is instructive that when a similar thing happened in the Namibian liberation movement,

---

7. *South African Communists Speak*, p. 402.
8. 'The Enemy Hidden Under the Same Colour', *ibid.*, pp. 400–17.

SWAPO, at almost the same time, the breakaway group similarly failed to attract support either in the ranks of the organisation or internationally, despite the strength of its arguments. The time was not ripe. South Africa attracted such strong feelings in the international community that any group fighting the South African government, whether it was the ANC or SWAPO, would always receive international support in the face of an internal revolt, and those in solidarity would instinctively condemn dissenters or critics. So it was inside South Africa too. It was easy to label the rebels as tools of Pretoria, no matter how justified their grievances may have been, and to ignore the substance of their complaints. Moscow, the most powerful international supporter of the ANC-Communist Party alliance, could be relied upon to put its full weight behind the SACP leadership.

All of the so-called 'Gang of Eight' faded into obscurity. In time, their former colleagues in the ANC came to regard seven of the eight without hostility. In 1987, on the occasion of the 75th anniversary of the ANC, there was a general amnesty to all those who had been expelled from the organisation over the years. Ambrose Makiwane continued to be remembered with some affection by the *Mgwenya*, veterans of the Luthuli Detachment of Umkhonto we Sizwe, who remembered with pleasure his celebrated quip: *'Ndibomvu, ndibomvu nomnqundu lo'* – 'I'm red, red, even my arse is red.' He was the only one of the Eight who is known to have been specifically invited to rejoin the ANC in 1987, which he said he would do only if he were restored to his position in the NEC.

There was special animosity towards only one of the Eight - Tennyson Makiwane. He found a job with the Food and Agriculture Organisation of the United Nations, which posted him to Swaziland as its representative. The ANC used its influence to block the appointment, perhaps fearing that Makiwane was of sufficient stature as to do it harm in such a position, or perhaps out of pure vindictiveness. Makiwane was fired by the FAO. Destitute, he moved to Lesotho, and there was contacted by an official of the homeland government of Transkei who persuaded him to come home. Later, ANC sympathisers arrested and interrogated by the Transkei Security Police reported to the organisation that the police seemed to be in possession of information which could only have come from Makiwane. It appeared to some in the ANC that he was not only a dissident but also a police informer. A unit from Umkhonto we Sizwe, acting on its own initiative and certainly without the knowledge of Makiwane's old colleague Oliver Tambo, hunted Makiwane down in Transkei and murdered him there in 1980. Tambo was furious and condemned the murder, but took no disciplinary action. In public, he denied ANC involvement. ANC intelligence chiefs today maintain that Makiwane was recruited as a South African spy as early as 1964, an intriguing allegation but one which remains unproven.

Makiwane failed in his bid to oppose communist influence in the

ANC and the application of sophisticated techniques of central control to stifle dissent, and he failed to have any impact on South African politics after that. But he left at least one important legacy. From the time of his disgrace and eventual murder until 1990, it was strictly taboo within the circles of the ANC, Umkhonto we Sizwe and the Party to refer openly to the role played by the Party within the alliance, or to question the principles of democratic centralism. Some in both the Party and the ANC considered that the Congress had adopted Stalinist methods, and that it had lost touch with its older tradition of free and open debate among the various individuals and schools of thought which had traditionally found expression in the organisation.

Internecine feuds involving dozens rather than hundreds of people, such as those which dogged the ANC throughout the late 1960s and early 1970s, are the stuff of which exile politics are made. The ANC survived this trial well in that it managed to avoid the sort of permanent split which it had suffered when the PAC broke away in 1959, or the total demoralisation which could tempt leaders simply to enrich themselves on organisational funds. Still, the bitter and highly personal quarrels of these years emphasised that the ANC ran the risk of losing all contact with what was actually happening inside South Africa and, like so many exile organisations, becoming fatally introverted. The quarrels in London, Dar es Salaam and Lusaka bore little relation to what was happening inside South Africa, where the tide of black politics was flowing in a different direction and where the intrigues and dialectics of the exiles were little known.

Umkhonto we Sizwe had been virtually inactive since the Wankie campaigns of 1967–8, and the ANC and the Communist Party were in danger of becoming irrelevant in South Africa. A new generation of black activists was emerging who seemed closer to the rival philosophy of Africanism than to the ANC's increasingly Marxist view that the South African question was mainly about class struggle and that the urban working class was the key constituency. Most of the ANC leaders in exile had learned their politics in the 1950s or before, and had left South Africa in the early 1960s. They had lost touch with the extent to which events at home had moved on. After the Rivonia arrests in 1963 apartheid had not stood still. The Pretoria government believed that it had defeated black radicalism and communism for good, and that all that remained was to encourage the development of a separate system of black politics, to be channelled through institutions designed by planners and politicians in Pretoria, whereby black South Africans could express themselves at no risk to whites. This was the doctrine of separate development, whose ultimate form was to be the creation of nominally independent black mini-states known as bantustans or homelands.

The bantustan idea is simple. South African law classified black people according to their supposed tribal identity, as Xhosa, Tswana, Zulu and so on. Each of these groups had occupied land at various periods of time in different parts of South Africa. In the nineteenth century the British colonial government had demarcated rural areas called Native Reserves, occupied by African farmers living under the immediate authority of chiefs who were the descendants of independent kings and traditional authorities of the time before the conquest. Their economy was traditionally based on farming. As South Africa developed an economy of modern mines, factories and services, young men in particular who needed paid work would move to the white cities, work for a season while their families stayed at home in the Reserves, and then go back to the family farm when their contracts were over. Employers paid low wages on the grounds that black workers did not need to support their families, who could live on subsistence farming back in the Native Reserves. The Reserves, in consequence, stayed poor.

After the victory of the National Party in the South African general election of 1948, the government developed this system. Officials paid close attention to the appointment of chiefs in the Native Reserves, intervening to impose their own candidates where necessary and weeding out the more independent chiefs like Albert Luthuli, the ANC President-General from 1952 to 1967. When chiefs were installed with obvious manipulation from Pretoria, they tended to be unpopular and regarded as illegitimate, and might be contested by other members of the local nobility.

The South African Communist Party, committed to the abolition of feudalism, always viewed the arcane politics of chieftaincy disputes with distaste, and generally rather despised the rural areas for their backwardness. Its view was the orthodox communist one that the urban working class was the one with real revolutionary potential. There were only some rural areas, such as the Transkei and Sekhukhuneland, where both the Party and the ANC had traditionally been strong and where communists maintained a close interest. The ANC was more closely attuned to rural politics, not least because it had always contained a number of leaders from prominent families who stayed closely in touch with the politics of their home areas, a good example being Nelson Mandela himself. This has given him a strong following in rural Transkei in addition to his overwhelming nationalist credentials.

For much of the 1950s one of the most prominent architects of apartheid, Dr Hendrik Verwoerd, was Minister of Native Affairs. Applying apartheid to the Native Reserves, he was the leading proponent of the idea of turning them into autonomous states, free to develop according to their own lights under the tutelage of the white race and the benevolent gaze of the Almighty. The theory was that every African person in South Africa belonged to a tribe, and that this tribe had a traditional homeland. (Whites, coloureds and Indians merely had separate 'group areas'.) It was only a question of identifying a person's tribal identity correctly and demarcating the appropriate tribal home. Eventually, every African person would have an identity which would tally with a given area of rural South Africa where he or she would have rights of citizenship. There would be no Africans at all with South African nationality or with permanent rights of residence in the Republic of South Africa. All could work on developing their own mini-states in conformity with their distinctive Xhosa, Zulu, Tswana or other culture. These Africans could find work in South Africa when jobs were available, but strictly on the basis that they were migrant workers.

That is a bald summary of the official theory. A more pointed way of putting it is that Africans would be moved further than ever from the towns and farms of white South Africa and put under the charge of collaborators of their own colour. This would reduce the threat of African people creating disorder, demonstrating or otherwise disturbing the peace in white South Africa and would decentralise the need for repression to places out of sight and out of mind. The only Africans in white South Africa would be either long-distance commuters or temporary migrants who would have to go home as soon as they had finished their contracts.

Although the bantustan policy was never accepted either by most South Africans or by the international community, it was not without its attractions to Africans who aspired to be politicians or who simply wanted to live comfortably. The homelands provided a rich source of patronage and a degree of power for a politician prepared to work within the system. The president or chief minister of a homeland government could build support by employing thousands of people on the government payroll in the ministries, universities, parastatal organisations, army and police which are essential to a modern state, even a pseudo-state. Members of homeland parliaments could compete for available funds to be channelled to their own areas, their own constituencies, or their own pockets. It was not uncommon for officials or politicians in Pretoria to receive a percentage of the proceeds as well. Homeland politicians could use the rhetoric of nationalist politics, appealing to the solidarity of the Zulu, the Xhosa, the Tswana and the rest, and even declare war on other homelands. There was always a touch of Disneyland about homeland politics, calculated to appeal to a white public eager to believe that apartheid was a system not devoid of benevolence and that they were helping to develop independent black states.

All the same, the politics of the homelands were deadly serious. Money and power were at stake. Each homeland authority was endowed with a police force. Some had development corporations to assist and subsidise foreign investment and channel aid money into development projects. In many cases, these turned into bottomless pits of corruption in which the homeland elites immersed themselves, sometimes with the connivance of ministers and officials in Pretoria and in the company of a motley collection of international contractors who scented easy money. The South African taxpayer picked up a large part of the bill run up by the huge development aid grants made by Pretoria.

The homelands offered jobs to black people unable to find decent work in white South Africa. There were openings for the elite of lawyers, doctors and other professionals, people who in earlier times might have been attracted to nationalist politics. In the early days, some black South Africans took at face value the offers of homeland independence and believed that the homeland governments would be allowed to run their own affairs without excessive interference from Pretoria. This turned out to be a naïve supposition, as any serious suggestion of real homeland sovereignty was soon crushed by Pretoria if it threatened the stability of the Republic of South Africa. Some homeland governments were taken over by dictators as corrupt as they were vicious, of whom the Matanzima brothers in Transkei and Lennox Sebe in Ciskei were probably the most notorious. Four homeland governments, Transkei, Ciskei, Bophuthatswana and Venda, opted for formal independence. Six others remained non-independent, and later had to resist pressure from Pretoria for them to accept independence. The case of the KwaZulu homeland was later to show just how meaningless the distinction between independent and non-independent homelands became over time, given that both were dependent on Pretoria and were unsuccessful in securing international recognition.

When Transkei, the birthplace of so many ANC leaders, became the first homeland to declare its independence of South Africa in 1976, many blacks decided that half a loaf was better than none. It was better to have a tinpot government of one's own than no freedom at all. The first President of Transkei was Botha Sigcau, the paramount chief of Eastern Pondoland. He was appointed to woo the Pondos who are important in Transkeian politics by virtue of their sheer numbers. Kaiser Matanzima, a nephew of Nelson Mandela by Tembu custom, but technically a third cousin once removed, became the Prime Minister and the real holder of power. After Sigcau's death, he became President and upgraded the role of his office.

Among the older generation, some former ANC and PAC activists who had grown demoralised after the Rivonia period decided to go and work in the homelands. But already a new generation of black radicals and intellectuals was emerging. Although the Verwoerd government had created a system of Bantu education specifically designed to prepare blacks for a status in life as hewers of wood and drawers of water, and separate Indian and coloured educational systems also greatly inferior to the white system, there remained possibilities for blacks to receive a decent higher education. Fort Hare, the *alma mater* of so many black nationalists in the 1940s and 1950s, still existed. It was still possible for blacks to receive an education at a number of white universities even after the imposition of racial restrictions, or through correspondence courses offered by the University of South Africa. There were other black universities too, pejoratively known as 'bush colleges', such as Turfloop.

The government's ambition was to acquire complete control of black education and subjugate it to the political will of Pretoria. The fact that this was never achieved was in part due to popular resistance movements in black communities, in trade unions, and in places of education. In addition, the complete suppression of modern education for blacks was not in the interests of South African business. Short of skilled labour, white businessmen lobbied the government with requests to provide training for at least some blacks who could fill vacancies as white-collar workers. Moreover, the homelands needed their own elite of professionals who, even if they were to be trained eventually inside the homelands themselves, for the time being could be formed only in South Africa proper. The government was obliged to concede with an increase in spending on black education.

It was at the black colleges and in the black student movement especially that a new school of nationalist thinking developed whose most important strand was the idea of Black Consciousness.[9] This was based on the belief that black people could not expect help of any sort from whites. They must work for their own self-improvement by their own efforts, first and foremost by regaining their self-confidence as a group and rejecting the inferiority which had been thrust upon them by the apartheid government and by whites in general. This new thinking came as a shock in white liberal circles where a paternalistic pride prevailed about the degree to which blacks had benefited from the efforts made by white liberals on their behalf. The National Union of South African Students, for instance, had always taken pride in its multiracial membership and its refusal to adopt apartheid norms. In 1969 a group of black students broke away from the mainstream students' union, insisting on the right of black South Africans to speak on their own behalf, and set up their own all-black South African Students' Organisation, SASO. Among the founders of SASO was a young University of Natal medical student, Steve Biko, who in time came to be considered the leading spokesman of Black Consciousness. He became famous internationally after his death partly through Donald Woods, a white journalist, who wrote extensively about Steve Biko and contributed to the making of the film *Cry Freedom*.

Much of the early influence on Biko and Black Consciousness came from America, where the civil rights movement had been followed by a fashion-conscious 'Black is beautiful' movement. Biko and his friends showed little interest in the ANC, which was effectively dormant inside South Africa, and still less in the Communist Party. If Biko had any knowledge at all of what was going on in the exiled

9. See Gail Gerhart, *Black Power in South Africa: The Evolution of an Ideology* (University of California Press, Berkeley and Los Angeles, 1978).

movement at this time, he showed little sign of it. He considered that the key to political organisation among black South Africans lay in understanding the psychological need they had to become assertive and to throw off attitudes of dependence on whites. Obvious attempts at radical political organisation would in any case rapidly have landed him on Robben Island. One of his prime aims was to restore to blacks a sense of self-esteem and self-confidence which had been severely dented by apartheid.

The reaction of white South Africans to Black Consciousness was frequently one of alarm. Black Conciousness seemed to many whites rather uncomfortably like apartheid in reverse, calling on the black majority to organise their own affairs. Black Consciousness lacked an explicit political programme at the beginning, due to its insistence on the primacy of the need for blacks to regain their cultural pride before they could formulate a strong challenge to the political status quo. Only towards the end of his tragically brief career did Biko begin to entertain ideas about the political order of a post-apartheid South Africa, including some which could be called socialist, and it was this which eventually helped to make Biko attractive to the exiled Communist Party and the ANC.

It was clear that some of the ideas of Black Consciousness were quite similar to the views of the PAC. The PAC position has always been hard to define precisely, but has been characterised by a stance of Africanist populism. When the PAC itself advocated an armed struggle to overthrow the Pretoria government, and made attempts to launch a guerrilla war, the organisation generally claimed that the way to liberate South Africa, or Azania as it called the country, was to concentrate on arming the people, who would then decide for themselves what form the struggle should take and how it should be organised. Under Maoist influence the PAC in exile took a close interest in the South African peasantry. No doubt land-hungry South Africans in the homelands would be attracted by the PAC proposition that the land of Azania belongs to the people, who must fight to retrieve it from the colonisers of the land. Perhaps the PAC's most consistent belief has been that the struggle cannot be led by representatives of the oppressors, which in South Africa means whites, although on one occasion at least the organisation has admitted a white to membership, namely Patrick Duncan.

Although the similarities in thinking between the Black Consciousness intellectuals and the PAC was not lost on officials of the Pretoria government, in the early days of Black Consciousness they hoped that this school of thought could be of service in helping to establish the homelands as legitimate. After all, the homelands were officially considered as offering precisely the opportunity for blacks to organise their own affairs which Black Consciousness adherents advocated. Only from the early 1970s did the state become really hostile to Black Consciousness, seeing that Biko and other student intellectuals of his persuasion were unsympathetic to the homeland governments and that Black Consciousness represented a potential security threat. The Security Police began to clamp down on Black Consciousness and detain its leaders, especially after a serious wave of strikes in 1973 had turned the attention of Black Consciousness activists towards the possibilities of trade unionism.

The instinct of the Communist Party, by now hardly existent inside South Africa, was to regard Black Consciousness as a new and dangerous heresy although, like any movement of resistance to apartheid, it offered potential for the grand nationalist alliance under Party leadership which was the aim of the Communist strategy. On the whole, there was little communication between activists inside the country and the Party or ANC apparatus outside. One of the rare exceptions was the communist Ahmed Timol, spirited out of South Africa for training in the Soviet Union before his murder by the Security Police in 1971. He was actually sent to the prestigious Lenin School in Moscow, which Party members generally believed to be the reason for his death. The Party, encouraged by the 1973 strikes, despatched Chris Hani to Lesotho in 1974, primarily with a view to using his station as a base to build the Party inside South Africa. Hani was already a member of the Central Committee and regarded as a man of the highest calibre. The pool of recruitment for the Party was to be ANC activists who had proven themselves inside the country, plus old Party stalwarts, some of whom had served time on Robben Island and who could be reactivated, as well as any other suitable elements. Umkhonto we Sizwe was incapable of mounting operations inside the country, where it was hardly visible, since it had attempted little since the Wankie campaign. Few recruits were leaving South Africa to join the armed struggle, although there was still a thin trickle. One group which came out of South Africa in 1974 included Keith Mokoape, whose brother Aubrey was a prominent Black Consciousness leader. Keith Mokoape and his fellow-recruits were sent for training in Egypt and the USSR, and the High Command in fact succeeded in infiltrating them back into South Africa on active service. One member of the group, Gwaza Twalo, known as 'Comrade F', a nephew of ANC Secretary-General Alfred Nzo, disappeared inside the country while on a mission. Another member of the same group, 'Comrade D', was blown up by his own bomb in Port Elizabeth. This group was of crucial importance in setting up underground structures inside the country before the Soweto rising of 1976 and in contributing to the later success of ANC operatives in Lesotho under Chris Hani.

There was, then, a small but very precious interaction between the ANC and the Party outside South Africa and the rising generation of young activists, among whom Black Consciousness was the doctrine with the most appeal. Although the exiled headquarters of the alliance was unable to organise on any sort of major scale inside the country, a connection continued to exist through an earlier generation of ANC or Party members, often emerging from prison and returning to the struggle. Joe Gqabi, for example, an early Umkhonto we Sizwe volunteer and a highly respected Party member, was released from prison after 12 years in 1975. He teamed up with other veterans from Robben Island such as John Nkadimeng in the Transvaal, who had become active in the Tobacco Workers' Union in 1948, joining the ANC in 1950 and the SACP in 1953. He was elected to the ANC's National Executive in 1955. Harry Gwala, also a veteran of the Party, was influential in his Natal base during a brief period out of prison between 1972 and 1975, when he was arrested and sentenced to life imprisonment on account of his Umkhonto we Sizwe activities. Gqabi helped develop the South African Students' Movement, a school-students' branch of SASO. He was soon arrested and tried on charges of working for the ANC, but he had played his part in keeping alive the contact between the banned organisations and the younger generation. In general, though, while there was no lack of interesting political developments inside South Africa, the influence of the exiled organisations remained marginal. As always, one of the Party's great strengths was its ability to view developments in their long-term perspective and to keep faith in the eventual, assured victory of the struggle.

While the 1973 strikes and the rise of Black Consciousness offered revolutionary potential, from the headquarters of the triple alliance in Lusaka, the view of the southern African landscape in the mid-1970s showed only one area of really outstanding promise, and this was the international arena. Here, events were working to unhinge the government of Pretoria roughly in line with the predictions made by the Communist Party and the ANC during the Morogoro Conference of 1969, and in a manner appropriate to the strategy mapped out by Joe Slovo in his Strategy and Tactics document and endorsed by the ANC.

The promise lay in the disintegration of the colonial governments on South Africa's borders. The only major European colonial power which remained determined to keep its colonies – after Britain, France and Belgium had all decided to decolonise – was Portugal. The government in Lisbon, one of the last of the European fascist dictatorships to survive, considered its vast colonies in Angola and Mozambique, and smaller possessions in West Africa, to be not overseas dependencies but provinces of metropolitan Portugal. The Lisbon authorities encouraged emigrants from poverty-stricken Portugal to seek their fortunes in Africa. After the Second World War hundreds of thousands of Portuguese had settled in the southern African colonies to try their hand at farming and even at relatively lowly urban trades, as hairdressers, bar-owners, taxi-drivers and so on. The settlers in Angola and Mozambique formed an anti-nationalist buffer to the north of South Africa. Between Mozambique and Angola was Rhodesia, technically a British colony whose British settlers had chosen to set up their own unconstitutional government which would continue white rule in defiance of Westminster. It too served as a buffer on South Africa's borders.

Nationalist movements had emerged in Mozambique, Angola and Rhodesia in the 1960s and turned to a policy of armed struggle, equipped by Chinese or Soviet governments interested in securing their own spheres of influence in Africa. Several systems of alliances connected the various nationalist guerrilla armies and outside powers. The ANC and the SACP had formed particularly close alliances with ZAPU in Rhodesia, under Joshua Nkomo, and with the Popular Movement for the Liberation of Angola (MPLA), the latter heavily influenced by the Portuguese Communist Party. MPLA intellectuals like Agostinho Neto enjoyed good personal relations with South African communists. Some MPLA and ANC people had become acquainted when they attended the same colleges, like Tony Mongalo of the SACP and José Eduardo dos Santos, later to be president of Angola. Both trained as engineers at the same school in the Soviet Union. Both ZAPU and the MPLA enjoyed the support of the Soviet Union, not least because of the recommendations which Soviet policy-makers received from South African communists, the regional allies most respected in Moscow.

Strategists in both the South African Defence Force (SADF) and in Umkhonto we Sizwe were well aware of the close connection between the liberation of South Africa and events in neighbouring states. Rhodesia, Angola and Mozambique were vital bulwarks defending South Africa itself against armed insurrection. The first time that the South African security forces gave military help to a northern neighbour in a war against nationalist guerrillas was during the Wankie campaign of 1967. The expertise in counter-insurgency developed by the South African security forces was to prove invaluable in later years when Angola, Zimbabwe and Mozambique had become enemies of Pretoria. The paramilitary unit Koevoet, which became notorious for its extreme brutality in torturing and killing villagers in the north of Namibia, was formed by South African policemen who had served in Rhodesia and had learned some of the gruesome techniques of counter-insurgency warfare from their Rhodesian counterparts. Not only did South African personnel gain first-hand knowledge of the terrain and conditions in neighbouring countries, but senior officers developed relationships which were to prove useful in the later destabilisation of Angola, Zimbabwe and Mozambique. Brigadier Charles van Niekerk of the SADF, for example, served as a liaison officer with the Portuguese colonial army in Mozambique in the early 1970s. After 1980 he became the liaison officer between the SADF and the anti-government Mozambique Resistance Movement (RENAMO) which was to be Pretoria's principal means of attacking Mozambique.

In 1974 the dictatorship in Portugal collapsed as a direct result of the financial and human cost of its African wars. It was evident that the new government in Portugal would have no choice but to call a halt to the wars in Angola and Mozambique, and that the colonial authorities would have to hand over the governments in Lourenço Marques and Luanda to one or other of the nationalist movements. In Mozambique there was only one serious nationalist movement, FRELIMO. In Angola, there were three, which complicated matters. In 1975, FRELIMO duly took over the government of independent Mozambique; in Angola, a fragile transitional government was shared between three nationalist parties, but collapsed before independence.

Black South Africans, even those who had never travelled and had only the vaguest knowledge of international affairs, could not help but be aware of the implications as they heard news of the unfolding events on their borders. Many naturally made a comparison between the nationalist victories to the north and their own aspirations. The triumph of the Mozambican liberation movement FRELIMO, in particular, inspired great interest and admiration among young black South Africans – not least, perhaps, because of the closeness of Maputo (the former Lourenço Marques) to the South African border, and because of the large numbers of Mozambicans who worked in South Africa's mines. Some young South Africans organised pro-FRELIMO rallies in 1975 which earned them prison sentences on Robben Island. They included Patrick 'Terror' Lekota, later to become a stalwart of the UDF and the ANC, Saths Cooper, later president of AZAPO, and Aubrey Mokoape, whose brother briefly served as deputy chief of military intelligence for Umkhonto we Sizwe.

In Pretoria, political and security chiefs braced themselves for the fall of their two Portuguese neighbours. Prime Minister Vorster and the secret service chief Hendrik van den Bergh devised a strategy of détente in preparation for what was to come. The idea was to develop a better relationship with black Africa as a whole, in the hope that they could then persuade the incoming governments of Angola and Mozambique to live in peace with South Africa, within the framework of a larger regional peace plan. They began an extensive round of diplomacy, part secret, part open, designed to implement the détente policy. Vorster and Van den Bergh made some progress, notably with Zambia's President Kenneth Kaunda, regarded as the key black leader in the southern Africa region since he played host to both the ANC and ZAPU, and was on reasonable terms with both the British and the Soviets.

In retrospect, Pretoria's exercise in détente was never a likely success. The combined international opposition was too strong. Nationalist movements throughout southern Africa, and like them, the Soviet government, were confident that white rule was doomed on the continent, and had little reason to come to terms with Pretoria. In the event, developments in Angola finally put the whole plan to rest and drew the USA directly into the equation for the first time. For the US government, 1975 was a disastrous year. First and foremost this was because of the fall of Saigon to the North Vietnamese Army and the realisation that the most powerful country in the world had not only lost a war against a Third World country, but against a Soviet ally. Hardliners in the US administration, led by Henry Kissinger, decided that it was necessary to demonstrate that the USA had not lost its resolve to fight.[10] It was a tragedy for the people of Angola that they happened to win their independence at this moment. Angola gained the unfortunate distinction of being the theatre in which the US government would begin to defend its reputation by demonstrating that it was resolved to resist further expansion by Soviet allies in the Third World. Without informing the US Congress, Kissinger ordered the CIA to support two of the Angolan nationalist movements, first the FNLA, the National Front for the Liberation of Angola, and then UNITA, the National Union for the Total Independence of Angola, so as to prevent the pro-Soviet MPLA from taking complete control at independence. When the FNLA collapsed, and the MPLA was on the way to gaining international recognition as the legitimate government of Angola, the CIA concentrated on backing UNITA in order to keep the new government under pressure. Already, even before Angolan independence, the UNITA leader Jonas Savimbi had made contact with South African Prime Minister John Vorster with a view to building an alliance. Now Cuba, anxious to uphold the cause of socialism in the world, and with the approval of the Soviet Union, sent an expeditionary force to fight in Angola on the side of the embattled MPLA. By the end of 1975, the superpowers were fighting a proxy war in Angola.

Washington encouraged the South African government of John Vorster to join this venture in spite of Vorster's reluctance to commit his army in Angola, hundreds of miles from the South African border. Vorster was eventually persuaded to do so only in the belief that he had enough support from Washington to make a rapid intervention effective. He had secured the cooperation of Kenneth Kaunda, the Zambian president who was also uneasy about the installation of a pro-Soviet government in Angola. With Zambia and the USA on his side, Vorster was confident that the SADF could carry out its task of installing a pro-Western government in Luanda.

In August 1975, while the CIA was arming its allies in Angola and almost at the same time that Prime Minister Vorster and President Kaunda were locked in secret talks in a railway carriage parked on a bridge over the Victoria Falls, the SADF crept over the border into Angola. Two months later a South African armoured column with air support headed for Luanda. Kaunda played his part by channelling arms to UNITA and even persuaded SWAPO, the Namibian guerrilla

10. An illuminating account of US official thinking on southern Africa at this time is provided by the former chief of the CIA operation in Angola: John Stockwell, *In Search of Enemies* (W.W. Norton & Co., New York, 1978).

movement then based in Lusaka, to cooperate, so that SWAPO and Pretoria actually found themselves fighting on the same side for a short time.[11] The same combination of interests included South Africa, Zambia, and the CIA, with the FNLA and UNITA as their local allies. Pitched against them were only the MPLA in Luanda, backed by Cuban forces and with Soviet support. Success seemed guaranteed.

It was at this juncture that the American government lost its nerve. Cuban artillery halted a South African column almost on the outskirts of Luanda. Meanwhile the US Congress, still unsettled by the fall of Richard Nixon and by revelations of illegal operations by the CIA, discovered that the CIA was involved in yet another secret war and ordered the intervention in Angola to cease. The US administration duly withdrew from the bargain it had struck with Prime Minister Vorster, leaving the SADF no alternative but to withdraw from Angola and leave Luanda in the hands of an MPLA government. Many South African army officers have never forgiven the USA for that betrayal to this day. The international intervention in Angola was to remain stalemated until 1988, and the civil war was to continue into 1991.

If strategists in Pretoria had foreseen the collapse of the colonial governments in Angola and Mozambique, so had Umkhonto we Sizwe strategists in the Revolutionary Council and the High Command. They had long predicted this development as a step towards the eventual liberation of South Africa itself. Although Umkhonto we Sizwe was still incapable of significant action inside South Africa, even before the Portuguese had packed their bags in Angola and Mozambique the Umkhonto we Sizwe High Command was putting in place its first really effective command structure on South Africa's borders. Chris Hani, not yet a member of the High Command but already with a reputation as a fearless fighter and a rising star of the Communist Party, established himself in Lesotho in 1974. In the same year he was appointed a member of the ANC's National Executive at an exceptionally young age. He demonstrated the bravado for which he was already well known by travelling right across South Africa to reach his new station in Lesotho. Joe Slovo, the Umkhonto we Sizwe Chief of Staff and leading strategist, installed himself in Maputo soon after Mozambique's independence. Due to its proximity to South Africa's industrial heartland in the Transvaal, it was considered the best site for an Umkhonto we Sizwe forward base from which the infiltration of South Africa would be masterminded. Other key Umkhonto we Sizwe personnel who set up clandestine networks in newly independent neighbouring states included Stanley Mabizela in Swaziland and Marius Schoon in Botswana. All were members of the Communist Party. All except Schoon were eventually to gain election to the ANC's NEC. Marius Schoon retired from the fray when he went

---

11. Andreas Shipanga, *In Search of Freedom* (Ashanti Publishing, Gibraltar, 1989), pp. 114–9.

to teach at the ANC school in Tanzania and thence was posted to Europe. His wife, also a leading activist, and their child, were blown up by a parcel-bomb in Lubango in 1984. The bomb was sent by a South African Police death squad, as one of its members later revealed.[12]

By the end of 1975 developments in the international sphere were inauspicious for the South African government. A radical and pro-Soviet government held the reins in Angola and was host to a sizeable contingent of Cuban troops. Angola shared a border with Namibia, which was clearly destined to be South Africa's next line of defence against attacks mounted from external bases. Mozambique was less of a worry because its government was heavily involved in fighting against Ian Smith's Rhodesians. South Africa and Rhodesia were now the last white states in Africa, while Namibia continued to be administered effectively as a province of South Africa in spite of its status as a United Nations' trust territory. And they were encircled by hostile states friendly to the South African liberation movements and armed by the Soviet Union.

12. *The Independent,* 20 November 1989.

4
From Soweto
to Angola
1976-9

Despite its failure to install a government of its own choice in Angola, and the generally ominous turn of events throughout southern Africa, John Vorster's government remained supremely confident of its internal position. Politicians and security chiefs believed that they had crushed the black nationalist movements, and black radicalism generally, in the previous decade. Hence the importance of neutralising the threat from without. If that too could be mastered, they thought, then South Africa would remain impregnable.

This confidence was widespread among white South Africans. In the previous decade they had seen remarkable economic growth, and the old antagonism between English-speaking whites and Afrikaners had lost much of its venom. Nevertheless, government stayed firmly in Afrikaner hands. The dominant political style was still not far removed from the old-fashioned, Bible-quoting Calvinist fundamentalism of D.F. Malan, the first National Party prime minister. Leaders of the National Party still liked to represent themselves as honest Afrikaner frontiersmen, simple and God-fearing, beacons of light and godliness in a dark continent. The fact was, however, that the South Africa of 1976 was governed by the leaders of a political party ensconced in power for 28 years, enjoying the fruits and privileges of power. Afrikaner politicians had become well-versed in the ways of international relations, so frequently marked by duplicity, so different from the values of Old Testament patriarchs. They believed that they had created the modern South Africa, but they knew well enough that the extraordinary economic growth their country had enjoyed since South Africa had acquired republican status depended on foreign investment and on the profitability of South African business, and that this in turn depended on cheap labour and political stability.

The leaders of the National Party realised, too, that an uneducated black public was easier to dominate than an educated one, but in spite of this the government had been obliged regularly to concede the demands of South African businessmen for more skilled labour and better job training for blacks. And yet so complacent had the white public become that political leaders and planners were confident they could tailor the black education system to their requirements without provoking any serious revival of the black nationalism which they had crushed in 1960–3.

Few people in positions of authority appreciated the depth of feeling which existed under the surface calm in black society, and especially among the younger generation. A new generation had arisen which had no personal memory of the nationalist movement of the 1950s and of the reverses it had suffered. Some were in the unstable position of having acquired just enough freedom of action and education to make them resentful of their circumstances and aware of some of their possibilities, but who could see little prospect of improvement through any official channel.

It was at this point, in 1976, that the government decided to introduce a new measure in black high schools, giving Afrikaans equal weight to English as a language of instruction in those areas where English only was in use. The person responsible for implementing this policy was an able and earnest former minister of the church, Dr Andries Treurnicht, the Deputy Minister for Bantu Administration and Education and a past Chairman of the Broederbond, the powerful secret society dedicated to the preservation of the Afrikaans language and Afrikaner nationalism. Treurnicht, today the leader of the Conservative Party, represented a strain of Afrikaner nationalism which was already looking old-fashioned in 1976. His ideology was, and is, based on a racialist interpretation of the Bible and a deep attachment to the Afrikaans language and Afrikaner nationalism.

Treurnicht's idea was to promote Afrikaans as a medium of instruction in black schools, even in sciences and technical subjects, so that a generation of black South Africans would grow up using Afrikaans rather than English as their common language. This conformed to the National Party and Broederbond programme of making Afrikaner culture dominant in South Africa, and not allowing the country to become anglicised in its speech. But Afrikaans was widely regarded, by those on whom it was to be imposed, as educationally disadvantageous and, moreover, as the language of the oppressor. The proposal provoked immediate resistance. According to opinion polls, the vast majority of blacks disagreed with the proposal to impose Afrikaans as a medium of instruction in schools which previously had taught in English.

The new language proposal provoked unrest especially among school students in the Soweto townships outside Johannesburg, a vast jerry-built city which was home to a million or more people, then living without security of tenure and often without the most basic amenities of water and electricity. Throughout May and early June, the Soweto schools were the scene of angry demonstrations. Policemen who went to the schools were attacked with stones. They responded in their usual muscular fashion.

The rioting which followed the first clashes between schoolchildren and policemen was splashed across the front pages of the world's newspapers and on television screens, the most damning images of South Africa since Sharpeville in 1960. Thousands of newspaper articles told of attacks by stone-throwing youths on the police, on other objects of hatred, or on random targets. Thousands more told of police counter-action, which included shooting into crowds with live ammunition. Participants told their tales. Among many accounts the following, from a boy named Petrus, then a Form II student at Madibane High School, could be considered fairly typical:[1]

A week before 16th June, the principal told us that we had to learn in Afrikaans. We felt angry because we did not understand Afrikaans well. How could we learn in Afrikaans? We had meetings at school. Then we decided to come together with other schools. All the students agreed – no Afrikaans.

On 15th June we went from school to school, telling students to join the march the next day. On the 16th we never went to classes. We went to meet the Morris Isaacson students. But they had to pass the Meadowlands Police Station and we had to pass the Orlando Police Station.

We never met. The police stopped the students from 'deep Soweto'. The Diepkloof students split up in Orlando East. Taxi drivers told us that the police had stopped the other students.

The next day we went to school, but we had no lessons. We got a message from the other Diepkloof schools to meet them. So we marched again. Some people wanted to attack bottle stores on the way. Students felt that liquor was killing our people.

But then some students said we must meet with the students from other schools. Together we must decide what to attack. So we marched to Orlando. On the way we stoned WRAB [West Rand Administration Board] offices. The police came. Some people ran away but others were caught.

I was caught.

On 16 June 1976 thousands of schoolchildren assembled in Soweto to march to Orlando West Junior Secondary School, where the main boycott had begun in the previous month. There had been more and more ugly incidents in the previous days, with police cars coming under attack from stone-throwing youths when they appeared on school premises to arrest strikeleaders. By 16 June the police had decided that the time had come to start shooting. A police cordon, armed with machine-guns as well as with the more usual riot equipment, opened fire on the schoolchildren's demonstration, killing 25 people and injuring 200, according to the police figures. The real totals may have been much higher.

Instead of dispersing to their homes, the thousands of youths who had been marching and demonstrating ran from the police lines and swept through Soweto, attacking government offices and bottle stores especially. Hundreds of citizens of Soweto lost property or were injured by mobs. Nevertheless, it was apparent that the insurgents were not utterly indiscriminate in their violence and were not motivated solely by criminal impulses, although there were no doubt

1. *Learn and Teach* (Johannesburg), 4, 1986.

plenty of young thugs who used the occasion as cover for looting. Many youngsters were convinced that they were making a revolution, and they singled out for attack the symbols of white domination. The schoolchildren had decided that they were not going to be like their parents' generation, resigned to their low status and powerlessness and drowning their sorrows in the cheap alcohol of the bottle stores and shebeens.

The Soweto police, overwhelmed by the ferocity of the 16 June demonstrations, called for reinforcements. Fresh police contingents arrived under the command of Brigadier Theunis Swanepoel, a Security Police interrogator soon to be dubbed by the press 'the butcher of Soweto' for reasons which need little explanation. It is worthy of note that, since his retirement from the police force, Swanepoel has gone into politics. He is one of several former security officers of that era who have since stood for public election as candidates for Dr Treurnicht's Conservative Party. Another is Hendrik van den Bergh, the former head of the secret service.

Throughout the second half of 1976, the riots spread to Cape Town, the cities of the Eastern Cape, and other urban areas – leaving only Durban, of all South Africa's cities, relatively unscathed. The students adopted more sophisticated tactics as time went on, switching to strikes rather than marches or stone-throwing. But they were no match for the riot police. By Christmas the trouble had died down. Probably about 700 people died between June 1976 and February 1977, and at least 4,000 were injured. Six thousand were arrested. Many of the insurgents, and consequently many of those killed, wounded or detained, were little more than children.

Images of insurrection and the response of the police were beamed from South Africa into living-rooms around the world. Viewers all over the Western world, initiated into real-life screen violence by the shocking newsreel coverage of the Vietnam war, were now introduced to a new battlefield about which they had previously known virtually nothing. The foreign investors who provided much of the money to keep South Africa's mines working became thoroughly nervous. Mining is a capital-intensive business which requires substantial initial investment, recouped only after a mine has been developed and has produced profits for some years. It is no business for exponents of short-term investment, and the image of political instability which South Africa presented was particularly harmful to the mining industry.

Not all businessmen in South Africa, or with money invested there, were concerned with the mining sector. During the boom of the 1960s and 1970s, the economy had diversified to manufacture goods for a consumer market not only in South Africa itself but throughout the countries to the north, as well as to provide services for the five million or so white South Africans and the rather smaller market consisting of blacks who had money to spend on consumer goods, leisure and services. Even in light manufacturing, investors will normally look for a return on their capital over a period of 10 years or more. It was evident to anyone watching the events in Soweto, even on television, that South Africa had serious political and social problems and that its political stability over the next decade was less than assured. There was an investment slump. Also oil prices had rocketted.

A great deal has now been written about the 1976 insurrection, quite apart from the newspaper reports which appeared at the time.[2] With every year that passes, and every new perspective offered on these events, their importance is confirmed as the point at which the economic boom of the 1960s began to look sluggish, and after which even the less perceptive could see that time was running out for the apartheid system. Black people had discovered their muscle and were never more to be as quiescent as they had been in the previous fifteen years. A generation of future activists had its first taste of action in 1976.

It is generally agreed that the 1976 rising was spontaneous and that it was sparked off in the first instance by the language issue. Claims that the rising was the product of a political conspiracy, whether made by those seeking to portray anti-government agitation as the result of external aggression, or by political actors claiming credit, provide little explanation. It is true that many of those taking to the streets had been influenced by Black Consciousness ideas, and that the philosophy of Black Consciousness and black pride were important in explaining the background to the rising. It is also true that individual ANC or Communist Party members still living inside South Africa had contacts in Soweto and may have been in touch with small groups of participants. The previous year a PAC underground cell had been arrested and was eventually convicted of preparing acts of sabotage, showing that the PAC had been active in some townships. But such contacts were only of minor importance in accounting for the turn of events. Few of those who took to the streets of Soweto seem to have had more than the most rudimentary awareness of organisations such as the ANC, the PAC and the Communist Party. Murphy Morobe, who was one of thousands of student activists in 1976 and who went on to become a leader of the UDF, maintained that 'We thought we were the first people to fight the government. We did not know about the Defiance Campaign and the school boycotts in the 1950s.'[3] That gives some idea of how completely the nationalist organisations had been eclipsed since they were forced into exile sixteen years earlier.

2. See, for example, Baruch Hirson, *Year of Fire, Year of Ash* (Zed Press, London, 1979); Alan Brooks and Jeremy Brickhill, *Whirlwind before the Storm* (International Defence and Aid Fund for Southern Africa, London, 1980). R.W. Johnson, *How Long Will South Africa Survive?* (Oxford University Press, New York, 1977) situates the Soweto revolt in its diplomatic and economic context.

3. *Learn and Teach*, 4, 1986.

The fact that the Soweto rising was spontaneous gave little cause of satisfaction to government security chiefs. They now realised that they had not destroyed black radicalism, as they had hoped, but that it seemed to have developed a hold on each new generation, developing new strains and becoming resistant to previous forms of treatment, like a virus. Black Consciousness was clearly a dangerous philosophy. Moreover, as with Sharpeville in 1960, the Soweto rising seemed to demonstrate the conjuncture of local and international events feeding off one another. The Soweto rising occurred less than one year after the victory of guerrilla movements in Angola and Mozambique. Schoolchildren were mouthing revolutionary slogans they hardly understood. The Portuguese 'Viva!' was co-opted by South African radicals and became part of the South African vocabulary.

For exiled political organisations, of course, the Soweto risings were enormously encouraging. At long last there were signs of real crisis inside the country, providing new material with which to work and new hope. The problem which presented itself to exiled revolutionaries was precisely how to make contact with the student insurgents, given the pervasive police repression, and how to recruit them to existing organisations and prevent them from channelling their energies into new directions, further splitting the nationalist or revolutionary movement. In as much as the insurgents of the Soweto generation had any political philosophy or organisation, it was Black Consciousness. And if there was any prospect of the students of 1976 joining one of the banned organisations, their natural home was the PAC. But the PAC had for years been riven by internal disputes and, since the arrest of Zephaniah Mothopeng and the core of its underground the previous year, it was in no position to welcome the students into any sort of organisation.

The ANC, on the other hand, was well organised and had a coherent strategy, thanks largely to the strategists and operatives of Umkhonto we Sizwe, and especially the communists who manned the Revolutionary Council and had set up Umkhonto we Sizwe offices in countries neighbouring South Africa. Within a short time of the riots erupting, Umkhonto we Sizwe officers in Lesotho, Botswana and Swaziland had begun to make contact with student activists, urging them to leave the country and join the ANC in exile. Teenagers who had taken part in the rising in Soweto, and had been detained, tortured or tear-gassed, wanted above all to get hold of guns and have some military training. The more thoughtful may also have realised that they needed to connect with an effective organisation which had a sense of broader strategy. As many as 4,000 men and women had left South Africa by early 1977, most of them determined to find arms and to return to the country as soon as possible to carry on the fight. The vast majority were steered adroitly in the direction of the ANC's headquarters in exile by Chris Hani in Lesotho, Marius Schoon in Botswana and Stanley Mabizela in Swaziland. Most believed that they would be back with Kalashnikovs within six months. At the beginning of 1991 many were still abroad, older and wiser, without having set foot in their homeland for 15 years.

The PAC missed a historic opportunity in failing to recruit the Soweto militants. That the ANC succeeded where its pan-Africanist rival failed was due to its superior organisation, connections and sense of strategy, which were in large degree the products of its alliance with the Communist Party. The independent governments of Angola and Mozambique had both allied themselves with the Soviet Union, which made them natural allies of the ANC and the SACP. As early as 1976, just one year after the independence of Angola, the ANC had acquired a training school for engineers in Luanda, and training camps for guerrillas at Fundo and Nova Katenga, to which it directed its new recruits. By 1978 it had opened additional camps at Viana, Quibaxe, Pango and Quatro in Angola, the latter used as a detention centre for ANC cadres who had transgressed the organisation's disciplinary rules. Thanks to the Party's contacts especially, it was possible to make agreements with governments in Eastern Europe for regular training-courses for new recruits.

At home, the Security Police began a campaign against the Black Consciousness organisations whose influence had helped inspire the 1976 troubles, detaining large numbers of activists and using torture on a scale greater than anything previously seen in South Africa. The experience of detention and torture further radicalised some, while the banning of their organisations sent them on a search for new political homes and new ideas. Some Black Consciousness firebrands eventually decided to align with the ANC, in most cases because it was simply the most solid organisation available. Many former Black Consciousness intellectuals in time also came round to the view that the ANC and the Communist Party were right in thinking that the South African problem was at heart one of class. Steve Biko had always been aware of the class factor existing alongside the race one, but he thought that the race issue had far more revolutionary potential. By the mid-1970s he, and many others, felt that the unity of the main black opposition organisations was a high priority, and he was working for this in the last years of his life. He was in communication with underground members of the ANC inside South Africa in the last months before he was beaten to death by the Security Police in September 1977. The Justice Minister who displayed such public contempt for Biko after his death, Jimmy Kruger, told journalists at the time that Biko was a communist.[4] It wasn't true.

There were several cases of activists formerly influenced by Black Consciousness aligning themselves with the ANC in the aftermath of the Soweto rising. Among the best-known was Curtis Nkondo, the first president of the Azanian People's Organisation (AZAPO), the

4. Recollection by John Burns, then the *New York Times* correspondent.

flagship of Black Consciousness after Biko's death. Nkondo had two brothers in the ANC and was appointed to the presidency of AZAPO as a popular figurehead by Black Consciousness adherents who thought he would adapt to their way of thinking. He was suspended after members of AZAPO grew suspicious of his ANC sympathies and accused him of retaining the presidency of the organisation only in order to try and steer it into alliance with the ANC. He was then banned by Pretoria and subsequently left the organisation. Jackie Selebe was another who rose through the strongly Black Consciousness Soweto civic organisations, but then joined the ANC and went into exile. In 1988 he was appointed to the NEC. Newspaper editor Zwelakhe Sisulu was another Black Consciousness intellectual who later declared his open support of the Freedom Charter, the symbol of ANC allegiance. Those who continued to espouse Black Consciousness and to reject the Freedom Charter were not only concerned for the independence of their organisations, but tended to see in the Communist Party the hidden hand of domination by whites, just as the PAC founders and the Gang of Eight had done in their time.

One of the most important political finishing-schools was Robben Island prison. Young Black Consciousness and pro-PAC militants arrived there to be confronted by the older prisoners, dominated by Nelson Mandela and his generation of activists. There were plenty of PAC militants who went to Robben Island in the 1960s and remained unswerving in their loyalties, later coming out of prison to constitute the internal leadership of the PAC. There were also Black Consciousness adherents, like Saths Cooper, who refused to align with the ANC, but rather more Black Consciousness supporters were won over to the ANC line and acceptance of the Freedom Charter, the basic manifesto of the Congress alliance, while they were on the Island. On occasion there were fist-fights between rival groups among the prisoners, just as there were later to be terrible battles between rival political groups in some townships. It was not unknown, either, for common-law prisoners to be converted to the ANC while on Robben Island. One such recruit was Joe Zungu, convicted and sent to the Island for membership of a gang of armed robbers known as the Big Five. Once on Robben Island, Zungu was converted by some of the ANC politicals, of whom the most active among the younger generation was Steve Tshwete, a Communist Party member later to be the political commissar of Umkhonto we Sizwe for a brief period. Tshwete converted Zungu into becoming an ANC supporter and in time Zungu became the leading ANC enforcer on Robben Island. After his release, Zungu, known on the Island as 'Main *Ou*' ('Main Man') because of his pugilistic skills, was made the ANC chief of security in Botswana. He was later asked to leave the country by the Botswana government and was appointed the head of the ANC security organisation, Mbokodo, in Lusaka. Here he acquired a new nickname, 'Joe my Baby', due to his habit of referring to female comrades as 'my baby'.

While Robben Island prison played a substantial role in forming a new generation of ANC members, the most important training was taking place in Angola. The problem facing the Party and the leadership of Umkhonto we Sizwe, after it had begun recruiting refugees from the 1976 rising as they fled abroad, was how to turn thousands of raw recruits not just into guerrilla fighters but into politically responsible cadres who would follow the political line laid down by the High Command and the Revolutionary Council. This had to be achieved without diluting the ideological purity which the SACP had attempted to instil in Umkhonto we Sizwe or, more prosaically, without provoking disagreements or splits which could take a particularly dangerous form once the rank and file were armed. The example of Tennyson Makiwane and the Gang of Eight was still fresh in people's minds.

The Party's and the ANC's response to this problem of education was to form a corps of political commissars, Communist Party members who would be attached to the various units and training centres of Umkhonto we Sizwe so as to teach new recruits that planting bombs or wielding an AK–47 was of no value unless it was in the service of a clear and coherent political strategy. The strategy in question was the one laid down by the ANC's Morogoro Conference, a watered-down version of the Party programme, guided by the principles of Marxism-Leninism. At the same time as the Party helped establish the system of commissars, it was on the lookout to recruit the most promising of the youngsters to its own ranks, with a view to sending them to Eastern Europe for special training.

This was not the first time that the ANC had appointed a political commissar. Flag Boshielo had been the Umkhonto we Sizwe commissar, the only person in the ANC to have that title, in the 1960s, but he was not immediately replaced after he had 'disappeared' in Rhodesia in 1970. Only in 1976 did the ANC create a post of National Commissar. The job went to Andrew Masondo, a member of the Communist Party Central Committee newly released from Robben Island. Masondo was a mathematician by profession, a former lecturer at Fort Hare, who had been imprisoned for membership of Umkhonto we Sizwe. He had had to endure exceptionally harsh treatment and humiliation during his time on Robben Island, but had borne his sufferings with dignity and fortitude.

Of the Angolan camps which the ANC had at its disposal, the most important was at Nova Katenga in southern Angola. So many new recruits were sent for military and political training there that it became known as 'the University of the South'. It was here more than anywhere else that the commissars had to ensure the correct development of their charges. The South African chiefs of staff were well aware of the importance of Nova Katenga Camp as a training ground for guerrillas. They destroyed it in an air raid on 14 March 1979.[5]

5. Recalled by camp inmate Amos Maxongo in a speech in London, 26 April 1991.

The person appointed as the first political Commissar of Nova Katenga, responsible for licking the new recruits into political shape, was Francis Meli. Born in East London in 1942, Meli was trained as a historian at the University of Leipzig in East Germany, choosing the history of the Comintern as his thesis topic, and had impeccably orthodox Marxist credentials. He combined the attributes of youth, background knowledge and ideological correctness – he was later a member of the SACP Central Committee – which would equip him to deal with the new recruits in Nova Katenga in a satisfactory manner. Already Meli had a reputation as an expert on the national question, in other words the problem of how to reconcile disparate national or ethnic groups in a socialist state. In this, as in many other things, Meli was a fervent disciple of Stalin. The SACP has traditionally considered that if there was one sphere in which Joseph Stalin may be said to have had the correct approach in the Soviet Union, it was in successfully incorporating all the diverse nationalities of the USSR into a socialist state. This belief was never shaken in the SACP until the outbreak of nationalist dissent in recent years indicated the limits of Stalin's achievement.

After a year in Nova Katenga, Meli was appointed editor of the ANC's theoretical journal *Sechaba*, one of the main vehicles for debate on the all-important national question. He went on to become one of the Party's leading theoreticians, usually writing under the pseudonyms Phineas Malinga and Nyawuza. Removed from the Party Central Committee on account of his alcoholism, and eventually put under investigation by a Party committee because of his lapses in preserving Party security, Meli died in Johannesburg in 1990, a broken man, just a few days after returning from exile. Meli was succeeded as the commissar at Nova Katenga by Mark Shope, formerly General Secretary of the South African Congress of Trade Unions, the trade union wing of the triple alliance which also included the ANC and the Communist Party. Later, Professor Jack Simons, one of the leading lights of the SACP for over half a century, came to assist with a special political programme.

The institution of commissars, or political officers, has a long pedigree in Marxist-Leninist theory. The idea was originally implemented by Lenin in the Soviet Union to dilute the influence of Czarist officers at a time when the Red Army was still young and of doubtful political loyalty. Revived by the ANC in Nova Katenga camp, commissars were soon being appointed throughout the ANC. Within a short time there were Communist Party commissars overseeing the whole spectrum of ANC life. Many ANC organs, student bodies or professional groups acquired their commissar, extending the Party's influence from the army to other parts of the ANC. As talent-scouts, the commissars were also looking for promising candidates for recruitment to the Party. Although the older generation of communists – people like Joe Slovo, Moses Mabhida, or Jack Simons – were well known as Party members, membership generally continued to be secret even to ANC members. As younger recruits were brought into the Party, it was not known to ordinary ANC members who was a Party member and who was not. The fact that it tended to be the best people who were asked to join the Party reinforced the Party's reputation in ANC circles as the elite, the secret society whose members were on the whole the best, the bravest and the most dedicated revolutionaries. They were subject to the Party's own code of discipline as well as that of the ANC as a whole. Party members were expected to lead exemplary lives, refraining from excessive drinking or sexual misconduct. This somewhat puritanical zeal also became a wider rule, so that the ANC, for example, reserved the right to approve marriages by its members in the camps and adopted a censorious official attitude to the personal lives of its cadres.

It was also in southern Angola that the ANC came into closer contact with SWAPO, the Namibian liberation movement which had been established by Namibian migrants in Cape Town in the late 1950s. Some of SWAPO's founders had been close to South African communists at first, and SWAPO, the ANC and the Party obviously had a good deal in common to the extent that they were fighting a common enemy. But, after the early days, South African communists had taken their distance from SWAPO because of the rather erratic positions it had adopted over the years and because, unlike other liberation movements with which the ANC was in alliance, it lacked a really solid Moscow connection. They may also have been rather jealous of the large sums of money SWAPO received from the United Nations, which made SWAPO financially independent. Sam Nujoma's organisation, at first based in Tanzania, had moved to Lusaka and compromised dangerously with the Vorster-Kaunda-Kissinger plan to invade Angola in 1975. Only after Angolan independence did SWAPO move to Luanda, partly as a result of interventions on SWAPO's behalf by Oliver Tambo and Joe Slovo, the latter being personally close to both the MPLA President Agostinho Neto and the MPLA's leading ideologue, Lucio Lara. The Angolans were angry over SWAPO's manoeuvres against the MPLA, and were unwilling to grant the organisation bases in Angola. They were persuaded to do so largely by these two senior ANC men, who realised the importance of having SWAPO harass the SADF in northern Nambia, diverting its energies and resources from the South African theatre. SWAPO was duly granted bases in Angola, and in course of time it adopted a Marxist rhetoric in line with that of its hosts.

It was in the military field that SWAPO seemed to offer the greatest promise as far as the ANC was concerned. With the liberation of Angola, SWAPO had the opportunity to set up bases in southern Angola and infiltrate its guerrillas into Namibia over a long border, and to get to grips directly with the enemy. The Namibian border was the weak link in South Africa's defences. Pretoria recognised this threat by systematically sending its most promising officers to command positions in Namibia where they could experience real war at first hand. The Namibian command became a stepping-stone to a top job as head of the South African army or even of the entire SADF.

The military line-up in Angola evolved rapidly after the abortive South African invasion of 1975. ANC and SWAPO guerrillas were welcomed by the MPLA, the most orthodox Marxist-Leninist party in power in southern Africa, backed by thousands of Cuban troops, with strong Soviet material support. Pretoria was often at loggerheads with the Americans during the years of Jimmy Carter's presidency, from 1976 to 1980. He was notably more hostile to South Africa and Rhodesia than his predecessors, although the US Department of Defence and the CIA continued to do their best to help the South Africans counter the pro-Soviet forces in Angola. Of the anti-government groups in Angola, the FNLA had collapsed. UNITA was small and confined to the south of the country.

The new situation in Angola, and the opening up of northern Namibia to SWAPO attack, provoked prolonged analysis by the staff officers of the SADF. Before the late 1970s, the regular armed forces had seen little action. The front line of the war against subversion was conducted inside South Africa by the Security Police, not by the army, and the overlord of all counter-insurrectionary activity was Hendrik van den Bergh, the head of BOSS. The task of the military was to safeguard South Africa from external attack, and in this, at least until the invasion of Angola in 1975, the SADF role had been limited to providing small contingents and liaison officers to help the Portuguese and Rhodesian forces. In the new scheme of things the soldiers could see that, if they did not play a more forceful hand in Angola especially, they would soon be faced with a serious guerrilla war in northern Namibia which, although technically a United Nations' trust territory illegally occupied by South Africa, they regarded as home turf. The top army officers were pressing to clear the decks for action. This meant honing their strategy and making sure that all branches of the South African security forces were pulling in the same direction. It also meant wresting control of policy from Van den Bergh and his organisation, which had restricted the military to a secondary role.

The results of this line of thought by the South African security chiefs were outlined in a defence white paper published in 1977. The paper argued that South Africa faced what it called a 'total onslaught' masterminded in Moscow. It was Moscow which was the principal ally and armourer of the new governments of Mozambique and Angola, as well as at least one of the guerrilla movements fighting for the liberation of Zimbabwe. Moscow lay behind the South African Communist Party, which in turn controlled the ANC, they believed. Moscow, or so South African military chiefs believed, was the ultimate controller of the Cuban troops now stationed in Angola in large numbers. The assault was at the same time military, political, psychological and diplomatic. The appropriate response was for South Africa to conceive a 'total national strategy' which would fight fire with fire. This was to be a 'comprehensive plan to utilise all the means available to the state according to an integrated pattern.'[6] The military view was based on first-hand experience gleaned in Angola, Mozambique and Rhodesia, and also on the study of counter-insurgency strategy in similar contexts, especially the French experience in Algeria.

In the hands of government propagandists, this vision of a coordinated Marxist attack went on to imply that liberal journalists, political activists and churchmen in South Africa, and throughout the Western world, who supported the southern African liberation move-ments were manipulated by the Soviet Union, quite possibly without realising it. It could be demonstrated by anti-communist propagan-dists that almost anybody or anything which opposed the South African government was, directly or indirectly, being controlled from Moscow. And indeed, it was undeniable that Moscow sought the overthrow of the South African government and supported an array of radical political and military organisations in the region.

The elaboration of the total strategy was closely associated with Pieter W. Botha, one of the old breed of Afrikaner politicians. Born on a farm in 1916, Botha became a full-time National Party organiser at the age of only 20. As a young man he gained a reputation as a bully-boy, a disrupter of opposition political meetings. Never in all his life did Botha have a full-time job other than as a party functionary or a politician. He is an Afrikaner and a National Party man to his bones.

Botha served as Defence Minister from 1966 until 1978, and in this long stint he formed a close relationship with the chiefs of the SADF. Like the military men, he had formed a deep dislike of Van den Bergh, the head of the secret service, and resented the way in which he had excluded the military from the leading role in security matters. The generals looked to Botha to implement the defence white paper at a political level. This he proceeded to do just when Prime Minister Vorster was failing and there was a battle opening up for the leadership of the National Party in which Botha could count on the powerful support of the military. The favourite to succeed Vorster was Information Minister Dr Connie Mulder. During 1977 and 1978 a scandal, eventually to be dubbed 'Muldergate' by the press, surfaced after the murder of a rising National Party politician sometimes tipped as a future finance minister, Dr Robert Smit. Journalists investigating the case began to uncover a vast network of corruption and other impropriety in the information ministry, and this was later confirmed by a commission of inquiry. The military men and their civilian supporters in Botha's entourage exploited the details of the scandal so

6. Joseph Hanlon, *Beggar Your Neighbours* (Catholic Institute for International Relations & James Currey Publishers, London, 1986), p. 7.

adroitly as rapidly to finish Mulder as a candidate for the premiership. The generals' favourite politician, P.W. Botha, got the job instead.

Behind the jockeying for the top political job lay a struggle between rival security services. The military chiefs were anxious to gain complete control of the security establishment, and to do this they had to reduce the influence of Van den Bergh, whose Bureau of State Security was independent of them. Van den Bergh had caused intense annoyance by styling himself a general in spite of his lack of police or military experience. More importantly, he had often clashed with the military chiefs and had undermined their operations in favour of his own schemes. Van den Bergh, too, became a victim of the Muldergate affair after it was revealed that his Bureau of State Security had operated illegal slush-funds for years, buying up newspapers and bribing journalists in South Africa, Europe and the USA in a bid to secure a better press for South Africa. Van den Bergh resigned and BOSS was emasculated. Eventually, after a couple of changes of name and an overhaul of personnel, it was to resurface as the National Intelligence Service under the direction of a young academic, Dr Lukas Neil Barnard, selected for the job by P.W. Botha. The essential point was that the wings of the civilian intelligence service had been clipped, to the advantage of the soldiers who proceeded to develop the Military Intelligence apparatus. As early as 1977–8, a colonel of Military Intelligence was based in northern Namibia and had the task of building up UNITA in Angola as a powerful South African ally. A permanent military mission, also led by a colonel, was despatched to liaise with UNITA at its headquarters in Jamba, southern Angola.

Once Botha was ensconced in power, the military men could clear the way for the implementation of their total defence strategy. The supreme organ of the new security apparatus was the State Security Council. Established by law as a body to advise the cabinet in 1972, it had not been very active under Vorster. Most of the work of overseeing security policy and advising the government had been done by Van den Bergh at the head of BOSS. Now, the State Security Council was upgraded to become the main instrument for policy-making on security matters, an arrangement which depended on the close relationship between two successive heads of the SADF, Generals Magnus Malan and Constand Viljoen and Prime Minister Botha. Both Malan and Viljoen had seen service in command of the Namibian border.

The State Security Council met weekly, normally just before cabinet meetings, to discuss business. Civilian politicians meeting in Cabinet were informed only later of decisions already taken by the State Security Council on matters falling within their brief. Some ministers felt that the real locus of power had shifted from the Cabinet of elected ministers to the security chiefs sitting in the Security Council, which reserved the right to discuss virtually any aspect of foreign and domestic policy.

Moreover, the State Security Council had its own secretariat which functioned independently of the main civil service and which was staffed largely by military men. Until 1985 the secretariat was headed by General A.J. van Deventer, who had led the South African retreat from Angola in 1975. On his retirement he was replaced by General Pieter van der Westhuizen, a former head of Military Intelligence. Many politicians and journalists agreed that the price of giving the Defence Force a free hand in defending South Africa's borders was to allow military men to take for themselves important spheres of decision-making. In time, even some government supporters felt that P.W. Botha's elevation to the premier's office was the basis for a transformation not far short of a legalised military takeover.

The new breed of security chiefs, who became known as 'securocrats', intended this apparatus as a means of ensuring the integrated defence of the state which they had outlined in the 1977 white paper, placing every single aspect of the affairs of state under a united and coherent command. In regard to political unrest in the townships, for example, the military were ready to move several steps beyond simply detaining trouble-makers. While the Security Police would continue in their task of identifying possible agitators, keeping them under surveillance and arresting or detaining them, the military wanted to evolve this into a more sophisticated counter-revolutionary strategy. The most urbane of the security chiefs were aware that the root problem of South Africa was apartheid, a grossly unfair system which was bound to generate opposition and protest and to fuel the forces of revolution for as long as it existed. In the long term, only good government could remove popular grievances and ensure stability. In the meantime, pending the creation of a fairer government, the securocrats could guarantee the maintenance of national security, provided they were given sweeping powers. Only the politicians could bring about the much-needed political changes which alone would remove the root causes of unrest. So it was that the soldiers urged the politicians to manage constitutional reforms which would create a new breed of black politician working within the system, while government departments concentrated on the economic improvement of black living conditions, concentrating on those areas where, in the view of the securocrats, the provision of electricity and water might undercut the appeal of political radicals. This sort of counter-insurgency strategy, the securocrats maintained, was twenty per cent military and eighty per cent political, a formula devised by the French general André Beaufre after his experience in Algeria.

The State Security Council also intervened in strategic economic matters, such as ensuring South Africa's continuing supply of arms and oil in the face of international sanctions. The first tentative steps by the international community to boycott supplies of strategic commodities or services to South Africa dated from the 1960s. Since then, Pretoria had not neglected the opportunity to study the problem closely when international sanctions were applied to Rhodesia. It had established its own arms manufacturer, ARMSCOR, to manufacture weapons for the SADF. ARMSCOR soon became so successful at developing and making weapons that it became a major exporter, especially of small-arms and light artillery pieces. But it never had the same success in developing and manufacturing such large and expensive items as high-performance aircraft. For research and development as well as for sales the ARMSCOR corporation relied heavily on secret cooperation with friendly countries acting in contravention of a total United Nations ban on arms sales to South Africa imposed in 1977, especially pariah states such as Israel. It was aided in this by elements in the security forces of NATO states. Here, the State Security Council and its apparatus could help coordinate all the different activities necessary to develop, buy and sell weapons in secret.

Oil, too, came under the umbrella of the State Security Council. South Africa had no natural oil supply of its own and had to import mostly from Middle Eastern countries which, in theory, applied a ban on sales to South Africa. Until 1979 the chief supplier was pre-revolutionary Iran, which considered South Africa a pro-Western ally on the shores of the Indian Ocean. After the fall of the Shah, there was a brief panic as planners in Pretoria worked to secure a new supply of oil. They were able to do so with relative ease by paying over the odds for middlemen to take up supplies from producing countries and ship them to South Africa under cover of false documentation. The smooth delivery of oil supplies was the task of South African state corporations, notably SASOL, which had also been working for years on techniques for extracting synthetic oil from coal, to reduce Pretoria's dependence on the outside world. It became a world leader in this field, although the resulting oil was so expensive as to be uneconomic to produce. Nuclear cooperation and trade in computers were also sectors deemed essential for national security and therefore of concern to the State Security Council. In all these fields South Africa could rely on help from friends in Israel, the USA, Britain, West Germany, France, Chile and elsewhere.

In the field of foreign affairs the securocrats came to wield extraordinary influence. Their aim was to seal and protect the borders of South Africa, including Namibia which was under South African administration. To do this necessitated aggressive external action. Acutely aware of the interdependence of South Africa and its neighbours, the generals considered that they had to persuade the rest of Africa of Pretoria's invincibility. Displays of South African military might would frighten neighbouring countries into seeing that resistance to South Africa's will was pointless and, in particular, would dissuade them from giving access to the guerrillas of SWAPO or Umkhonto we Sizwe. They would learn that any act hostile to Pretoria's interest, even an indirect one such as hosting a guerrilla organisation, would bring swift and ruinous retribution. It was imperative, in the securocrats' view, to do this while maintaining an appearance of normality and non-aggression for the sake of both domestic and international opinion. Foreign military adventures had to be secret. The war for South Africa was to be fought not only outside the borders of the Republic but with many South Africans hardly aware that there was a war in progress at all.

In purely military terms, the generals knew just how difficult it is to defeat a guerrilla army once it has managed to set up a secure base and solid lines of supply. The essential thing, from the point of view of counter-insurgency strategists, was to prevent SWAPO or Umkhonto we Sizwe from establishing a base within striking distance of South African territory. The method of persuasion was a mixture of incentive and dissuasion. The incentives took the form of induce-ments to cooperate with Pretoria: preferential trade arrangements, customs agreements, development aid, and so on. The dissuasion took the form of trade sanctions, sabotage, the sponsorship of anti-government banditry or rebel movements, and, in the last resort, invasion. This coercive aspect of South African policy towards its neighbours was christened 'destabilisation' by General van der Westhuizen and his staff.

In this type of warfare, conventional forces were required compara-tively rarely. The only theatre in which the SADF systematically deployed its arsenal of tanks, aircraft and troops fighting in regular order was in southern Angola. There, after the fiasco of the 1975 invasion, the SADF intervened almost annually to destroy SWAPO or Umkhonto we Sizwe bases and training camps within striking distance of the Namibian border, judged to be a distance of several hundred miles, so as to keep the guerrillas bottled up in central Angola. From time to time, too, the SADF had to deploy to defend its Angolan ally, UNITA, against Angolan government offensives. Although UNITA had developed into a formidable force with South African and American equipment and advice, it lacked the resources to defend itself against the tanks and aircraft of Angolan government forces, backed up by Cuban and Soviet equipment, advice and manpower. To counter armoured offensives, UNITA relied on the SADF. South Africa was always reluctant to deploy its conventional forces in Angola, even though it did so on many occasions. For one thing, it was very expensive, requiring the maintenance of sophisticated weapons in the field and long lines of supply and communication. It risked attracting international attention and condemnation of what was, in fact and in law, the invasion of a sovereign state with which South Africa did not even share a border, since Namibia was not legally considered a South African territory. And the deployment of white conscript troops carried the risk of casualties, which would awaken the white South African public to what was happening in Angola and might create a reaction. How many white parents would really be willing to lose a son in a vicious bush war whose motives were unclear and whose existence was not officially acknowledged?

In most theatres other than Angola, the SADF came to rely on the highly unconventional soldiers of the Special Forces. The idea of this type of soldier is probably as old as warfare itself. They are scouts and raiders, sent behind enemy lines in small parties to spy, to kill and to sabotage. Much of the training and technique of the SADF Special Forces derived from the experience of commandos used by both sides in the Second World War and developed in the so-called 'low-intensity conflicts' which pitted armed forces against guerrilla armies in Asia and Africa in the 1960s and 1970s. Much, too, was gleaned from Mao Ze-Dong's theories of guerrilla warfare. Mao's fighters had served as a model for Third World guerrilla armies fighting in rural areas against conventional occupying forces. The aim was to move among the peasants like fish in water. The technique of Maoist-influenced guerrillas was to infiltrate villages and mix with the people if they turned out to be friendly. The villagers would advise the guerrillas of the presence of enemy troops and would hide and feed them. Young men would provide a source of guerrilla recruits. The guerrillas would gain knowledge of local conditions. If the villagers turned out to be hostile, the guerrillas would simply terrorise them into acquiescence and maim or murder anyone suspected of collaborating with government forces.

Properly applied, the Maoist technique of warfare makes life difficult for a counter-insurgency force which finds it almost impossible to distinguish between peaceful and innocent villagers, those who sympathise with the guerrillas, and those who are simply so terrified by living between rival armed forces that they collaborate with whichever side is in the area at any one time. If the army of occupation resorts to terror tactics, as it invariably will, this simply alienates the people still further and makes them more susceptible to the guerrillas' propaganda.

Maoist tactics had been deployed by nationalist guerrillas in Zimbabwe, especially, and the Rhodesian security forces had developed the most ruthless techniques yet seen in Africa for countering them. Especially fearsome were the Rhodesian Special Air Service, closely related to its British parent and employing a large number of ex-British Army mercenaries, and the Grey's and Selous Scouts. These units operated with a high degree of autonomy, often leaving senior military staff in ignorance of their activities. Small groups of mixed black and white troops would penetrate deep into guerrilla-occupied territory. They might aim to sabotage a specific target. More often, they sought to acquire information and to counter their enemies by any means possible.

The methods adopted by the Selous Scouts in particular were unspeakably atrocious. They would torture any prisoner whom they thought might have useful information. They would also, for example, disguise themselves as nationalist guerrillas, enter a village, and see what sort of reception they received. If the people fed them, they would then take reprisals against the village, sometimes indiscriminately, on the grounds that its people were pro-guerrilla. They became expert at bushcraft, living off the land and tracking. They also developed a particular interest in poisons. The Rhodesian secret services developed a form of nerve gas which could be impregnated into clothing, and they would then leave this clothing in places where it would be picked up by likely nationalist guerrillas who, wearing the clothing and absorbing the poison through their skins, died in their hundreds. The Selous Scouts poisoned rivers and food supplies behind enemy lines, or used poisons in individual assassination attempts. This knowledge of poisons was later passed on to the South African Security Police, which manufactured poisons for use against ANC members.

Although the Rhodesians pioneered this form of warfare, it was soon developed by the Portuguese colonial forces once they had discovered that conventional forces could make little progress against their Angolan and Mozambican nationalist enemies. They created their own ruthless death squads, the Grupos Especiais. And it was the Portuguese who pioneered a new tactic which, in turn, was adopted and perfected by the Rhodesians, although it had also been used by the British during the Mau Mau emergency in Kenya. This was the use of so-called 'pseudo-terrorists', units of black Africans employed by the colonial government to live exactly like the nationalist guerrillas, to move far behind enemy lines and gather intelligence. In time, such units could also be used for sabotage and counter-terror, even committing atrocities which would then be blamed on the enemy, the aim being to cause the maximum confusion as well as the maximum number of casualties. The most infamous such force created by the Rhodesians was the Mozambique National Resistance (MNR or RENAMO), originally developed as a scouting unit which could provide the Rhodesians with intelligence from deep behind nationalist lines in Mozambique, but later developing into an autonomous military force, one of the most fearsome outfits ever seen in southern Africa. There are good grounds for considering RENAMO primarily as a bandit force, in spite of its scale. The nature of banditry is of course akin to guerrilla fighting in that it is an irregular form of warfare. But at the heart of true guerrilla warfare is the element of popular support, whereas RENAMO did not originally stem from any popular political movement. While the nationalist armies of southern Africa have mobilised by political means, as well as military ones, RENAMO in particular has spread its influence mostly by terror and massacre.

From the time of the first joint Umkhonto we Sizwe-ZAPU campaign in 1967, South African personnel had gained experience of a modern bush war and learned from the experience of their Rhodesian and Portuguese allies. One of the first South African detachments to fight in Rhodesia was led by Colonel Jan Breytenbach, brother of the leading

Afrikaans poet and anti-apartheid political activist Breyten Breyten-bach. Colonel Breytenbach later went back to South Africa and helped to create several units modelled on the Selous Scouts. Several Security Police officers later accused of heading South African government death squads similarly received their first training in Rhodesia.

The white members of these ferocious units were trained by the normal commando techniques. They underwent a physical training so punishing as to result in occasional deaths from exhaustion.[7] Foreign mercenaries, particularly ex-Rhodesians after 1980, were also employed in special units. But the rank and file of special units consisted mostly of black Africans, and some, such as RENAMO as it evolved at the hands of South African Military Intelligence, were even composed exclusively of blacks with just a few white advisers and liaison officers. In time RENAMO became completely indepen-dent and developed into an authentically Mozambican force.

To some extent, black recruits to Special Forces units or other surrogate forces were motivated simply by the pay they received. But South African officers discovered that the best recruits in their most lethal and successful units were very often nationalist guerrillas from SWAPO or Umkhonto we Sizwe who had been 'turned' and recruited into the SADF or one of its auxiliary units. Sometimes, the remnants of former guerrilla armies could be recruited into South Africa's service *en masse*. This was the case with 32 'Buffalo' battalion, largely manned by black Angolans who had fought in one of the armies contesting the prize of Angolan independence in the 1970s. These men, after the MPLA victory in 1975, had joined the South African armed forces because they had nowhere else to go. Other units used individual nationalist guerrillas who had been captured and 'turned' to fight against their old colleagues. Their loyalty was assured by an induction period of extreme brutality, which had the required psycho-logical effect, and also by obliging the recruits to commit such atrocious murders as to make them pariahs anywhere outside their military unit. Guerrilla fighters who had been 'turned' in this way fought in several units. Koevoet, a highly efficient outfit developed in Namibia to fight against SWAPO, gained an especially atrocious reputation for brutalising and murdering villagers whom it suspected of harbouring SWAPO fighters. And yet many of Koevoet's rank and file consisted of captured SWAPO guerrillas who had been turned against their former comrades. Similarly the Security Police in South Africa used former Umkhonto we Sizwe guerrillas, known as Askaris, to hunt down and kill their former comrades. Askaris and security policemen formed the nucleus of the death squad known as the Civil Cooperation Bureau, which operated throughout the 1980s and came under the authority of the head of Special Forces, at one time Major-

7. Interviews with former members of Special Forces in Britain and the Netherlands, 1987–8.

General 'Kat' Liebenberg – the current head of the SADF – and, most recently, Major-General Eddie Webb. It was typical of the Special Forces' style that they should spawn such a unit without senior officers and officials necessarily being informed of its precise activity.

The use of these techniques, combined with the right-wing political views of most white South African soldiers, came to produce a distinctive variant of the theory of counter-revolution in southern Africa. Many white South African and Rhodesian soldiers came to believe that guerrilla warfare was all technique and no politics, in other words that Africans were prevailed upon to support and fight for SWAPO or Umkhonto we Sizwe because unscrupulous Marxist leaders, trained in Moscow or Beijing in the latest techniques of warfare and political indoctrination, bullied the hapless African masses into doing so. If Pretoria could bully even more – so the logic went – then they could beat the Marxists at their own game. It was a theory of terror versus counter-terror which contained no room for politics whatever, in the sense of people acting from a genuine identification of their self-interest or out of conviction. It is ironic that this approach should have developed under the command of officers who had it drilled into them at staff college that counter-insurrection was eighty per cent politics and twenty per cent war.

One of the consequences of the total mobilisation of the South African state for counter-revolution, and of its preference for making war by clandestine means, was a significant increase in official corruption. The securocrats established networks to supply RENAMO and UNITA, to evade international sanctions, and to pay bribes. RENAMO and UNITA paid for their supplies with ivory, diamonds, and whatever other commodity was to hand. These networks were hidden from the South African Parliament and public on the grounds that they had to be kept secret for reasons of state security. Inquiries about front companies, proprietary airlines and strange relationships were met with a knowing smile, a remark about the need to continue trading, and a refusal to communicate. Unscrupulous international traders and Pretoria's secret servants shared commission payments and developed vested interests in illegal trades in ivory, guns and even drugs, often doing business through the homelands where surveillance was less strict. In this way, South African death squad operators, Special Forces and intelligence men developed autonomous sources of funding which made them semi-independent of the government and created a considerable obstacle to normalisation when at last President F.W. de Klerk tried to bring that about.

This was the type of military organisation and strategy which confronted Umkhonto we Sizwe in the phase of its war which began when the youth of Soweto arrived in Angola for training and when the generals in Pretoria formulated their total defence strategy. As early as 1977, Umkhonto we Sizwe had received and trained enough new recruits from inside South Africa, recent veterans of the Soweto rising, as to mount almost the first series of military operations inside the Republic since the bombings of the early 1960s. The 1977 operations were small-scale, but the fact that they occurred at all marked a milestone in the war. The first fighter from this new wave to be captured and executed by the government was Solomon Mahlangu, who went down in ANC mythology as the first of the new breed of guerrilla martyrs. The ANC named its school in Tanzania in memory of him.

Although the 1977 infiltration achieved little for Umkhonto we Sizwe of military significance, the symbolic importance of launching some sort of military offensive in the wake of the Soweto insurrection was obvious. At last Umkhonto we Sizwe could claim to have overcome the difficulties it had encountered in the post-Rivonia period and to have reached the threshold of a new phase, whereby young South Africans, trained outside the country, would be sent back to do sabotage work inside the Republic.

Seeking ideas and inspiration on how to develop this new phase of the war, in 1978 leaders of the ANC and Umkhonto we Sizwe including Army Chief of Staff Joe Slovo, Oliver Tambo, Army Commander Joe Modise and Cassius Make, the deputy secretary of the Revolutionary Council, travelled to Vietnam to learn from the legendary General Giap, the architect of victories over both French and American armies, on how to fight a guerrilla war. The most important lesson which Giap impressed on the Umkhonto we Sizwe High Command was the importance of long-term planning. As well as paying attention to military strategy, logistics and training, a successful guerrilla army must fit all its activity into a long-term political and military programme whose objectives are precisely defined.

On their return to Africa, the Umkhonto we Sizwe leaders, and most notably Joe Slovo, its leading strategist, tried to apply what they had learned in Vietnam. They produced a three-year plan in which military tactics were to be part of a wider political strategy. This they termed 'armed propaganda'. It was based on the perception that Umkhonto we Sizwe was in no position to base its fighters permanently inside South Africa or to maintain a sustained series of attacks. That could come about only at a later stage. The aim of armed propaganda was to help mobilise the population, preparing it for the more intensive and arduous phase of People's War. A campaign of armed propaganda could be carried out by launching attacks from bases outside South African territory, infiltrating armed and well-trained guerrillas into the country. Their targets would be the most spectacular ones possible, designed not so much to strike at the South African war effort – that was beyond their means – as to inform all South Africans that Umkhonto we Sizwe was in business. This would be combined with a political offensive whose purpose was to inform South Africans of the existence of the ANC's guerrilla army and to imbue them with a few basic slogans. Thus, the ANC declared 1979 to be the Year of the Spear in commemoration of the victory of a Zulu army over British redcoats at Isandhlwana exactly 100 years previously. 1980 was the Year of the Charter, a slogan designed to spread knowledge of the Freedom Charter, the basic manifesto of the ANC which was then 25 years old but which was not widely known inside the country. The other purpose of armed propaganda was that of recruitment, embodied in the slogan 'Swell the ranks of Umkhonto we Sizwe' which was widely heard at this period. The phase of armed propaganda was planned to end with the Year of the Youth in 1981 and to be replaced by a phase of People's War. In the event, the three-year programme was highly successful and turned Umkhonto we Sizwe – 'MK' – into a household name. Spectacular attacks were launched on Moroka, Orlando and Booysens police stations in 1979, the latter in a white suburb. All three targets had gained notoriety during the 1976 rising as torture centres, and were thus very powerful symbols of the return of the Children of Soweto. Later attacks in 1980 and 1981 were better publicised. All played their part in encouraging recruitment into Umkhonto we Sizwe which did not dwindle until after the 1984 uprisings. Then the emphasis shifted from joining the army in exile to concentrate on People's War, which envisaged the formation of locally based defence units, grenade squads and street committees which were to be the nerve-centres of the rising.

At the end of the 1970s, the ANC's military and political operations came under the supervision of the Revolutionary Council in Lusaka. Its Secretary, after the demise of Joe Matthews, was Moses Mabhida, followed by John Nkadimeng, with Cassius Make as Deputy Secretary. All were prominent Party men. Maputo, from 1976, was at the cutting edge of Umkhonto we Sizwe planning and infiltration operations. By far the bulk of the army's manpower was in rear bases in Angola. The Mozambique region was under the command of Joe Slovo. Botswana, also a forward military base, was under Joe Gqabi and seemed particularly promising. Gqabi's men managed to smuggle entire lorry-loads of arms across the border into South Africa which, they hoped, would be cached by comrades inside the country. Only later did it emerge that the Umkhonto we Sizwe apparatus had been penetrated by enemy agents so thoroughly that these lorry-loads went straight to the military authorities in Pretoria and were stockpiled in Defence Force arsenals. Pretoria later made good use of its stock of captured Soviet weaponry to arm allied organisations like RENAMO, enabling the South African government to fend off accusations of complicity by pointing to the Eastern European origin of RENAMO weaponry.

While the Namibian border was still the one place where South African soldiers clashed with nationalist guerrillas head-on, albeit only rarely, the real front line of the struggle for South Africa was actually north of the Limpopo River, in Rhodesia. By the late 1970s it was clear to strategists in Pretoria and abroad that Ian Smith's government could not hold on for much longer. Smith conceded the principle of black rule by inviting black ministers led by Bishop Abel

Muzorewa into the government in 1979, but this did nothing to placate the nationalist forces led by Joshua Nkomo and Robert Mugabe. ZANLA, the military wing of Mugabe's ZANU party, operating out of independent Mozambique, had succeeded in occupying large areas of land and creating liberated zones where it was ZANU's writ which was effective, and where the Rhodesian security forces could penetrate only in armed columns. The South African government decided that it had to put pressure on Smith to give up while there was still a chance of handing power through the ballot box to a moderate black government under Muzorewa. The alternative would be to keep fighting and see Rhodesia eventually fall to more radical nationalists who, having taken power by force rather than through negotiation, would be more difficult to deal with. It was important for South Africa to stabilise this important northern border, more so as Pretoria now hoped to establish a Constellation of Southern African States, a regional grouping which would recognise South Africa, a South African-supervised internal settlement in Namibia, and the homelands in return for peace and South African aid. Throughout 1979 South Africa wanted to avoid upsetting this diplomacy by any undue aggression towards its neighbours. Apart from periodic attacks on southern Angola, therefore, Pretoria refrained from overt hostility to its neighbours.

The ANC, too, was anticipating the climax of the Zimbabwean war. In 1978 Umkhonto we Sizwe sent some fighters into Zimbabwe on detachment with Nkomo's ZIPRA army, traditionally its closest ally in Zimbabwe. Some of them were to stay inside the country until after the declaration of Zimbabwe's independence in April 1980.

In the end, all the key players wanted an end to the Zimbabwean war except possibly the Smith government, which was inclined to fight to the bitter end, and the guerrilla leaders, who knew that if they kept on fighting they would eventually win an unconditional victory. But neither Smith, nor Mugabe, nor Nkomo could resist outside pressure to negotiate. Smith was dependent on South African support to keep going, and South Africa now wanted to settle in the hope of establishing a moderate government in Salisbury. Mugabe's ZANLA guerrillas were dependent on their bases in Mozambique, and a warweary government in Maputo was putting pressure on them to settle. After some dexterous British diplomacy, all sides reached an agreement signed at Lancaster House in London on 17 December 1979 with a promise of free and fair elections the following April. All the main parties to the Zimbabwean conflict believed they had struck a good bargain and that their side could win an election. The South African government was rooting for Muzorewa. The ANC, the SACP, and Moscow had their money on Joshua Nkomo's ZAPU.

5
Destabilisation
1980-3

The first independence elections in Zimbabwe, on 4 March 1980, were a shock to a lot of people. Robert Mugabe's ZANU party scored a landslide victory where international diplomats and pundits had tipped either Muzorewa or Nkomo to do better. Perhaps the best explanation was that ZANU had won the reward for its whole-hearted military effort. Mugabe's soldiers had occupied large parts of the country before the ceasefire. The thousands of camouflage-clad guerrillas were there for all to see, and they made it plain that they had not fought all these years to be robbed by an election. The message to the Zimbabwean people was simple: if you want peace, vote for the winners. A vote for Muzorewa was a vote for further bloodshed.

Nkomo's ZAPU did surprisingly badly at the polls. To some extent this may have been because the ZANU forces were predominantly Shona, and Shona-speakers were a majority in Zimbabwe. But it was also the case that the ZAPU armed forces, although well-equipped and well-trained, had had a tendency to hold back from an all-out military assault. They occupied less ground than their ZANU rivals by polling day.

The Soviet government, the SACP and the ANC had all backed the wrong horse. They had maintained a solid alliance with Nkomo's ZAPU, which they considered to be more sound ideologically, and closer to Moscow, than the rival ZANU. During the war ZANU leaders tried hard to persuade the ANC to shift its stand on Zimbabwe and to adopt a policy of neutrality between the rival guerrilla armies, but in vain. Mugabe and his ZANU colleagues became extremely frustrated by the ANC which, under Communist Party influence, had been instrumental in isolating them from the mainstream of revolutionary movements in Africa. The ANC, through its communist alliance, held the key to Soviet acceptance and respectability in the revolutionary world, especially after China had lost interest in African affairs in the late 1970s.

Some of the Umkhonto we Sizwe fighters who had fought alongside ZAPU since 1978 stayed on after the Lancaster House agreement. They were only spotted when, coming in from the bush to the assembly points where the nationalist guerrillas were supposed to gather, some were identified by members of the British monitoring force as South Africans. Soon after independence they were sent back to Zambia, and from there many returned to the miserable Angolan camps where conditions were harsh and life was both difficult and tedious. Others managed to stay on in secret, passing themselves off as ZAPU men or going underground, forming the nucleus of an Umkhonto we Sizwe presence in Zimbabwe which was unknown even to Mugabe's security. It was not too difficult for Umkhonto we Sizwe guerrillas, especially if they were Zulu-speakers, to pass themselves off as Ndebele loyal to Nkomo's ZAPU party. The Ndebele are a people of South African origin, whose language is closely related to Zulu. When Mugabe's government later discovered what had happened, ministers and officials were livid with anger.

Throughout the early 1980s the situation in Zimbabwe remained tense. The independence elections had merely increased rivalry between the rival nationalist forces, ZANU and ZAPU. Mugabe feared a coup mounted by fighters from Nkomo's ZIPRA army, cheated of power by the election results, and with possible backing from Moscow. The ZIPRA Military Intelligence chief Dumiso Dabengwa was later found in court to have written to the head of the KGB in Moscow, Yuri Andropov, on the very eve of Zimbabwe's independence. When this correspondence was uncovered by Zimbabwean security men, at the same time as they discovered arms caches, Dabengwa and another former ZIPRA commander were detained. Dabengwa was an old friend of Chris Hani, whom he had known since the Wankie campaign of 1967. Prime Minister Mugabe was faced with the nightmare of a ZAPU coup, with ANC assistance and Soviet backing, in order to snatch the victory lost at the ballot-box in 1980. To make matters worse, within a year of Zimbabwean independence Pretoria's Special Forces and Military Intelligence were doing their best to destabilise Zimbabwe and were recruiting disgruntled ex-ZAPU fighters for sabotage operations inside the country.

For Pretoria, there was at least one windfall as a result of the collapse of Rhodesia and the independence of Zimbabwe, declared on 18 April 1980. Thousands of battle-hardened Rhodesian soldiers, including Muzorewa's personal troopers and many from the Selous Scouts and the SAS, went south. The Rhodesian security chiefs also handed over to Pretoria control of RENAMO, the 'pseudo-terrorist' outfit which had been performing scouting duties inside Mozambique for the Rhodesians. It was a rather small-scale operation and seemed to have little left in it when its Rhodesian paymasters handed it over intact to South African Military Intelligence.

The many Rhodesian soldiers who wanted to continue in the army joined South Africa's Special Forces, now re-organised to assimilate the newcomers and deploy them in the destabilisation campaigns which were now being mounted. At the heart of the Special Forces were six Reconnaissance Commando units, each having a specialised role. Five Recce, for example, was based at Phalaborwa in the eastern Transvaal and had as its main task the destabilisation of Mozambique in conjunction with RENAMO. Its 750 personnel included some 500 blacks, most of them of Angolan, Mozambican or Zimbabwean origin, the remnants of the many defunct guerrilla armies which had been formed and dismantled in southern Africa in the past 20 years. Four Recce specialised in sea-borne operations in Angola, and so on. Black Angolans, Mozambicans and Zimbabweans working for South Africa were invaluable in destabilising their countries of origin since their operations could not easily be detected or identified as being under South African command. Special Forces headquarters was at Durban with its high command at Voortrekkerhoogte, near Pretoria.

Despite the ANC's dismay that Nkomo's ZAPU had failed to become the dominant power in Zimbabwe, there was no doubt that, on balance, the liberation of the country was an asset to the ANC and a blow to Pretoria. Zimbabwe had great potential as a base for guerrilla operations inside South Africa, since the two countries shared a common border.

Umkhonto we Sizwe was now getting into the stride of its armed propaganda campaign, advertised by a most successful 'spectacular'. On 1 June 1980, personnel from the Umkhonto we Sizwe Special Operations force launched a simultaneous attack on four installations of the South African Coal, Oil and Gas Corporation (SASOL) inside South Africa, including oil storage tanks and a refinery. The fires which blazed for the best part of a week after bomb explosions at one of the oil storage tanks could be seen for miles. It was the underground army's most successful operation to date and in some respects its best ever. The financial cost to the state was variously reckoned at figures between R7 million and R70 million, up to £45 million.

The attack on the SASOL oil facilities was timed to cause maximum nervousness in government circles. SASOL had been created and developed as part of the government's drive to become self-sufficient in all strategic sectors. In addition to importing foreign-produced oil, the government had been planning for eventual sanctions ever since the early 1960s, and had, with considerable pride, developed technology originally acquired from Germany to extract oil from coal. The only problem was that, even at the very high oil prices obtaining in the late 1970s, it was far more expensive to manufacture oil from coal than to import it. What the plant represented more than anything else was white South African ingenuity and determination. It was this showpiece which Umkhonto we Sizwe attacked at just the moment when South Africa was facing a cut-off in supplies after the revolution in Iran and when an oil shortage seemed like a real possibility for the first time.

The Special Operations force which hit the SASOL facilities was Umkhonto we Sizwe's crack unit, under the overall command of Joe Slovo, although the actual operation was carried out by a team under Motso Mokgabudi, known as Obadi. A Communist Party member like many of the top Umkhonto we Sizwe cadres, Obadi had undergone extensive training at a school in the Soviet Union where he specialised in artillery and especially the use of rockets. After his return to Angola, Obadi was put in charge of Fundo camp, used by the ANC for intensive training courses in sabotage, bomb technology and artillery. It was run jointly with advisers from the Soviet military mission to Angola. Some of those trained at Fundo were also taken for further specialised instruction by members of the Irish Republican Army working out of an anonymous apartment building in Luanda. The IRA men were experts in the construction of bombs and booby-traps, and passed on their know-how to ANC specialists, including Obadi. The IRA connection, which began in late 1978, has always been one of the ANC's most closely-guarded secrets. It is not clear what later cooperation there may have been between the two organisations, although some British sources[1] were to claim in the late 1980s that it continued, and that officials of the ANC's Military Intelligence department had visited the IRA in Northern Ireland.

Obadi and others from the unit which attacked SASOL returned to base without being intercepted, but South African intelligence soon learned the identities of the saboteurs. Some months later, Obadi was detained in a swoop by security men in Swaziland, who held some suspected ANC operatives without knowing exactly who they were. Only when Pretoria learned of the arrest, and offered the Swazi government a R1 million ransom for Obadi, did the Swazis realise that they had detained someone too hot for comfort. Fearing the ANC's possible reaction, they panicked and handed Obadi back to the ANC in Maputo.

For a time there was little reaction from Pretoria to the SASOL attack. There was one attempt on the life of Chris Hani, planned by the Security Police in Bloemfontein. They entrusted the operation to an informer, a young Lesotho national who was close to Hani, the leading Umkhonto we Sizwe operative in Lesotho, where he had built up an effective command and intelligence structure.[2] The agent made a mistake while he was handling the bomb and it blew up in front of him, bursting his eardrums and damaging his legs. Probably, Pretoria was afraid of the adverse consequences of taking aggressive action against the countries which gave sanctuary to the bombers at a time when world attention was still focused on newly independent Zimbabwe, and while Jimmy Carter, who had done so much to push for Zimbabwean independence, was still in the White House. Only towards the end of a bleak year did Pretoria receive its first piece of good news on the international front. In November 1980, Ronald Reagan was elected president of the United States. He was sworn in on 20 January 1981. Just ten days later, South African commandos launched the first of their new-style cross-border raids.

1. Notably the Conservative Party MP, Andrew Hunter.
2. *Vrye Weekblad,* November 1989.

The target of the 30 January 1981 raid was the Maputo suburb of Matola, where a number of buildings contained the operational headquarters of Umkhonto we Sizwe. The invaders drove the 70 kilometres from the South African border and attacked three ANC houses, killing 13 people. Among the dead was Obadi, who had commanded the attack on the SASOL installations the previous June; a SACTU official and ex-Robben Islander, William Khanyile; and the commander of Umkhonto we Sizwe's Natal machinery, Mduduzi Guma. He had been a respected lawyer in Durban, leaving the country in the aftermath of the 1976 rising. All three were top members of the Party, Guma being particularly valued. He had single-handedly translated the Party Programme, *The Road to South African Freedom,* from English into Zulu and was very close to the Party General Secretary, Moses Mabhida. Other ANC fighters were also killed in the raid. The attackers also killed a Portuguese engineer who had the misfortune to bear a striking physical resemblance to Joe Slovo. For some hours the jubilant South Africans believed that Slovo was dead. Some of the ANC men managed to fight back, killing two South African soldiers. One of the dead was wearing a helmet bearing the slogan 'Sieg Heil'. He turned out out be a Briton, Robert Hutchinson, who had served in the Rhodesian SAS before moving south in 1980.

The timing of the raid, just ten days after President Reagan had been sworn in at the head of a new and fiercely anti-communist administration, was surely no accident. The US government failed to condemn the incursion, and in fact the Maputo government, tipped off by East German intelligence, believed that the local CIA station in the US embassy was working closely with the South Africans.

From Pretoria's point of view, the Matola raid was a success marred only by disappointment when the returning unit learned that it had missed Joe Slovo. The Mozambican government expelled all the CIA agents from the country and shut down the local CIA station, which brought relations with Washington to a new low. Oliver Tambo, delivering the funeral oration for the ANC men killed in the Matola raid, made a speech in which he appeared to threaten all the whites of South Africa with racial violence. If the possession of a weapon made someone a legitimate target as the South African army seemed to believe, he said, then almost the entire white population had to be included in this category since so many of them kept firearms in their houses.

This success, and especially the lack of American reaction, encouraged the South African military chiefs to plan raids against ANC bases elsewhere in what had come to be known as the front line states.[3] Throughout the rest of the year there was a spate of cross-

---

3. Joseph Hanlon's *Beggar Your Neighbours* gives a full account of destabilisation in the early 1980s. Much of the material in this chapter is based on Hanlon's book.

border operations by the Special Forces, now augmented by thousands of ex-Rhodesians who were in effect continuing the war against African nationalism, temporarily suspended after the independence of Zimbabwe, in a new uniform. Mozambique was subject to at least twelve attacks by the SADF in the next three years. Worse by far, South African Military Intelligence started to relaunch RENAMO as an armed force charged with destroying Mozambique's infrastructure, and it began to take on a spectacular life of its own. According to a former Military Intelligence clerk, by 1982–3 South Africa was sending some 60 tonnes of weapons per month to RENAMO, by air and sea. In Angola, President Eduardo Dos Santos reckoned that in the first 11 months of 1981 there were 53 SADF incursions onto Angolan territory and 100 bombing raids. South African Military Intelligence was also aiding UNITA on a massive scale and maintained a permanent military mission at UNITA headquarters in Jamba. In Zimbabwe, ANC representative Joe Gqabi was assassinated in July 1981. South African agents made a series of bomb and sabotage attacks against the Zimbabwean government. The most serious, in December 1981, was the bombing of ZANU party headquarters in Manica Road, Harare. A bomb exploded above a conference room where a meeting of the Central Committee, fortunately postponed, had been scheduled to take place. This chance alone prevented the bomb from claiming the lives of several Zimbabwean leaders. Even the distant Seychelles was subject to an attack by a band of supposed mercenaries in November 1981. In fact, most of the mercenaries were soldiers from Five Reconnaissance Commando at Phalaborwa. Their aim was to seize control of the strategically important islands. According to some of those involved,[4] the plan had received approval at very high level in South Africa.

The SADF was equipping itself to fight a series of clandestine wars making particular use of the reorganised Special Forces, which were authorised to conceive and execute their own operations independent of the main army command, and whose members enjoyed an effective immunity from prosecution. Former Special Forces officers have described how they operated on a need-to-know basis, withholding information from anyone who was not required to know for operational purposes. Even senior officers and political authorities were only vaguely informed of some operations, which allowed them to plead ignorance in response to embarrassing questions. Military Intelligence also set up a new, ultra-secret unit which worked closely with Special Forces. This was the Special Tasks' Directorate under the overall command of Brigadier van Tonder, who had experience re-equipping UNITA in 1977–8. Van Tonder's office was divided into four sub-sections, responsible for the destabilisation of Zimbabwe,

---

4. Members of the Seychellois opposition in exile, in conversation with Stephen Ellis.

Mozambique, Lesotho and Angola respectively. The Mozambique desk, which had responsibility for supplying and liaising with the MNR, was under Colonel Charles van Niekerk, who had served on detachment with the Portuguese in Mozambique ten years previously. The Zimbabwe desk was under Malcolm 'Matt' Callaway, an ex-Rhodesian intelligence officer, while Lesotho was under another ex-Rhodesian, Colonel May.

Calloway was one of several senior intelligence officers who had worked as double agents in Zimbabwe. The explanation for this lay in the nature of the transfer of power in Zimbabwe. When Robert Mugabe took over the reins in April 1980, he was determined to encourage the white community to stay in the country and to avoid the chaos which had attended the exodus of whites in Mozambique. One of his first acts was to ask the head of Rhodesia's Central Intelligence Organisation (CIO), Ken Flower, to continue in his post with the new government. This was intended as a way of ensuring continuity in the security service and of reassuring whites that there would be no settling of scores now that the nationalists had taken over power. Flower accepted, and remained loyal to his new master. Many other whites in the Zimbabwean intelligence and security services also stayed at their posts but transferred their real loyalties elsewhere. Pretoria was able to recruit white sympathisers from the very heart of the Zimbabwean intelligence establishment.

At the time of Zimbabwe's independence, Calloway was working for the CIO and was stationed at Dett, where he was responsible for organising an assembly-point for guerrillas from the ZIPRA army coming in from the bush. In fact, he was already in contact with South African intelligence.[5] He became acquainted with the ZIPRA commander who knew the whereabouts of arms caches in the area. Later, when ZIPRA Military Intelligence chief Dumiso Dabengwa was accused of caching weapons, the young ZIPRA commander appeared as a prosecution witness. In 1982 Calloway's double-dealing was discovered and he left Zimbabwe and went to work for the SADF's Special Tasks Directorate in Pretoria. He was put in charge of recruiting agents from his old patch in Matabeleland. His speciality was recruiting disaffected former soldiers of Nkomo's guerrilla army whom he converted into saboteurs, known as 'super-ZAPU', for use in destabilisation operations in Zimbabwe and Botswana.

A similar case was that of Kevin John Woods, who also worked for the CIO after independence as the senior administrative officer for Matabeleland. He was recruited by the South African security services in 1983 and became a spy on their behalf. Among his duties for his Zimbabwean employer was the preparation of intelligence reports on the threat from so-called 'dissidents', mostly disaffected former ZIPRA fighters, for the attention of Prime Minister Mugabe.

5. *Southscan,* 16 November 1990.

Calloway was helping run dissidents into Matabeleland at one end of the operation, in Pretoria, while Woods was preparing reports on the resultant activity at the other end, in Zimbabwe. Both were in fact taking orders from South Africa. The maintenance of a dissident threat in the region enabled Pretoria to keep the ANC's old friends in ZAPU out of power in Zimbabwe and to create suspicion between crucial elements of the Zimbabwean armed forces and intelligence. Woods was eventually arrested in Zimbabwe in 1988.

Not only was there no American reaction to the escalation of the southern Africa conflict marked by the cross-border operations, but there were signs that the anti-communist ideologues who infested the Reagan administration in Washington were encouraging South Africa to fight Moscow's allies in the region, in Angola and Mozambique especially. CIA director William Casey saw South Africa as a vital regional ally which could do the sort of anti-communist work which he was not always free to do under the watchful eye of Congress. In time he constructed an elaborate – and illegal – system of multiple alliances in which several other US allies played a role without actually involving CIA agents and without running the risk of reprimand by Congress. Thus one US ally, Morocco, gave weapons to UNITA in Angola with funds from another ally, Saudi Arabia. South Africa received oil from the conservative Gulf States and sold arms to Iran, and so it went on.[6] South African pilots were even identified flying arms to the Nicaraguan contras, suggesting that there had been a comprehensive deal on secret military collaboration between the USA and South Africa.[7] South Africa's secret servants were no doubt delighted to be of service to such a system, since it conformed to their own perception of the need to combat the total Marxist onslaught and cemented close relations with the USA.

Umkhonto we Sizwe, of course, could not command anything remotely similar to the resources of such interests as the CIA or the SADF. The USSR was able to equip Umkhonto we Sizwe fighters with weapons via Angola, Zambia and Tanzania. According to Oleg Gordievsky, who was deputy chief of the KGB station in London in the early 1980s, Soviet intelligence passed funds to the South African Communist Party and the ANC through its London embassy. In six months at the end of 1982 he handed R270,000 for the Party and R578,000 for the ANC to the chairman of the SACP, Yusuf Dadoo. Gordievsky claims that Dadoo used to call at the Soviet embassy in a once-elegant London mansion, write out a receipt, and then stuff banknotes into every pocket of his clothing. Dadoo was impeccably honest, and led an ascetic life while handling such large amounts of money. Funds were also distributed via the Soviet embassy in Lusaka,

6. Interviews with Sam Bamieh, 1988.
7. Stephen Emerson, *Secret Warriors. Inside the Covert Military Operations of the Reagan Era* (G.P. Putnam's Sons, New York), p. 222.

the main Soviet diplomatic and intelligence base for southern Africa.[8] Other communist governments, including East Germany, provided the ANC and the Party with forged dollar and rand notes printed on government security printing presses. This simultaneously financed the armed struggle and helped destabilise the South African and US economies.

In spite of its limited resources, Umkhonto we Sizwe was able to stage at least one major operation in 1981. The elite Special Operations unit carried out another successful 'spectacular', launching a rocket attack on the headquarters of the SADF at Voortrekkerhoogte near Pretoria. The attack was prepared by two white agents who had infiltrated from Maputo and rented a house at Mooiplas, close to the military complex. A team of black ANC guerrillas, posing as servants and labourers, then brought in piece by piece a Soviet-made rocket launcher and small arms. More white operatives supplied cars for the attack party. The five ANC guerrillas who had been detailed to carry out the attack took up residence in the farmhouse and on 12 August 1981 launched five 122 mm rockets against the military complex some four miles away. Four only exploded. In less than a week the five guerrillas were back in Maputo.

The attackers were convinced that their four rockets must have caused extensive damage and casualties inside the base, although press reports claimed that little damage was done, and that the only casualties had been black workers inside the base. But, as in the SASOL attack carried out by the same unit in the previous year, the intention was mainly to demonstrate to the people of South Africa that Umkhonto we Sizwe was alive and operative.

South African military chiefs took Umkhonto we Sizwe very seriously, in spite of its small size and modest achievements, because they knew its potential if ever it was allowed to build proper supply lines. In addition to the major attacks carried out by Slovo's Special Operations unit, the ANC-Communist Party guerrilla army was managing to infiltrate a trickle of fighters into South Africa with the aim of building an underground inside the country. The problems facing them were immense. It was generally impossible to smuggle into the country any weapon larger than a few hand-grenades. To stay underground, guerrillas had to carry into the country enough money to be able to exist in a township for weeks or months, buying their own food and other needs. Unlike the fighters of earlier wars in Zimbabwe or Mozambique, they could not live off the land in the rural areas, not least because Umkhonto we Sizwe placed its priority on winning over the urban masses. The death-rate for guerrillas entering the country was alarmingly high and incoming fighters knew they had little chance of getting out alive. In 1980 one fighter, Petrus

8. Gordievsky and Andrews, *KGB: The Inside Story,* quoted in the *Sunday Times* (Johannesburg), 28 October 1990.

Jobane, cornered by the police in Soweto, blew himself up with his own grenade rather than be taken alive. ANC propaganda hailed Jobane as 'the lion of Chiawelo' and the Communist Party, of which he was a member, glorified him as the model of a fighting communist. The Umkhonto we Sizwe fighters romanticised this type of self-sacrifice. They had little sympathy for any of their comrades who allowed themselves to be captured, expecting fighters to take their own lives rather than surrender.

Anyone who was captured knew that they would be extensively interrogated, probably tortured, and forced to reveal information, but perhaps most frightening of all was the prospect of being 'turned'. The Security Police had now perfected this technique. When a captured guerrilla had been squeezed dry of information, an attempt might be made to 'turn' him and either to send him back into the ANC as a double agent working for the Security Police, or to convert him into an Askari, a trooper with one of the Special Forces or police units working undercover on assassination and sabotage duties. There were cases of Umkhonto we Sizwe guerrillas who were captured and turned into double agents, but who promptly reported this to ANC security when they were sent back to their Umkhonto we Sizwe units. To prevent this, the Security Police developed the technique of forcing 'turned' guerrillas to murder an ANC activist inside South Africa, thus preventing them from ever double-crossing their new masters. It was by this means that the murder squads which hit the headlines in South Africa in late 1989 were developed.

A typical, and important, example of a government death-squad at work was the murder of the ANC lawyer Griffiths Mxenge in Durban. Durban had been largely untouched by the student rising of 1976. Support for the ANC in the city and its townships was not solid, since the Inkatha organisation of Chief Mangosuthu Gatsha Buthelezi, Chief Minister of the homeland of KwaZulu, wielded considerable influence. Buthelezi aimed to tread a middle path between cooperating with the Pretoria government, in his capacity as a homeland leader, and proclaiming his sympathy for the ANC. Although Buthelezi had come to be regarded as a collaborator by radical activists in the late 1970s, Tambo, ever the diplomat, had consistently cultivated him and met him and other Inkatha leaders with a small delegation from the ANC's National Executive outside South Africa in October 1979, much to the annoyance of Mxenge, one of the leading ANC sympathisers in Durban. During the meeting Buthelezi represented himself as the popular representative of the ANC's domestic constituency. There were inevitable differences on the questions of the armed struggle and sanctions, and it led to a public break in the middle of 1980.

One of Buthelezi's skills was to invoke Zulu history. The powerful Zulu kingdom which had arisen in the early nineteenth century had resisted conquest by either Afrikaner trekkers or British imperial armies longer than any other African state, even inflicting a major defeat on British redcoats at Isandhlwana in 1879. As late as 1906 there had been an important Zulu rising against colonial rule. Perhaps more readily than any other black South African people, the Zulu could be mobilised around an ethnic identity rooted in the historical existence of a centralised Zulu state.

Born into a leading family which had traditionally supplied prime ministers to the Zulu kings, Buthelezi had been a member of the ANC Youth League and had been expelled from Fort Hare University, apparently for political activity.[9] In 1954 he had taken over the leadership of the Buthelezi clan and had been recognised by the Pretoria government as the legitimate chief of the clan three years later. After the banning of the ANC in 1960, Buthelezi stayed in his home base in Natal, and developed a strategy of identifying openly with the ANC while at the same time using whatever opportunities came his way to build up his political base in rural Zululand. He criticised the government's homelands policy, but at the same time was elected head of the Zululand Territorial Authority in 1970 and the KwaZulu Legislative Assembly in 1972. In 1975 he revived a defunct Zulu cultural organisation, Inkatha, and began to develop it into a Zulu political party. Buthelezi showed impressive skill in adopting a measured anti-government stance, refusing for example to accept nominal independence for the KwaZulu homeland, while at the same time using the power and patronage offered by his control of the KwaZulu government. He was no puppet of Pretoria. In fact, Tambo was to reveal in 1985 that the ANC in exile had encouraged Buthelezi to join the homeland government of KwaZulu as a way of keeping influence inside the system. Many inside the ANC ascribed this decision to the ANC's general distaste for mobilising support in rural areas. Cultivating Buthelezi, with his base in rural Zululand, was seen as a short cut to winning rural support. For years he was spared from the scorn habitually poured on homeland leaders by the ANC in exile, which saw him as a homeland leader of a special type. Partly as a result, his power base grew.

His refusal to accept independence, and his sympathetic stance towards a strike movement in Durban in 1973, actually brought Buthelezi close to being toppled by Pretoria. The Durban strikes were championed by one of Buthelezi's ministers, Barney Dladla. Dladla became popular as a result, and though he was later demoted and eventually fired from the KwaZulu administration, by that time many Durban workers had come to be quite well-disposed to the KwaZulu government. Buthelezi managed to survive Pretoria's hostility at this time and enticed into Inkatha the Zulu king, Goodwill Zwelethini, giving himself added legitimacy in the eyes of rural Zulus and clan chiefs. Claiming to be the authentic representative of the ANC which

9. Mzala, *Gatsha Buthelezi: Chief with a Double Agenda* (Zed Books, London, 1988) is the main biography. The author was an SACP member.

he had known in the 1940s but which had now been hijacked by Tambo's Lusaka mission in exile, Buthelezi built a formidable local power base and began to compete for a national role as the leading internal nationalist.

The first significant challenge to Buthelezi from the left occurred shortly after the murder by the Security Police in September 1977 of Steve Biko, the Black Consciousness leader. Biko's disciples disrupted a speech by Buthelezi at the predominantly Indian University of Durban-Westville. His response was to remind his listeners of the 1949 Zulu-Indian clashes which had resulted in numerous Indian deaths. Shortly afterwards, in March 1978, Buthelezi was publicly humiliated by being jeered by a hostile crowd at the funeral of PAC founder Robert Sobukwe. His bodyguard had to intervene to save him from attack by the crowd. It was clear after these events that there was no more common ground between Buthelezi and activists of the ANC and other anti-government organisations.

In 1980 a wave of strikes swept through the schools in various parts of the country, and especially in Natal and the Eastern Cape. This came at a difficult time for Buthelezi. The year began with mobilisation by the ANC for the celebration of the 25th anniversary of the Freedom Charter, followed by a signature campaign for the release of Nelson Mandela. Three ANC guerrillas were killed in a shoot-out during a bungled operation at Silverton, and then came the spectacular Umkhonto we Sizwe attack on SASOL. Buthelezi believed that a major Umkhonto we Sizwe campaign was beginning and he was determined to stand against it. The first targets of his counter-attack were striking schoolchildren who were forced back to their desks by *impis*, groups of Zulu Inkatha supporters armed with spears and clubs. Buthelezi went on record to condemn the SASOL attack and the Mandela signature campaign. In a speech delivered in London in June 1980, ANC Secretary-General Alfred Nzo attacked Buthelezi personally, confirming the rupture between the ANC and Inkatha. The speech was reported in the South African press, but without identifying Nzo by name. Buthelezi angrily replied that he would expect Tambo himself to respond to the questions of unity that he, Buthelezi, had raised during the London meeting the previous October. Tambo duly issued a public reply at a Lusaka press conference on 23 July 1980, when he said that Buthelezi had 'emerged on the side of the enemy against the people'. Mxenge and other ANC leaders in Durban supported the strikes and the anti-Buthelezi movement. Buthelezi, a man hypersensitive to criticism and with a sharp tongue, dismissed Mxenge as a 'Xhosa lawyer'.

Griffiths Mxenge was murdered in Durban on 20 November 1981. His body bore 45 stab-wounds. The first public claim to inside knowledge of Mxenge's murder came from a man called Butana Almond Nofomela, shortly before he was due to be hanged in October 1989 for the murder of a white farmer. His execution was halted after he had stated in an affidavit that he had been a member of a death squad which killed at least nine government opponents, including Mxenge, in South Africa and neighbouring states. He named senior Security Police officers who had allegedly paid him and others to kill Mxenge in 1981. Eventually, a government commission of inquiry into the death squads was to cast doubt on some of Nofomela's evidence, but not without confirming sufficient details as to give a striking impression of this aspect of counter-revolutionary warfare.[10]

Nofomela's allegations were confirmed both by his former commanding officer in a special death squad, Captain Dirk Coetzee of the Security Police, and by David Tshikalange, a former member of the same unit. Dirk Coetzee said he had knowledge of, or had taken part in, the assassinations of several suspected ANC members inside and outside South Africa. He described how the deaths of victims who had been taken prisoner were kept secret by their being poisoned or shot and their bodies burnt. He also said that letter-bombs had been used by the Security Police to kill anti-apartheid activists such as Ruth First in Mozambique in 1982 and Jeanette Schoon in Angola in 1984. Although the official commission of inquiry discounted much of the evidence from Coetzee and others, there remains strong evidence that death squads formed by members of the security forces may have been involved in the murders of at least 60 opponents of the government between 1979 and 1989. Several appeared to have strong connections to the Special Forces and to the Security Police.

According to Coetzee, the Security Police in Durban decided to murder Mxenge in November 1981. They knew that the lawyer served as a conduit for ANC funds but were unable to prove it and were unwilling to take him into custody for fear of a repeat of the Biko affair, when a murder in detention had caused an international outcry. So a Security Police brigadier contacted Coetzee who was known to be in command of a death squad and asked him to arrange for Mxenge's murder. Coetzee duly delegated the task to four men in his squad, telling them to disguise the murder as a robbery. After being given information on Mxenge's movements by the Durban Security Police, the four killers went to the lawyer's house at night, poisoned his dogs and ambushed him in the road outside. They took him to the Umlazi sports stadium where they stabbed him to death, slit his throat and cut off his ears to keep as trophies. They then took his wallet and personal effects. Each of the murderers was paid R1,000 for his work.

Officially, Mxenge's death was an unsolved crime, but ANC supporters were convinced from the start that it was a murder carried out with official complicity. Since Buthelezi was one of the key authorities in Natal, they blamed him. After such a murder there was no possibility of a police agent ever getting close to the ANC or

10. Patrick Laurence, *Death Squads. Apartheid's Secret Weapon* (Penguin Forum Series, London, 1990).

abandoning his handlers, as the ANC would certainly have killed him for committing such a crime. Thus his loyalty to his handlers was assured. This technique was now widely used by the security forces to retain the loyalty of agents or double agents. According to Captain Coetzee, few of those agents who were 'turned' ANC men, or Askaris, were ever really committed to police work, and many eventually returned to the ANC in spite of their deeds. Coetzee has testified that, during his time in charge of a death squad, Ben Lucky Zwane and the brothers Johannes and Chris Mnisi all returned to the ANC. Others were murdered when their handlers thought they were about to defect.

The use of Askaris was just one means by which the security forces combated Umkhonto we Sizwe, the ANC and the Communist Party. They were also highly effective in recruiting or placing spies inside the ANC and even the ultra-cautious Communist Party, and not all such spies were motivated by this sort of coercion. In March 1981, the ANC Intelligence and Security organ uncovered the most important spy network it had ever found. To the consternation of its intelligence officers, the spies they identified had been in action for a long time and seemed to have done major damage. Worse still, they were uncovered by accident, which did not bode well for the effectiveness of the ANC's counter-espionage machinery. Security officials stumbled upon this spy network due to the erratic behaviour of a man known as 'Piper', an ANC official and a member of the Communist Party. Based in Lusaka, Piper suddenly made an attempt to flee to South Africa and was stopped and questioned by the Botswana authorities who handed him to ANC Security in Zambia. He confessed that he was working for Pretoria and that he had panicked and tried to escape after he thought that he had been discovered. In fact, the ANC had had no suspicions about him and would not have detained him if he had kept his nerve. Under interrogation, Piper claimed that Pretoria was running two major spy rings inside the ANC, one of which was tasked with penetrating Umkhonto we Sizwe, the other with penetrating the ANC's National Executive Committee. Piper himself had been staggeringly successful. He admitted to being a professional officer of the Security Police who had joined the ANC with the sole aim of infiltrating it. He had been recruited into the Communist Party and had even been selected to study at the Lenin School in Moscow. On his return to southern Africa from the Soviet Union, he had been elected to the internal committee of SACTU and was well on the way to achieving his goal of becoming a member of the NEC.

Acting on the names given by Piper, ANC Security men arrested some other senior Umkhonto we Sizwe officials who, under interrogation, confessed to being spies also. Their identity was staggering. One was Kenneth Mahamba, the commander of the Umkhonto we Sizwe camp at Quibaxe in Angola. One of the thousands who joined Umkhonto we Sizwe in 1976, he confessed to having been recruited as a police spy while he was still at home in Pretoria. Another of those named by Piper and who confessed to spying was one 'Sticks' or 'Stix', who was no less than the head of Umkhonto we Sizwe Security in Angola. A third spy alleged to have penetrated the ANC army was Comrade Justice, another who had joined up in 1976 and had been considered one of the best recruits of his generation. Justice confessed that, while he was undergoing training at Nova Katenga in southern Angola, he had succeeded in poisoning the food of camp inmates. Cuban doctors were on hand to cure the victims, and there were no deaths. By the time Justice was uncovered in 1981, he was working in Umkhonto we Sizwe Security in Maputo. Others from this ring had been based in Botswana. It was they who for months had successfully diverted arms shipments destined for the underground in South Africa to their handlers in Pretoria. The Botswana spies managed to escape to South Africa after Piper's arrest. The whole ring was said to have been handled by a Security Policeman called Slow.

The spy-ring in Umkhonto we Sizwe whose discovery was claimed by ANC Security in March 1981 appeared to have infiltrated every stage in the conveyor belt along which fighters were to proceed from the base camps in Angola, through headquarters in Lusaka, up to the forward areas on South Africa's borders and then into the Republic itself. Kenneth Mahamba later died at the ANC's Quatro prison camp. 'Stix' was released some years later after the ANC's security organ had failed to prove his guilt conclusively.

ANC Security officials are adamant that Piper was a genuine spy. They learned of the existence of Slow, the South African spy-master, only from Piper and Kenneth Mahamba, and on the basis of that information they made an attempt on Slow's life. Mahamba too was certainly an agent, in the opinion of the same ANC Security officials. Before his discovery, he had been highly successful in damaging and destroying Umkhonto we Sizwe equipment, including trucks and film projectors. The idea was to hold up deliveries of food, medicine and so on to the Angolan camps. The destruction of film projectors led to acute boredom in the camps, which resulted in increased use of *dagga* and home-brewing of liquor. Both brewing and *dagga*-smoking were disciplinary offences. Mahamba, as a camp commander, was also able to curtail some promising Umkhonto we Sizwe careers by suggesting that some of the more able recruits were enemy agents, when they were in fact innocent of the charge. Some people were kept under suspicion for years as a result of Mahamba's false allegations. One such case was Mzwandile Mabopane. A gifted and articulate man, his talents were spotted by Mahamba early on. Mahamba suggested to Security personnel that Mabopane was a possible enemy agent, and for years he was under scrutiny, frequently being questioned and urged to confess. As one of the most promising cadres, he would normally have been sent to the Soviet block for advanced training. In fact he was passed over again and again, while his less able contemporaries went abroad. Eventually his name was cleared, and he was duly sent to a political school in Bulgaria, but the damage had been done, and he had become bitter and suspicious. Mabopane was later appointed military commander of the Eastern Cape. He died in 1986 in a shoot-out with the police, after holding at bay an enemy unit for over ten hours near Sterkspruit, killing several of them. Others in Mabopane's position, innocent men put under suspicion as a result of trickery, even took their own lives.

Although ANC Security men were adamant that Piper and Mahamba were indeed spies, who had operated in their midst for years and caused immense damage, there is no doubt that the climate their unmasking created was used by some in the ANC for blatantly personal and political purposes, and to rid themselves of rivals. Some senior military leaders, who had been faced with rank-and-file opposition ever since the Wankie campaign, used the occasion to send for investigation their old adversaries. One such was Comrade Boyce, a Wankie veteran. In 1981 he was sent to the Viana camp in Angola on the pretext that he was a suspected spy. He came back in 1982, and was made ANC deputy representative in Lusaka the following year. Some of those who were interrogated by members of the ANC Security department in the months following Piper's and Mahamba's unmasking have given a harrowing account of events.[11] On the receiving end of the rumours and accusations set off by the incident, they came to believe that the spy scare was an invention by unscrupulous Security officials unnerved by the restiveness of fighters in ANC camps in Angola. In effect, at the same time as the Party was successfully installing political commissars under the control of the National Commissar, Andrew Masondo, in every ANC unit, it was also reinforcing the Security department. Masondo encouraged the Security men and commissars in his fief of Angola to maintain an iron grip on the camps and to interpret any type of criticism as treachery. The discovery of the spy network provoked a suspicion so general as to cast doubt on the loyalty of any ANC soldier, notably those who publicly called for an ANC conference to discuss questions of strategy and to air a range of grievances in the camps.

ANC Security chiefs claimed that the discovery revealed a need to study matters of security in detail and to overhaul the entire machinery. The ANC's senior leadership gave to its Security department, known as Mbokodo, 'the boulder which crushes', wide-ranging powers to investigate. Mbokodo men set to work detaining anyone suspected of espionage, of connection with Mahamba and Piper, or simply perceived as acting in a suspicious manner. They were given full powers to beat and torture suspects. In the pervasive atmosphere

---

11. Bandile Ketelo, Amos Maxongo and others, 'A Miscarriage of Democracy: the ANC Security Department in the 1984 Mutiny in Umkhonto we Sizwe', *Searchlight South Africa*, Vol. 2, No. 1.

of suspicion, almost any action by a cadre based in the Angolan camps could become grounds for investigation. Men and women who complained about the quality of food in the camps, or who complained about the lack of military activity in South Africa itself, were labelled as suspects and held for interrogation. In April 1981, commissions to investigate security and discipline were established in every ANC camp, supervised by security officers. They launched a major campaign against *dagga*-smokers, with suspected users being interrogated and beaten, the normal mode of punishment being to leave offenders tied to a tree for a three-week period. No suspected drug-user was actually executed, although one man named Reggie died while he was being tortured and interrogated about the drug network in Quibaxe camp. Although his death was not intended, the fact that his torturers went unpunished seemed to convey the message that Security had a free hand in dealing with *dagga*-users. A man named Mahlatini, a musician with the ANC cultural ensemble, Amandla, died in similar circumstances.

Some of those who suffered at the hands of Mbokodo, such as Amos Maxongo, a young guerrilla who had left Port Elizabeth in the late 1970s, claim that the need to punish offences against elementary discipline was used as a pretext to eliminate known critics of the ANC leadership, and this indeed seems to have been the case. Some of those detained as alleged *dagga*-smokers were in fact interrogated by Security men about their political opinions and their reasons for demanding an ANC conference.[12] Mbokodo went about its house-cleaning responsible to no one except the Security directorate in Lusaka, which had overall control of the two separate organs, Intelligence and Security.

South Africa's own intelligence and security services, well aware of the confusion and suspicion reigning in the ranks of Umkhonto we Sizwe, chose this moment to launch an offensive. On 8 December 1981, a South African undercover unit murdered two leading commanders of the Special Operations unit in Swaziland. The two Umkhonto we Sizwe men were ambushed while they were driving in their car and killed. Under pressure from Pretoria, the Swazi government expelled some ANC men. The following February, the Swazi king signed a secret security pact with Pretoria.

In Botswana, Umkhonto we Sizwe commander Joe Modise and head of Ordnance Cassius Make were arrested by the local police after a Security Police infiltrator inside the ANC had passed information to the authorities. The police caught these two senior officials in possession of a plan of military operations for the year 1982 which they were taking to a top-secret meeting with operatives from inside South Africa. They also had in their possession two pistols and over 60,000 rands in cash. All of these finds, including the

12. Interview with Amos Maxongo, London, 26 April 1991.

operational plan, were later exhibited in court when the two men were charged with illegal possession of firearms.

The cumulative effect of all these setbacks was to paralyse Umkhonto we Sizwe's offensive strategy. The trickle of operations inside South Africa nearly dried up as officials were grounded pending investigations by the ANC Security branch. The rank and file were marooned in their Angolan camps, in poor conditions and thoroughly demoralised by the detentions and beatings which were now commonplace. The ANC fighters, most of them young men and women who had left Soweto in 1976, had now spent more than five years in the difficult conditions of Angola. There was every reason for them to want to return to their home country on missions to get to grips with the enemy.

The atmosphere of intimidation created by the grip of the Party's political commissars and by the work of security men trained in Eastern Europe spread from Angola to other sections of the ANC. There were increasingly frequent cases of Security officials or senior ANC officials using the spy scare as a means of neutralising their opponents, usually by either detaining them at Revolutionary Command headquarters in Lusaka or sending them to the ANC farm in Angola's Malanje province. Some senior commanders were using the security crisis to purge the Umkhonto we Sizwe rank and file. One of those ordered into exile at the Malanje farm was a man known as Wellington, a veteran of the 1967–8 Wankie campaign. Wellington resisted the order of transfer whereupon a senior official, later to rise to one of the top positions in ANC Military Intelligence, was ordered to shoot him. Wellington was wounded; as soon as he had recovered, he was bundled into a military transport and sent to Angola. The camps became a dumping ground for any ANC member whom the leadership wished to silence or whose presence somewhere else had become awkward.

A good illustration of just how pervasive the intimidation exercised by Mbokodo became in the fullness of time concerns Pallo Jordan, the ANC's Director of Research, who is today head of the Department of Information and Publicity. In June 1983, Jordan was detained for six weeks after a dispute with a Communist Party member who was a senior official of Intelligence and Security. The Security men made Jordan write his biography again and again in an effort to find a contradiction. No one in Mbokodo really thought Jordan was an enemy agent. The ritual of writing and re-writing his biography was an attempt to humiliate him, to subject him to their will rather than to find contradictions. It was meant to send a message to all and sundry that if a man as senior as Jordan could be detained, then no one was safe. Less than a year before this Jordan had survived an assassination attempt by agents of Pretoria, having been injured by the blast that killed Ruth First in Maputo in 1982. Jordan was eventually rescued only by the intervention of Oliver Tambo and by the overall head of Security and Intelligence, Mzwai Piliso, who had been away on business at the time Jordan was detained. Although it was generally agreed that the Security man whose path Jordan had crossed had gone beyond the limits of his responsibility in his treatment of Jordan, he was not punished after this incident. It is not surprising that others in the security apparatus drew the conclusion that they were immune from punishment.

Another case concerned Jacob 'Mavili' Masondo, a respected former member of the Revolutionary Council and former head of Umkhonto we Sizwe's Ordnance department. Masondo also argued with the same Security chief who had persecuted Jordan, was detained and then exiled to the ANC farm at Malanje, and died there as a result of his diabetes late in 1983. The death of such a respected figure in these circumstances sparked an outcry against the abuses of the security organ. Even Jack Simons, a Party leader, was moved to protest, but again no correction was forthcoming.

The intellectual and ideological leadership which the Party had asserted over the revolutionary alliance since the Morogoro Conference was now being accompanied by an increasingly tight control of administration and security as a result of the introduction of political commissars and the security crackdown following the unmasking of Piper and Kenneth Mahamba. Many of the rank and file in the ANC resented the growing rigidity of the organisation. However, few conceived this in terms of a conflict between ANC nationalists and the Communist Party. In part, this was because membership of the Party remained a closely kept secret even inside the ranks of the exiles. Some leading personalities were known to be Party members, but other ANC officials who were also Party members were not identified as such. Moreover, Party members generally enjoyed a high reputation for competence, quality and dedication. Those who suffered from the growing use of authoritarian methods inside the ANC were far more prone to identify the problems of the leadership in terms of personality than by reference to political allegiance. Joe Slovo, for example, although known to be a communist, remained popular with the rank and file of the ANC and Umkhonto we Sizwe throughout these difficult times. No one questioned his commitment and no one doubted his personal integrity. The same could not be said of some other leaders of the ANC, communist or not, who were regarded as self-serving, corrupt or brutal, and were held responsible for the hardships of the rank and file. Officials with responsibility for security and political education tended to be most frequently blamed.

One of the few whose reputations were enhanced in the early 1980s, as Umkhonto we Sizwe struggled with the problems posed by South African espionage, real and imagined, and by South African attacks, was Chris Hani. Since his escapades during the 1960s, becoming a spokesman for the rank and file in their criticisms of the leadership and leading a unit in the Wankie campaign in 1967–8, Hani had carved himself a mighty reputation within the army and the Party. He was appointed to the ANC's NEC in 1974, although the appointment was not announced for some years. From his base in Lesotho Hani had personally recruited many of the youngsters fleeing from South Africa after the Soweto rising of 1976, and he rarely missed an opportunity to push the brightest and most promising of them into key posts, gaining a reputation as the patron and godfather of many of the best cadres. His occasional sorties into South Africa itself, and his escapes from several attempts on his life, testified to his undoubted courage.

Hani was also making his mark inside the Party, still dominated by the older generation. Moses Kotane died in 1978 after 39 years as the Party General Secretary. At an extended meeting of the Party Central Committee held in East Berlin at the end of 1979, another veteran, Moses Mabhida, was elected to replace him. Brian Bunting, Ray and Jack Simons, Dan Tloome, Joe Slovo and other leading communists had all made their mark in the Party in the 1930s or 1940s. Other highly capable and respected communists had died in the struggle, like Joe Gqabi. Of the younger generation, the brightest of the rising stars were Hani and Thabo Mbeki.

Mbeki was born in the same year as Hani, 1942, and like him had attended Lovedale High School. Unlike Hani, he was the son of a famous father, the ANC and Communist Party veteran Govan Mbeki, one of those sentenced to life imprisonment at the Rivonia trial of 1964. Thabo had gone into exile in the early 1960s, had acquired a master's degree in economics from the University of Sussex in England, and had then studied at the Lenin School in Moscow. He appears to have joined the Party at an early age, no doubt under the influence of his father.

When Mbeki came back from Moscow he had a golden future in the Party in front of him. A brilliant theoretician, charming and highly articulate, his often unorthodox ideas were received with interest in a Party generally hostile to dissent. No doubt this was largely out of respect for his family background, which made his loyalty unquestionable. Mbeki climbed swiftly, winning his way to membership of the Party's Politburo, the true seat of power in the Party, which generally contained only seven or eight members. It was a major achievement to be elected to this body, dominated by the generation of Yusuf Dadoo, the Party chairman, born in 1909, or Jack Simons, born in 1907, or his wife Ray, born in 1913. Mbeki's espousal of unorthodox positions, and his growing closeness to the Swedish Social Democrats who, under Prime Minister Olof Palme, were among the ANC's most loyal foreign supporters, were considered unsound by the most orthodox Communists, including Slovo and Jack and Ray Simons. In 1981 the hardliners succeeded in removing him from the Politburo on the grounds that he had failed to attend Party meetings, replacing him with Chris Hani. Mbeki remained an ordinary member of the Party but moved closer to the Swedes than ever. He retained a following among officials of the ANC and some members of the Party, on account of his intellectual skills and his political acumen. Moreover his closeness to Oliver Tambo, whose principal speech-writer and aide he became, made him a dangerous foe.

Hani's elevation to the Politburo was the start of a further rise in his political fortunes in an organisation highly respectful of age and seniority. The following year, 1982, Hani was appointed Political Commissar of Umkhonto we Sizwe, the second-ranking position in the military hierarchy. He was already popular with the lower ranks, and could count on the support of a growing number of protégés. His new position gave him increased scope for exercising the patronage necessary to build an unassailable power base. In May 1982, Hani left Lesotho and moved to Maputo to work directly with Joe Slovo, the army Chief of Staff. He became very close to Joe Slovo and also to Moses Mabhida, the Party General Secretary. Hani's future seemed assured in the Party, in the army, and, through them, in the ANC as a whole.

6
Mutiny
1984

The Umkhonto we Sizwe High Command was determined to replace the strategy which it called armed propaganda – sabotage attacks carried out to advertise the presence of the ANC army – with the next strategic phase, People's War. According to the plan elaborated after the 1978 visit to General Giap in Vietnam by Slovo, Tambo, Make and Modise, this was due to begin in 1982. In the new scheme, there would be less emphasis on spectacular, high-profile sabotage attacks carried out by the Special Operations unit, like those at SASOL and Voortrekkerhoogte. Instead, Umkhonto we Sizwe planned to put in place the administrative machinery to stockpile arms in the Frontline States, and to spirit weapons and trained saboteurs from there into South Africa, where they would stay for locally planned operations. The next wave of fighters would then be able to attack and melt back into hiding places in the townships, where they would depend on support networks in the local community. There would be no more need for what the Security Police disparagingly called 'commuter bombers', coming into the country and then fleeing back over the border once their mission was accomplished.

There were a number of weak links in this chain. It was possible, at any rate in theory, that the ANC's arms-suppliers might refuse to provide more hardware. The ANC, never a wealthy organisation, would have difficulty buying replacements on the open market. In the circumstances of 1982 this possibility looked extremely remote. The USSR and its Warsaw Pact allies remained committed to the overthrow of the government of South Africa through armed struggle, and there was every reason to believe that the supply of weapons and training from this source would continue for as long as it might take to seize power. No one suspected or foresaw that Mikhail Gorbachev would come to power in the Soviet Union, and that he would end the Cold War which put southern Africa in the front line of the struggle between the communist and the capitalist worlds. The SACP, believing to the depth of its being that the Soviet Union was the true home of international socialism, considered that betrayal from this source was unthinkable.

An area of greater concern to the Umkhonto we Sizwe strategists was the states in the front line on South Africa's borders. These were the vital forward bases, where Umkhonto we Sizwe needed to deploy its officers and stockpile its arms. This could be done on a large scale only with the approval of the governments in Harare, Maputo, Gaborone and elsewhere. Although no one doubted that these governments universally detested apartheid, they could sustain only so much pressure. The securocrats in Pretoria had concentrated their efforts on forcing the Frontline States to refuse sanctuary to Umkhonto we Sizwe. The liberation of Zimbabwe had provided an important asset to the struggle throughout southern Africa. But weaker governments like Mozambique, Lesotho and Swaziland were so vulnerable to destabilisation by South Africa, and had already suffered so greatly, that there had to be at least a question-mark over how long they could continue in their present course.

Finally, there was a doubt about the ANC apparatus itself. Even if Umkhonto we Sizwe could establish an efficient channel for the supply of arms and trained manpower, could it trust its own members? The spy drama which had unfolded in March 1981 suggested not. ANC security men became preoccupied with rooting out real or imaginary spies in their own ranks. The disruption caused by the arrest of Kenneth Mahamba and Piper, and the witch-hunts which swept through the camps in Angola, in conjunction with the cross-border operations by Pretoria's Special Forces and Security Police, and the capture of the plans for 1982, had set back the timetable. 1982 saw Umkhonto we Sizwe still unprepared to launch a People's War.

Throughout the year, South African operations against Umkhonto we Sizwe and its hosts in the front line continued at an intense level, using all the methods available to the State Security Council – cross-border raids, assassinations and sabotage, sponsorship of rebel movements like UNITA, RENAMO and 'super-ZAPU', as well as trade sanctions and so on. For the time being Maputo remained the guerrilla army's real nerve-centre. The Security Police were more than ever determined to kill Joe Slovo, the Chief of Staff whom they correctly identified as the single most important strategic brain behind the Special Operations force. A parcel bomb sent by a government death squad to Maputo on 17 August 1982 killed Slovo's wife, Ruth First. There were occasional assassination attempts against other senior figures too, notably Chris Hani.

The South African defence minister, General Magnus Malan, believed that destabilisation was working, and he estimated that within five years the ANC would have been completely expelled from the Frontline States. But destabilisation was not without political cost to South Africa. Even a generally supportive US government was concerned by the impact on international relations of South African hostilities against neighbouring countries. In late 1982, the US director of Central Intelligence, William Casey, met South African leaders including P.W. Botha, Foreign Minister 'Pik' Botha, General Malan and senior military men. He is reported to have urged them to revert to more diplomatic methods, believing that Angola and Mozambique especially had been weakened to the point that they would be prepared to expel Umkhonto we Sizwe in exchange for peace and a South African promise of neutrality. Casey and others in the US government were particularly concerned about the massive Cuban presence in Angola. They argued that as part of a general political settlement between South Africa and the Frontline States it was possible to negotiate the departure of Cuban troops from Angola in exchange for a South African agreement to leave Namibia.[1] Officials of the South African foreign ministry led by 'Pik' Botha generally shared this analysis.

There was also concern about the cost of destabilisation in South African business circles. The policy of destabilisation was good for those in the transport business, since the sabotage of rail and other transport facilities in southern Africa obliged landlocked countries like Malawi, Botswana, Zambia, Zaire and Zimbabwe to export and import goods via South African railways and harbours. This was a source of profit to South African freight companies and to South African Transport Services, which received additional revenue from the volume of business transferred from Mozambican and Angolan railways. But it was disastrous for those South African businessmen with interests in the Frontline States. For companies which traded there, destabilisation was destroying their markets. For those, like the mining giant Anglo American, who also invested in production in the Frontline States, it was damaging their output.

At the close of 1982, South African security forces launched a blitz on ANC personnel in Lesotho which some took to be a signal from hardliners in the security establishment that they were not prepared to bow to pressure from other quarters in their own government. On the night of 9 December, a force of over 100 South African commandos attacked several houses in Lesotho known to be used by the ANC. They killed 42 people including 30 members of the ANC. Among the dead was Zola Nqini, chief ANC representative in Lesotho, a former Robben Island prisoner. Some of the attackers, returning with their mission accomplished, lost their way home in the dark. A phone call from Pretoria to the Lesotho government in Maseru convinced the local authorities that they would be well advised not to obstruct the return of the commandos. The Lesotho army kept well away. So provocative was the raid that even the US government supported a resolution of the United Nations' Security Council condemning the attack. Umkhonto we Sizwe responded to the raid on 20 December, the day the Maseru dead were buried, by exploding three bombs at the ultra-sensitive Koeberg nuclear research station.

One reason why the casualty-list was so long was that the victims of the Maseru massacre were unarmed. The ANC in Maseru had

---

1. Joseph Hanlon, *Beggar Your Neighbours,* pp. 34–5.

hardly any weapons, so difficult was it to provide a flow of weapons from outside into Lesotho, an enclave entirely surrounded by South Africa. And if the ANC could not get weapons even into independent Lesotho, it was infinitely more difficult to smuggle them into South Africa itself. One of the most persistent themes of rank-and-file critics inside Umkhonto we Sizwe was that not enough was being done at the war-front. They would prefer to die fighting inside South Africa than to kick their heels in squalid camps in Angola.

To maintain some sort of military activity in the face of these difficulties, the Umkhonto we Sizwe High Command decided that, in the absence of suitable preparations for the People's War which it had envisaged, it would launch another spectacular sabotage attack on the scale of the SASOL and Voortrekkerhoogte operations. This time the method used was a car-bomb placed outside the headquarters of the South African Air Force in Pretoria on 20 May 1983. The bomb killed nineteen people, including the two people who planted it,[2] and more than 200 people were injured. Among the dead were eleven officers of the South African Air Force including a brigadier. Whatever the public reaction to the bombing, which provoked outrage in white South Africa, no one could fail to note that it struck near the heart of the South African military establishment. The Pretoria bomb was the work of the Special Operations unit working out of Maputo, now under the command of a Communist Party member code-named Rashid. The South African Air Force, feeling honour-bound to reply in its own name, launched a retaliatory bombing raid on Maputo three days later. It missed any ANC target and hit only a jam factory, killing a number of Mozambican workers.

The ANC was now ready to unveil the new machinery for the direction of the People's War which it was confident would still develop. The old Revolutionary Council, formally established at Morogoro in 1969, was abolished. It was replaced by a new body called the Political-Military Council (PMC), whose task was strikingly similar to that of the State Security Council in Pretoria. Charged with coordinating the armed struggle with activity on the labour and political front, the PMC consisted of representatives from the army, the Intelligence and Security department, and the political and labour wings of the triple alliance formed by the ANC, the Communist Party and the South African Congress of Trades Unions. Since SACTU was effectively an emanation of the Communist Party, it meant that communists dominated the PMC in any one of a number of capacities. A Party member could sit on the PMC as a representative of the ANC, of the army, of SACTU, or of the Party itself.

The PMC's chairman was Oliver Tambo in his capacity as President-General of the ANC. Its vice-chairmen, serving *ex officio*, were ANC Secretary-General Alfred Nzo (who was also a member of the Party

2. *New York Times*, 3 August 1983.

Central Committee), ANC Treasurer-General Thomas Nkobi, Communist Party General Secretary Moses Mabhida, and SACTU General Secretary John Gaetsewe (also a Party member). The PMC was the direct successor to the old Revolutionary Council, which had first been led by Joe Matthews, and then by Moses Mabhida until 1981 when his other role as General Secretary of the Communist Party obliged him to give up the job. John Nkadimeng, another veteran communist, then succeeded him until 1983, when the Revolutionary Council was transformed into the Political-Military Council. In all these years, Joe Slovo served the Revolutionary Council as its chief theoretician, writing documents on People's War and insurrection which became the official ANC approach to armed struggle. His pamphlet *No Middle Road* was for years the handbook of ANC revolutionaries of every political hue.

The Revolutionary Council had been the means by which the Party had been able to take control of the armed struggle in spite of the continuing interdiction on non-African membership of the ANC's governing body, which excluded from membership such important Party thinkers as Joe Slovo and Mac Maharaj. In 1983, when the PMC was established to replace it, its first Secretary was a non-communist, Joe Nhlanhla. This was a crucial post, since the Secretary serviced meetings and ran the secretariat. Nevertheless, in terms of power and stature Nhlanhla's post was much diminished from the position the communist chieftains Mabhida and Nkadimeng had wielded as Secretaries of the Revolutionary Council in the old days. The new-look PMC supervised a decentralised structure with disparate approaches and resources. Real power lay with the newly-established military headquarters, consisting of Hani, Modise and Slovo, and the political headquarters, comprising Nkadimeng, Mac Maharaj and Josiah Jele. All of these were leading communists, with the exception of Modise.

While these changes were taking place at the top level, the army rank and file were becoming increasingly restive, especially in the Angolan camps where the bulk of Umkhonto we Sizwe fighters were housed.[3] The origins of their dissatisfaction went back to the late 1970s when trained guerrillas had been sent to a camp in northern Angola called Fazenda, where fighters were to undergo three-month courses in survival techniques. Conditions at Fazenda were harsh, supposedly so that inmates could learn how to adapt to spartan conditions. Even food and water were scarce, which was a reflection not only of the extreme hardship of daily life in war-torn Angola, but also of the notion that the Fazenda inmates were learning how to live in the bush, in preparation for their eventual infiltration into South Africa.[4] As the months rolled by, the Fazenda guerrillas became

3. The following passage relies heavily on the account by a number of former ANC guerillas in *Searchlight South Africa*, No. 5, July 1990.
4. Interviews by Stephen Ellis with guerillas who had experience of Fazenda. Lusaka, May 1990.

frustrated by their meagre existence and the consuming boredom. They wanted to see the action they had been trained for, and to be pitched into South Africa to meet their enemy. Meetings of Fazenda inmates became angry. By 1979, three men from Fazenda had become so disillusioned that they travelled to Luanda to hand in their resignations to the ANC representative there. In Luanda they were detained by ANC and Angolan government security men and transferred to the newly constructed detention centre near Quibaxe in northern Angola known as Quatro, meaning 'four' in Portuguese. It acquired this nickname by reference to a notorious prison in Johannesburg known as Number Four. In Quatro, beatings, starvation and torture were commonplace. One of the three was released in 1981, a second only in 1984, and the fate of the third remains unknown. To head off further discontent, the Fazenda inmates were among the contingent of Umkhonto we Sizwe personnel sent to fight alongside ZAPU on the eve of Zimbabwean independence. Fazenda was closed down.

It was in these circumstances of growing tension in the Angolan camps that the spy scare arose in March 1981 following the unmasking of the alleged spies Piper and Kenneth Mahamba. Among those detained on suspicion of espionage was a group of guerrillas who had called for an ANC conference to discuss the problems in the camps. Others who criticised the excesses of the ANC security organ were detained in turn. The general clampdown on all expressions of dissent and on anyone suspected of criticism of the ANC leadership spread from Angola to other ANC establishments. At ANC headquarters in Lusaka, Zambia, detention centres were set up, including one at the old Revolutionary Council headquarters known as RC. Similar detention centres existed in Mozambique and Tanzania.

Oliver Tambo toured several of the camps to inspect conditions and hear grievances, and in September 1982 issued instructions to all army units that they should submit their grievances and proposals to the leadership. The papers which were duly produced by the camp personnel criticised the excesses of the security organisation and called for a general conference of the ANC, the first since Morogoro in 1969, at which there could be a full debate and the election of a new leadership. In response, Tambo rejected the request for a conference and appealed for patience, citing the exceptionally difficult circumstances in the host countries. He suggested that Umkhonto we Sizwe might be deployed in support of the military effort in Angola and Mozambique, where the host governments were hard-pressed by civil wars or insurgencies supported by Pretoria. The ANC's National Commissar, Andrew Masondo, who was also a member of the NEC and of the Party's Central Committee, toured the Angolan camps to express his disappointment at the memoranda which had been submitted by the occupants in response to Tambo's request for proposals. He was especially disappointed by the response from Pango and Viana camps, whose submissions were, he suggested, unreadable. Masondo, by this time, was deeply unpopular in the ANC camps, since he was held responsible for the excesses of the political commissars under his command and was generally regarded as utterly unsympathetic to the condition of the rank and file.

The abolition of the Revolutionary Council and its replacement by the PMC in April 1983 were intended partly as a response to these criticisms from below, but this administrative reshuffle inspired little enthusiasm, especially when it was learned that there was to be no reorganisation of the army High Command. Some army leaders were criticised for corruption. Rumours abounded that a clique within the leadership was involved in smuggling into and out of South Africa, using army personnel to take drugs into the Republic and bring out stolen cars, which were then sold in Mozambique or elsewhere for personal profit. Some senior ANC figures were said to have grown rich on rackets of this type, and to be investing their money in Zimbabwe especially.

Quite apart from the ANC's own administrative and political shortcomings, conditions in Angola were lamentably bad as a result of the continuing civil war between the MPLA government and its Cuban allies on one side, and Jonas Savimbi's UNITA backed by South African forces and US aid on the other. Goods were in short supply. Road convoys were at risk of ambush. Throughout 1983 the ANC base camps in the Malanje region were under constant pressure from the UNITA rebels, and the Angolan government was putting pressure on the ANC to earn its keep by helping in the war against UNITA, as SWAPO was doing already. Mindful of the pressure from their Angolan allies, and also of the need to give the soldiers some combat duties so as to keep them from boredom and disaffection, the Umkhonto we Sizwe High Command decided to launch a campaign against UNITA with the object of clearing the Angolan rebels out of the Malanje region. This may also have been calculated to postpone the dissidents' demand for a congress, which would have been politically embarrassing at that time.

The ANC marshalled an entire brigade to throw into battle against UNITA in August 1983, before the onset of the rainy season. In order to muster the maximum strength, the commanders released from the penal centre at Quatro some of the suspects who had been swept up in the search for traitors since the March 1981 discovery of Kenneth Mahamba and Piper. Those who were released to join the ANC offensive against UNITA had either repented of their errors or been cleared after investigation. The ANC units were led into battle by Chris Hani, now the Umkhonto we Sizwe political commissar, Timothy Mokoena, who was later to succeed him in that post, and Lennox Zuma, the former Umkhonto we Sizwe Chief of Staff who had fought with FRELIMO in Mozambique against the Portuguese as well as commanding units during the Wankie campaign.

In their first encounters with UNITA the Umkhonto we Sizwe guerrillas, eager for battle, performed well. While demoralised Angolan government conscripts broke and ran in the face of UNITA attacks, abandoning their equipment to the enemy, the ANC fighters did well enough to impress the Soviet military advisers who helped plan their campaigns. After pushing UNITA from its positions and forcing them to retreat, Hani left for Maputo. The increasingly confident ANC brigade began to make forays deep into UNITA territory. It was then that they started taking losses and falling into ambushes. The more the casualties mounted, the more the troops asked themselves why they were fighting black Angolans, hundreds of miles away from South Africa, in a war which was not theirs, and why they could not fight their real enemies in South Africa. They noted, too, the low morale of the Angolan government troops, and the apparent hostility of some people in Malanje to the government which Umkhonto we Sizwe was defending. Those who had survived the purges swapped stories with others who been mistreated after being caught up in the March 1981 security sweep. Dissatisfaction turned into insubordination.

By January 1984 the discontent had grown to the point of open mutiny at the battle front in Malanje, starting with a military unit which had just returned from fighting UNITA without food for four days. An important meeting of Umkhonto we Sizwe headquarters was due to take place in Luanda, Angola's capital, that month, and the soldiers knew that their entire leadership would be present. Responding to the calls coming from Malanje province, on 12 January 1984 a delegation from the ANC's NEC, including Oliver Tambo, arrived at Caculama, the main Umkhonto we Sizwe base in Malanje. The mutineers, based at Kangandala some 80 kilometres away, sent word to Tambo and his delegation that they were demanding an immediate end to operations against UNITA and the opening of a campaign in South Africa; the suspension of the ANC security apparatus and an investigation of Quatro; and that Tambo should come to their camp at Kangandala to address them personally and listen to their grievances. Tambo decided that he would not submit to the mutineers' demands, and left for Luanda that evening without going to their camp.

Far from quelling the spirit of mutiny, Tambo's refusal to meet the mutineers caused it to spread throughout the ANC camps in Malanje, to the extent that within a few weeks as many as 90 per cent of personnel were to join. The mutineers decided they would go to Luanda to put their demands to the ANC's top brass in person. Hundreds of armed fighters duly commandeered trucks to take them to Luanda to lay siege to the ANC leadership, then in the city for an extended meeting of the Military Headquarters. As they approached Luanda they were diverted to Viana, a transit camp for both ANC and SWAPO fighters on the outskirts of the capital, where the ANC hoped to isolate the mutineers. The camp was hastily evacuated to make room for them. The mutineers refused to disarm, and turned Viana into their headquarters. Despite attempts to isolate Viana, people from other ANC establishments in Luanda made their way to the camp to join the mutiny. Later, anyone found to have been in Viana at the time of the mutiny without permission was to be categorised as a mutineer.

At this stage, the mutineers' main demand was that they should be deployed in South Africa to engage their real enemy, and not to be thrown into battle against UNITA or any other force with whom they had no fundamental quarrel. Ironically, the main subject on the agenda for the meeting of the military headquarters which had been planned for January was a paper on People's War by Joe Slovo, a blueprint for the intended onslaught against South Africa. The mutineers called for the resignation of the entire ANC leadership, although they were still sufficiently loyal to express confidence in a handful of the most senior leaders, including Tambo, as President of the ANC, Hani, Slovo – not yet a member of the NEC, but a visible part of the leadership – and Moses Mabhida, the General Secretary of the Communist Party. They accused all the rest of betraying the revolution and being too comfortable in exile, no longer interested in engaging the enemy in battle. They reserved their sharpest criticism for Joe Modise, whom they went so far as to accuse of being an imperialist agent, Andrew Masondo, the National Commissar whose men imposed the Party line in the camps, and Mzwai Piliso, the head of the Security and Intelligence organ. Although some of those who were personally criticised were leading communists, such as Masondo, his political allegiance was not an issue of concern. Modise, as hated as Masondo, had never been a communist, and Piliso had already left the Party.

Some 900 mutineers, ensconced in Viana camp, received a recommendation from Chris Hani that they should elect a smaller number with whom negotiation would be possible.[5] They duly held an election to decide who among their number should represent their views. This produced a ten-person body known as the Committee of Ten. The Ten promptly deposed the administration of Viana camp and took control themselves.

The chairman of the Ten was known in ANC circles as Zaba Maledza. Like most people in the ANC he had adopted a pseudonym on joining the organisation, which he used in preference to his real name, Ephraim Nkondo. Zaba was the brother of Curtis Nkondo, the former president of the Azanian People's Organisation who had been suspended from the Black Consciousness movement on account of his ANC sympathies. Curtis Nkondo was chairman of the National Education Union of South Africa and was one of the leaders of the United Democratic Front tried for treason in South Africa in 1984. Zaba Maledza, too, had started out as a Black Consciousness activist,

5. Interview with Amos Maxongo, London, 26 April 1991.

but had left South Africa after 1976 and joined the ANC. He was one of those who had been held at Quatro in the early 1980s for disciplinary reasons, then released in 1982. Immediately before the mutiny he was the ANC's chief propaganda officer in Angola. He was the companion of Lindiwe Mabuza, a diplomat who was later to be the ANC's representative in Sweden and subsequently the organisation's first permanent representative in Washington.

Sources diverge on the names of other members of the Committee of Ten, mostly because they were known by such a variety of names, some underground operatives assuming a whole string of aliases. One member of the committee has been variously named as Moses Thema or Mbulelo Musi. His real name appears to have been Moss Mafaji, the brother of Aaron Mafaji, director of the ANC farm at Chongela in Zambia. Moss Mafaji was a graduate of the elite Lenin School in Moscow who had quarrelled with the Party leadership and was later expelled from the Party. Sidwell Moroka was a former bodyguard to Oliver Tambo and Umkhonto we Sizwe Chief of Staff for the Luanda region. He was put in charge of security matters within the Committee of Ten. Another of the Ten was Jabu Molofo or Vilakazi, the Commissar of the ANC's Amandla Cultural Ensemble whose leader was later nominated for a Hollywood Oscar after composing the music for the film *Cry Freedom*. Others of the Committee of Ten included Kate Mhlongo, also known as Nomfanelo Ntokwana, a leading activist from Port Elizabeth, where she became a household name on account of her work for the banned Congress of South African Students. In Luanda she had a role in women's mobilisation and was also on the staff of the ANC radio station, Radio Freedom. Another of the Ten, Grace Mofokeng, was also attached to the radio staff.

Represented by an elected leadership, the mutineers formulated three formal demands. First, they called for the immediate suspension of the ANC security department and the establishment of an inquiry into its activities, with terms of reference to include a study of Quatro camp. The second demand was for a review of policies affecting the armed struggle and an identification of the reasons for its failure to prosper. Third, they demanded a conference to debate policy matters and elect a new leadership.

The mutineers, under arms, were occupying Viana camp while the targets of their criticism attended an extended meeting of the Military Headquarters a few miles away in Luanda. Army commander Joe Modise was despatched to talk to the mutineers. The dissidents would not even allow him within the gates of Viana camp. The ANC leadership then consulted the Angolan authorities who despatched the Presidential Guard under the command of Colonel Antonio dos Santos França 'Ndalu', later to become army Chief of Staff. The Angolans shot a sentry whom the mutineers had posted at the gate of the camp. Two Angolan soldiers were also killed when they entered the camp in an armoured vehicle, which the mutineers attacked with a hand-grenade. These were the first casualties of the mutiny. The furious Angolans withdrew and issued an ultimatum: they would storm the camp if the mutineers did not lay down their arms.

Shortly before the expiry of the Angolans' ultimatum, the Umkhonto we Sizwe leadership sent Chris Hani to reason with the mutineers. Hani was one of the few senior leaders respected by the army rank and file, not least because of his reputation for physical courage and his own history as a champion of rank-and-file soldiers. He talked his way into the camp and persuaded the mutineers to allow him to address them, calling on them to put down their weapons before he spoke. Hani gave one of the finest speeches of his life, persuading the rebels to surrender and hand over their weapons without firing a shot.

Meanwhile further risings had broken out in Malanje, and more mutineers were heading for Viana. Angolan armed forces and ANC security men invested the camp, whose inmates were now defenceless. Later Joe Modise and Andrew Masondo arrived, together with five people sent from ANC headquarters in Lusaka to inquire into the mutiny. According to some survivors of the mutiny[6] these five were James Stuart, a veteran trades unionist and Party member, Sizakele Sigxashe, the chief intelligence analyst and later head of ANC security, who had joined the ANC in 1959 and the Party shortly afterwards, and had acquired a doctorate from a Moscow university; Aziz Pahad, a Party member and intelligence officer usually based in London; Tony Mongalo, also a Party member who had trained in the Soviet Union at the same school as Angolan president José Eduardo dos Santos; and Ruth Mompati, who had worked with the Tambo-Mandela law partnership in Johannesburg in the 1950s. None of the members of the commission was a member of the ANC National Executive Committee at that time. One source names the fifth member of the Stuart commission as Mbuyiselo Dywili.[7]

The following day, 16 February 1984, some of the leading mutineers were taken to the maximum security prison in Luanda. Others were transported to two Umkhonto we Sizwe camps in the north of Angola, Pango and Quibaxe. The interrogation of the mutineers at Luanda prison was accompanied by beatings, and in mid-March the prisoners went on a hunger-strike which ended when about 11 of the prisoners, including Zaba Maledza, were transferred to Quatro. Some survivors of the mutiny remained in Luanda prison until 1988. In February 1985 they received their first visit from a group of ANC leaders, including Chris Hani, the man who had persuaded the Viana mutineers to surrender.

While the leaders of the mutiny were detained in Luanda, where they were shortly interviewed by the Stuart commission in its effort to

6. *Searchlight South Africa,* No. 5, July 1990, p. 47.
7. *Ibid.*

unravel the causes of the mutiny, the bulk of the mutineers were required to follow a course of what was termed reorientation in the northern Angolan camps. It was apparent that the ANC leadership was attempting to repair the damage caused by the mutiny by isolating the leaders and suggesting to the rank-and-file guerrillas who had elected the Committee of Ten that they had been misled by a handful of politically irresponsible people. Hence the logic of requiring a political reorientation course. Some of the former mutineers agreed to be reoriented, but there was still widespread loyalty to the Committee of Ten. One group of former mutineers refused to attend a reorientation course and demanded the release of their leaders. On 13 May 1984, a group of those recently transferred from Viana camp mutinied for a second time, storming the armoury at Pango camp and disarming the guards, killing some of the camp guards as they overran the administration block. This time, the mutineers were led by Ronald Msomi Hoyi, the son of Inky Hoyi, a prominent chief in the Ciskei homeland. Ronald Msomi Hoyi was held in particularly high esteem by his comrades on account of his exploits in the campaign against UNITA.

When news of the new rising reached Military Headquarters in Luanda, Chris Hani and Timothy Mokoena assembled a force which Mokoena was to lead to recapture the northern camp. The loyalist forces arrived in the north on the sixth day of the mutiny, and attacked at once. During the pitched battle which followed several mutineers and some of the loyalist forces were killed while others, including Hoyi, were captured. The loyalist forces set up a military tribunal, composed mostly of security men, which sentenced seven people to be publicly executed by firing squad. The condemned men continued to call for a conference and the release of their colleagues until their execution. Groups of Pango mutineers who had left the camp during the mutiny were rounded up over the next few days. Zaba Maledza died in a punishment cell at Quatro a few days after the public executions; he was later said to have committed suicide, although many in the ANC have never accepted this version of events, believing he may have been executed.

The findings of the Stuart commission were never released, but it was widely known that the investigators attributed blame for the mutiny on the excesses of the security department, poor political education, poor recreational facilities and quality of food, and the yearning to go home and fight. The main single scapegoat was National Commissar Andrew Masondo. At the first decent opportunity, he was dropped from the ANC and Communist Party leadership and banished to the post of director of the Solomon Mahlangu Freedom College, the ANC school in Tanzania. The post of National Commissar was abolished and has never been revived. All the members of the Stuart commission were elected to the ANC's National Executive Committee the next year, which was generally interpreted as recognition of their work.

Although news of the Angola mutiny, known as *Mkatashingo,* spread throughout the ANC, and was certainly reported to the South African government by its intelligence services, little information reached the general public in South Africa or elsewhere. Only in early 1990, after the unbanning of the ANC, did a group of survivors of the mutiny contact the British press. They subsequently returned to South Africa and gave a press conference describing conditions at Quatro, and alleging that the ANC was still holding large numbers of political prisoners. Nelson Mandela and Albie Sachs both confirmed that abuses had taken place and that the organisation was still holding prisoners.

While these tragic events were taking place in Angola, the external environment in general was taking a turn for the worse as far as the ANC and the Communist Party were concerned. The pressure on the Frontline States from South Africa was intolerable, and one by one their governments began to crack under the strain. The first to surrender was Mozambique. Independence had come in 1975 at the end of a vicious war, but since then the country had known no peace. It had served as the main base for Robert Mugabe's ZANLA forces in their fight against Ian Smith's Rhodesians, and had suffered crippling Rhodesian raids. The economy had foundered under the pressure of Rhodesian measures and some absurdly over-ambitious socialist planning. It was widely expected that things would improve for Mozambique after Zimbabwe's independence in 1980, but in fact they got worse. South Africa's directorate of Military Intelligence helped RENAMO to develop into a fearsome engine of destruction, raiding throughout central Mozambique in particular, killing indiscriminately in pro-government areas, destroying roads, railways, hospitals, schools, shops, and virtually anything else connected with the government. Despite RENAMO's appalling record, and its origin as the creation of the Rhodesian secret service, there was a possibility throughout the 1980s that right-wingers in the US Congress and the White House might persuade the government to support RENAMO as anti-communist freedom fighters, on the same basis as the Afghan mujahedeen, the Nicaraguan Contras, or Jonas Savimbi's UNITA.

By late 1983, Mozambique's President Samora Machel had realised that he could not afford to go on giving strong support to the ANC and sticking to a strongly pro-Soviet line. He began to regret some of his previous errors. As he once told Robert Mugabe after the Zimbabwean leader had made a particularly fiery speech, 'I used to talk that way. Look at me now.'[8] Machel, working especially through one of his senior ministers, Jacinto Veloso, began to improve US–Mozambican relations, which gradually recovered after the low point when Maputo had expelled CIA agents in 1981. US intelligence chiefs, unwilling to be seen dealing directly with Marxist Mozambique,

---

8. Quoted in *Africa Confidential,* Vol. 27, No. 25 (1986).

encouraged Britain to do so in their stead. The British Lonrho company, well-connected in Africa, began to invest in Mozambique, while Samora Machel visited Western Europe to win support.

Finally, on 16 March 1984, Machel signed a non-aggression pact with South Africa at Nkomati, binding both parties to cease from helping each other's enemies. Mozambique told Umkhonto we Sizwe to pack its bags, leaving only an ANC diplomatic presence in Maputo. Lennox Zuma, the Umkhonto we Sizwe Chief of Administration who had especially close ties with FRELIMO since he had fought with them against the Portuguese, left Maputo, and with him went other military chiefs including Joe Slovo, Ronnie Kasrils and Chris Hani.

Unknown to Machel, and possibly even to P.W. Botha, some elements in South Africa's Military Intelligence had no intention of abandoning RENAMO. Before President Botha had put his signature to the Nkomati Accord, they had given the organisation sufficient arms and ammunition to keep them in the field for several months. And before the end of the year, the hawks in the directorate of Military Intelligence had resumed supplies, some by parachute-drop, believing that the time had not yet come to cease support for RENAMO. The Military Intelligence personnel who carried out this operation appear to have believed that those in government who wanted to make peace were naïve in believing that it was in South Africa's interest to give up RENAMO. On the contrary, they argued, it was a key asset since it was RENAMO which had driven FRELIMO from the Soviet and ANC camp into a more neutral position, and only RENAMO could prevent the FRELIMO government from backsliding. Besides, RENAMO was useful not just as a means of putting pressure on Mozambique, but also as a way of continuing to blockade Zimbabwe and the other landlocked Frontline States. To give up the alliance with the Mozambican rebels now would be to fail to press home an advantage. It was one of the most striking features of National Party politics in this period that factions within the government and the security forces were able to operate their own foreign policies with impunity. At what point President Botha and his foreign ministry learned of the continuing resupply of RENAMO is unclear, but once they had they permitted the policy to continue.

For the time being, however, in the run-up to the American presidential election of 1984, P.W. Botha was operating in diplomatic rather than military mode. He visited Europe and was received by Margaret Thatcher. On the other side of Africa, South Africa signed another non-aggression pact with Angola, promising not to invade the country again and to refrain from aiding UNITA. Before leaving southern Angola South African troops burned villages and killed livestock to drive people away and create a free-fire zone. Like the Nkomati Accord, the Angola agreement broke down within months, not least because Ronald Reagan was re-elected to the White House. The South African military men persuaded P.W. Botha, whose constitutional title was changed from Prime Minister to State President in 1984, that they should continue to apply military pressure to the Frontline States.

Other South African neighbours began to waver in their commitment to the struggle against apartheid, wondering for the first time whether victory was really inevitable as they had always believed, and whether the costs of destabilisation were worth the prize. Kenneth Kaunda of Zambia toyed with the idea of signing a similar treaty. In Lesotho, Prime Minister Leabua Jonathan refused to buckle in his commitment to the ANC but many in his inner circle had doubts. Julius Nyerere of Tanzania, now reconciled to the ANC after the disagreements which had arisen in earlier years, took the lead in canvassing his fellow-presidents, attacking the Nkomati Accord and urging them to stand firm on behalf of black South Africa. He succeeded in stiffening the resolve of both Zambia's Kaunda and Lesotho's Jonathan. The latter demoted Foreign Minister Evaristus Sekhonyane and his permanent secretary Tom Thabane after Jonathan discovered that they were negotiating a security pact with Pretoria behind his back. Nevertheless, Jonathan did not fire them but simply moved them to different departments, installing as his new foreign minister Vincent Makhele, a radical who headed the thuggish Basotho National Party Youth League. The Youth Leaguers began to receive training from North Korean instructors.

For the ANC and the Communist Party, the Nkomati Accord was a major disaster, especially since it coincided with the mutiny in the Angolan camps. It virtually shut down Mozambique as an infiltration route and took out of action probably the most useful of all the Frontline States from the military point of view. Once the flurry of diplomatic activity in early 1984 had abated, a quick glance at the map confirmed the ANC's lack of progress. On the Angolan front, the SADF continued to hold the Namibian border and to support UNITA. The Namibian guerrilla movement SWAPO was paralysed by repeated purges of alleged spies, the scale and ferocity of which made the ANC's problems in Angola pale into insignificance by comparison. The effect was that Namibia continued to be relatively well insulated against attack, with all of southern Angola offering no safe haven for Pretoria's enemies.

Even Zimbabwe was virtually useless as an infiltration centre. The South African side of the border was occupied by white farms whose owners were well armed and equipped, and had been brought into the government's security network. Moreover, the Harare government's fear of its former guerrilla rival, ZAPU, degenerated into systematic violence in 1983–4, encouraged by South African double agents who were still working for Mugabe's Central Intelligence Organisation, the old Rhodesian security outfit which continued to operate with many of its white personnel. The Harare government, fearing the continuing threat posed by a ZAPU party unreconciled to its electoral defeat in 1980, and continuing to claim the allegiance of numbers of former guerrillas, launched a murderous purge in ZAPU's Matabeleland stronghold, killing thousands of people in the process. Robert Mugabe's government discovered the existence inside the country of a secret Umkhonto we Sizwe underground, including fighters who had been living under cover inside the country since before independence, in contravention of an understanding that the ANC would inform the Zimbabwean security services of the identities of its operatives. Much as the Zimbabwean government disliked South Africa, it was hardly going to permit Umkhonto we Sizwe to channel more men and arms into Zimbabwe in these unsettled conditions. Zimbabwean security chiefs were particularly opposed to the idea of allowing Umkhonto we Sizwe free rein in their country, and they even used to have regular meetings with their South African counterparts, the only forum for formal bilateral meetings between the two neighbours.

Swaziland, Botswana and Lesotho were the only other states which shared a border with South Africa and from which Umkhonto we Sizwe could hope to command a guerrilla war inside the Republic. In some ways, the most promising of these was Lesotho. Although it was an enclave inside South Africa, and therefore difficult to link with the ANC's international supply network, the government of Prime Minister Leabua Jonathan, a former worker in the South African mines, had become quite friendly to the ANC over the years. The country shared a long border with the nominally independent homeland of Transkei. Umkhonto we Sizwe operatives had cultivated good relations with Lesotho security men and had even managed to penetrate Transkeian security to some degree from bases inside Lesotho.

Swaziland was the scene of one minor incident in the post-Nkomati period which was all too typical of Umkhonto we Sizwe's relations with the Frontline States. This came about when an Umkhonto we Sizwe fighter known as Bruce went to a disco in downtown Manzini and invited a local woman he met there to accompany him back to his house. When she refused, Bruce produced a pistol and forced her to go back with him. Later in the evening, she managed to escape and reported the attempted abduction to the Swazi police. Some policemen duly escorted the woman back to the house where she had been taken by Bruce, expecting to find perhaps one man armed with a pistol. Instead they were met with a hail of bullets from automatic weapons. It emerged that Bruce was a member of the Umkhonto we Sizwe Special Operations unit and that the house where he had taken his reluctant girl-friend was a safe house belonging to the Special Operations unit. Among its occupants was none other than Barney Malakoane, a leading guerrilla commander who had taken part in the attacks on SASOL and Voortrekkerhoogte. There followed a gun battle between the ANC men and the Swazi police in which several policemen were killed. Naturally, this was to provoke reprisals by the Swazis against the ANC.

From a security point of view, for an underground operative to attempt to take a girl-friend back to a safe house by force was a very elementary lapse. And yet incidents of this sort were quite commonplace. Time and again ANC cadres, even those who had undergone extensive training from East German, Soviet and other top security establishments, made the mistake of adopting far too high a profile in their southern African hideouts. They took with them into exile the macho culture of the South African townships which has become a distinctive part of the ANC style and the identity of the ANC young. Although the Communist Party tried hard to instil a puritan sense of conduct into its own members and into the ANC at large, it remained a feature of the communist style too. Too many Umkhonto we Sizwe guerrillas, once equipped with some money, a gun and a car, could not resist the temptation to put on the style at their supposed underground hideouts in Swaziland, Lesotho or Botswana. The young men liked to show off their designer clothes and their expensive habits to impress the girls. Too often it was easy to pick out an ANC underground man in the discos of Manzini or Maseru. He was the one with the fashionable clothes and the BMW who boasted of his trips abroad. Nor did this kind of behaviour stop in southern Africa. There were incidents in Bulgaria where ANC trainees, subjected to racist taunts in a bar, had killed their Bulgarian tormentors. Even in Cuba, ANC trainees warned to stay away from beaches frequented by Western tourists could not resist the temptation to visit the best beaches on the island in contravention of their orders. ' 'n moegoe is 'n moegoe', the ANC men used to say, 'even if he's from Cuba'. South African machismo reigned supreme.

The strain put on Umkhonto we Sizwe's already shaky logistical network after the Nkomati Accord induced a near kamikaze spirit among the volunteers. Fighters who did manage to get inside South Africa did so knowing that their chances of leaving again were slim. The likelihood was that they would be killed in action, tried and executed or, most horrible of all, turned into Askaris and sentenced to a life as pariahs. Their philosophy was to live hard and die young.

7
Rising
in the Townships
1984-5

For the ANC, the outlook in early 1984 was bleak indeed. One of the most important of the Frontline States, Mozambique, had dropped out of the fight. Umkhonto we Sizwe was reeling from the effects of the mutiny in its Angolan camps. The brightest spot on the horizon lay in a rather unexpected quarter – inside South Africa itself.

The pendulum of black politics inside the country had swung yet again. The days when the government aspired to eliminate black politics altogether had long gone, and been replaced by the comprehensive counter-revolutionary strategy advanced by the securocrats and articulated by their political spokesman, P.W. Botha. The military men assured Botha of their ability and preparedness to guard South Africa against the sort of externally based assault which had eventually brought down Rhodesia, by destabilising the Frontline States until, one by one, they sued for peace and agreed to expel Umkhonto we Sizwe. At the same time they were aware that South Africa's most fundamental problem was an internal one. Securocrats and politicians had to find a way to create African, coloured and Indian political parties, and a constitutional framework in which they could operate, which would be able to win the allegiance of a significant part of the population and which would gain international recognition.

In order to achieve this internal goal, it was necessary to tolerate or even encourage a limited measure of black political activity. This was not a new approach. Pretoria had created some limited space for black politics in the 1960s and 1970s in the hope that the homeland system might take root. Invariably, any space of this type was exploited by radicals, whom the government then attempted to curb in a never-ending game of cat and mouse. Thus, Steve Biko and the Black Consciousness movement which had so influenced the 1976 generation had originally been able to develop partly because the government at that time, concerned with channelling support away from the ANC and into channels of separatist thinking which it hoped would underpin the creation of the homelands, had allowed Biko and his friends the political space in which to develop. Only in 1977 did the police crack down really hard in an attempt to smash Black Consciousness. This in turn created an opening for the re-emergence of pro-ANC forces and forced some Black Consciousness activists into the arms of the ANC. Black Consciousness radicals, alarmed to find that some within their ranks were closet ANC admirers, began a search for ANC sympathisers who might undermine the ideological purity of their organisations.

ANC leaders inside South Africa therefore decided that, if they could not exist peacefully inside the Black Consciousness organisations, they should set up structures of their own. They began with celebrations for the 25th anniversary of the Freedom Charter in 1980, and set up a series of campaigns around the icon of the imprisoned Nelson Mandela. There was a Release Mandela signature campaign and a Release Mandela committee. To provide symbolic leadership for these campaigns, activists appealed to people with ANC family connections, such as Archie Gumede (the son of Josiah Gumede, the man who had first put the ANC and the Communist Party on speaking terms) and Albertina Sisulu, the wife of the imprisoned former ANC Secretary-General. The government tolerated this resurgence of activity by people known to be close to the ANC because P.W. Botha's securocrats, as part of their total strategy of counter-revolution, wanted to introduce piecemeal political reforms. As Botha told his white constituents, they must 'adapt or die.' Repression on its own was stupid and, ultimately, unworkable.

The centrepiece of Botha's reforms was to be a new constitution which would give some degree of political expression to coloureds and Indians – but not Africans – at the national level. Government strategists believed it was possible to win support from the bulk of the coloured and Indian communities, and in time middle-class Africans too, for a government dominated by the National Party. To this end, the government began an effort to 'sell' its proposals to the public prior to the presentation to the white Parliament of the draft proposal for a new constitution in August 1983.

The various manifestations of pro-ANC sentiment, and even the creation of organisations by ANC sympathisers, gained momentum. Late in 1981 there emerged a Charter Movement of more than 100 organisations of all races that endorsed non-racialism and the Freedom Charter. In January 1983, the radical coloured churchman, Reverend Allan Boesak, proposed a coalition to fight the government's proposals, and such an organisation eventually came about in the form of the United Democratic Front. Strongly suspected by the government of being an ANC front, the UDF soon attracted to its leadership ANC stalwarts like Archie Gumede and Albertina Sisulu. They were later joined by veteran ANC members and communists coming out of prison, like the firebrand from the Eastern Cape, Steve Tshwete. It was a sign of the times that some of the prison graduates like Patrick 'Terror' Lekota – named after his prowess at football, not his political methods – and Murphy Morobe had gone to Robben Island as Black Consciousness devotees but had been persuaded to adhere to the Freedom Charter by Nelson Mandela and other leaders.

In the course of time, the government was to charge some leading lights of the UDF with treason on the grounds that they had conspired with the ANC and the Communist Party to bring down the government. Three trials in particular may be said to have involved prominent UDF people: the trial at Delmas of Terror Lekota, Popo Molefe and others; the Pietermaritzburg trial of Albertina Sisulu, Curtis Nkondo and others, and the trial of Moses Mayekiso and four other civic leaders in Alexandra.

The UDF, not so much an organisation as an umbrella for hundreds of separate groups ranging from ethnic associations to single-issue lobbies, was launched nationwide in August 1983. The timing of the launch and indeed the whole rationale of the UDF was to contest with the government the political ground staked out by Botha's reformers. The new Parliament was to consist of three segregated chambers, one each for whites, coloureds and Indians. The Coloured and Indian chambers had virtually no power. When the new constitution was actually imposed in August 1984, few people other than the white electorate were seduced by it, either at home or abroad, and the UDF was triumphant in persuading coloured and Indian voters to boycott the polls.

While this battle of wills was fought between government managers and opposition politicians, rent strikes were under way in a number of townships in protest against poor conditions and the lack of essential services, especially in the industrial heartland south of Johannesburg known as the Vaal Triangle. In September 1984, the Vaal townships exploded into unrest. Crowds went out on the streets demonstrating and throwing stones and were met by the police with their usual brutality. The movement spread like wildfire, joining the political sophisticates who had organised the UDF with a wider constituency motivated by the eternal hatred of apartheid and protesting over specific material grievances. No government prosecutor was able to demonstrate that the Vaal uprising was a planned act of subversion, and, indeed, the most serious unrest inside the country since 1976 was to a considerable degree a spontaneous event.

But once the masses had gone out on the streets, political activists were able to come to the fore and articulate the views of the many. In some townships, the unrest became so endemic that local leaders were able to organise informal street committees to enforce rent strikes and commercial boycotts. The UDF leaders had to tread a tightrope between openly calling for the overthrow of the government, which would guarantee arrest, and articulating the feelings of angry township youth. Gangs of youths known generically as 'comrades', armed with sticks, stones, home-made weapons and petrol bombs, attacked government targets and rooted out informers, developing in the process a horrific new weapon, the necklace or petrol-filled tyre, used to burn victims to death. The Security Police information system began to dry up as police informers left the townships in fear of their lives and as the young comrades, with the fanaticism of extreme youth, even pre-adolescence, refused to wilt in the face of the worst the police could do to them. In time, some townships became no-go areas where the police were afraid to patrol other than in force, leaving control of the streets to groups of young comrades.

The composition and political allegiance of the comrades varied widely from one area to another. Generally, they could be placed somewhere within a spectrum ranging from disciplined allegiance to an organised leadership, to sheer anarchy, to membership of an organised criminal gang. Many street leaders were allied, at least in name, to one of the national bodies which claimed to represent South African blacks, usually the UDF. In other places, they claimed allegiance to one of the Black Consciousness organisations such as AZAPO or the Azanian Students' Movement (AZASM). Statistics on membership of black political organisations have to be treated with the greatest caution, since none of them was in any position to organise in the manner of a conventional political party with card-carrying members, and all had an interest in exaggerating the numbers of their adherents. AZAPO had 86 branches by 1986 and claimed 110,000 members, compared with the UDF's 700 affiliate organisations and millions of members. AZASM, which claimed 80,000 members, was particularly radical. Elsewhere, the streets were taken over by strictly criminal operators only barely disguised as political activists. Around Durban, groups adhering to Buthelezi's Inkatha operated under local pro-Inkatha bosses, some of whom were members of the Inkatha central committee but were known to some sections of the press as warlords on account of their propensity for organising large units of Zulu men armed with traditional weapons, which they employed against opponents. A measure of the degree to which the 1984–6 uprising which began in the Vaal Triangle was aligned to the UDF was that, of some 24,000 people detained in 1986, some 80 per cent were estimated to be UDF sympathisers and five per cent aligned with AZAPO. Inkatha, which was generally pro-government, suffered not at all from these detentions.[1]

For the ANC and the Communist Party, these developments were a godsend. It was Thabo Mbeki, often the ANC and the SACP's most original thinker, who was credited with inventing the slogan which was to be frequently repeated in the next couple of years. The ANC would 'make South Africa ungovernable', ANC officials told journalists. ANC spokesmen sometimes liked to create the impression that the Vaal uprising had been masterminded by the ANC, which was not the case, or that the young comrades all owed allegiance to the ANC, which was also not true. It was rather a case of the ANC exploiting an opportunity for which it had waited patiently.

The situation provided just the environment which Umkhonto we

1. *Africa Confidential*, Vol. 28, No. 2 (1987).

Sizwe needed in order to work inside South Africa in a way it had not managed since the early 1960s. The strategists of the guerrilla army had always conceived of the liberation of South Africa taking place as a result of an urban insurrection, in which, under the influence of the ANC–Communist Party–SACTU alliance, with its armed and trade union wings, the oppressed people of South Africa would finally cease collaboration with the government and big business totally, and would be prepared to turn to violence *en masse*. The Vaal uprising in 1984 brought this vision much closer to reality. Radicals leaving the country and making contact with the ANC abroad supplied the names of likely sympathisers in the townships. Instead of encouraging these people to leave for military training abroad, as they had in 1976, Umkhonto we Sizwe officers now wanted them to stay. They would be useful as contact points for trained guerrillas who could infiltrate into the country and connect with the street leaders whose names were being reported to ANC Intelligence. At last, the era of People's War seemed to have arrived. Circumstances now favoured an Umkhonto we Sizwe strategy of concentrating on building a network of support inside South Africa instead of attempting primarily to influence events from outside, as it had done ever since the Rivonia trials of 1964.

The SACP was quick to take stock of the changed outlook and to be infected by the new political optimism stemming from the rising inside South Africa. In December 1984, the Party held its Sixth Congress in secret in Moscow. Considering that the Party needed a significant adjustment to its strategy, the Congress decided to expand activity inside South Africa, at a low level since the early 1960s, and especially to concentrate on building up Party membership there, rather than directing its recruitment efforts very largely at ANC exiles as it had done previously. It did not alter its overwhelming commitment to the use of violence and remained confident that, in the fullness of time, the armed struggle would result in the overthrow of the Pretoria government.

The 70 or so delegates to the Sixth Congress also proceeded to elect a new Central Committee, a highly secretive activity. During the years in exile, ordinary Party members were not informed of the identity of all the members of the Central Committee and the Polit-buro which are the highest organs governing the Party. The most junior Party members might know the identities of few fellow-members outside the basic cell to which they belonged. Only at higher levels of the apparatus, in a system where various levels of organisation chose delegates to represent them at a higher level, might the identity of the Party leadership be known.

At the 1984 Congress, Chris Hani was re-elected to the Politburo in triumph, receiving the highest number of votes jointly with the veteran trade unionist Ray Simons. Ray Simons was one of the Party's intellectual and political heavyweights, and Hani was close to the same tendency within the Party, which could be said to include Jack

Simons, Joe Slovo and Mac Maharaj. The delegates also elected Thabo Mbeki to the Politburo, returning after his reverse in 1981, when he had been dropped. Mbeki's election was a mark of his recognition by delegates as the most able politician in the Party and one of its most accomplished ideologists, even though the purists regarded him as little more than a Social Democrat and were highly suspicious of his good relations with Sweden. Although Mbeki could not be said to lead anything which could be labelled a faction within the Party, his personal and political skills were known to be particularly appreciated by some other Central Committee members, including, for example, Aziz Pahad and Francis Meli, considered the Party's leading expert on the national question. The Sixth Congress dropped from the Central Committee Meli and also Andrew Masondo, the latter held responsible for the Angola mutiny.

The Politburo, therefore, represented a spread of political opinion, including the orthodoxy of Hani, Slovo, Maharaj and Jack and Ray Simons, and the iconoclasm of Thabo Mbeki. Another tendency was identified with Party General Secretary Moses Mabhida, a man not noted for intellectual fireworks, but endowed with a deep understanding of South African politics. Mabhida rarely made concessions to white or Indian communists, sometimes, for example, insisting on speaking Zulu even in the presence of a mixed-race audience. At the same time, he was on warm personal terms with Slovo and other whites. He was no crude chauvinist, but was proud of his Zulu culture and highly sensitive, just as Kotane had been, to the dangers posed to the Party if white and Indian members were seen to dominate. The person most closely identified with an Africanist approach within the top levels of the Party was Mabhida's close associate and fellow-Zulu Josiah Jele, also elected to the Politburo in 1984.

The Party's confidence that the Vaal uprising represented the beginning of the end for the white government naturally led to contemplation of the future. If it was true that the liberation of South Africa was close at hand, then the day was approaching when the aims of the Party and of the ANC might diverge. After all, the Party had been committed since 1928 to a national democratic revolution as a first step towards socialism. The ANC was officially committed only to majority rule, and not to socialism, although since going into exile the ANC had been heavily influenced by Marxist-Leninist thinking. Broadly speaking, there were at least two possibilities for the post-liberation period which many militants thought to be not too distant. It was possible that the ANC mainstream, who were not Party members but who had come to know the Party intimately in the course of the struggle, might have been so influenced by the Marxist vanguard as to regard a democratic revolution as merely the forerunner of a socialist transformation. In that case, the Party and the ANC could continue to work in harness for the foreseeable future. But that was not a guaranteed outcome. It was also possible that many in the ANC might regard their task as having been completed once they had won freedom for all South Africans, without reference to socialism. The Party had to be ready to stand on its own feet and to recruit its own members independently of the ANC. Hence the membership drive launched in December 1984 as a result of the deliberations of the Moscow Congress. The Party had never completely lost contact with a small, and very valuable, number of internal cadres. Resolving to build up the Party's strength inside the country, the Sixth Congress laid special emphasis on the labour movement. The aim was to open up a terrain of political struggle in the workplace, profiting from the increasing strength of trade unionism, and so increase the proportion of Party members inside the country, in preparation for the day when the Party would eventually be legal once more.

In the meantime, the SACP continued to view the alliance with the ANC as the cornerstone of its strategy, as it had been ever since its suppression in 1950. In a vaguer sense, the two organisations had been destined to work together ever since the day in 1928 when the Comintern ordered Sidney Bunting to work with the ANC towards the goal of an independent black republic. Senior members of the Party, led by Joe Slovo, regarded it as imperative that the ANC allow whites, coloureds and Indians to become full members of the ANC leadership in order to bind the two organisations even more closely and forestall any eventual parting of the ways.

The Party could make powerful use of an appeal to non-racialism. Since the ANC stood for a non racial, or even anti-racial, future, and a South African constitution in which no significance would be attached to race, was it not logical for the ANC itself to be colour-blind? A powerful counter-argument, never rehearsed in formal ANC meetings since the downfall of Tennyson Makiwane and the Gang of Eight, was that it would alter still further the balance of power between the ANC and the Party, by allowing Party members further to dominate ANC organs in various capacities. Virtually all non-African members of Umkhonto we Sizwe were Party members. The admission of whites, coloureds and Indians to the NEC would therefore automatically tend to increase the proportion of communists. It would also alarm the considerable number of ANC members who, while not anti-communist as such, still thought that the ANC should have a distinctively African identity separate from the Party. If membership restrictions were lifted completely, Party members could surface in key positions in any one of a variety of roles, for example as members of the ANC, as Party members, as army officers, or as SACTU officials. And yet every Party member knew that Party rules and discipline meant that a comrade was always a communist first, and that in the event of a clash of interests, the interest of the Party would always have priority over that of the ANC as a whole. Some ANC members in the 1950s had had similar reservations, when the ANC was still legal inside South Africa, about the role of the other congresses within the Congress Alliance.

It would be unthinkable for the Party to enter any major meeting of the ANC without having prepared its own position beforehand, knowing it could count on its members to advance the Party's line, without necessarily identifying it as such, in a larger ANC assembly. Having prepared its own positions at its Moscow Congress, the Party threw its full weight behind demands for the ANC to hold a full conference, the first since 1969, at which the membership question would be at the top of the agenda. The ANC, in deference to the demands of the Angola mutineers, had already announced that it would hold a consultative conference the following year, 1985.

The Conference was eventually convened at Kabwe in Zambia in June 1985.[2] The chairman of the Conference was Professor Jack Simons, who was given the honour of upholding the symbolic continuity of authority during the brief period between the dissolution of the old NEC and the election of its replacement. Each of the ANC's regional organisations sent delegates, mandated by their local units to speak on the conference agenda. In some cases at least, delegates were chosen by Party units without consultation with the ANC rank and file. There were also numerous officials, including security personnel, who attended *ex officio*, and who were granted voting rights, giving the leadership and the Party and ANC bureaucracy effective control of the conference. It was dominated by Party members, with Jack Simons being the overall chairman, and Politburo members John Nkadimeng and Dan Tloome chairing various sessions. The number of delegates from Umkhonto we Sizwe, largely a communist fief, also buttressed the Party's effective control of the conference.

Even before the meeting, there was intense lobbying. One prominent NEC member, John Motshabi, argued strongly for the retention of racial barriers to ANC leadership. Motshabi was a former member of the Communist Party, who had been expelled from the Central Committee in 1981 on account of his alleged chauvinism. He had protested at what he claimed to be the dominance of whites and Indians in the Party. He also had a rather meaningless title as convener of the PMC, a post which carried no identifiable responsibilities. Now he produced a pamphlet known as 'the green document' which he circulated widely. Motshabi pointed out the preferential treatment accorded to non-Africans in the ANC. Most ANC members in Zambia, he said, lived in Lusaka townships like Lilanda and Chilenje, whereas the whites and Indians were to be found in the comfortable suburbs of Roma, Kabulonga and Woodlands. The small number of whites within Umkhonto we Sizwe were trained in Europe or at special camps in Angola run by Cubans and Russians. The mass of black fighters trained in squalid camps in Angola. He also alleged tribalism in the ANC, claiming that the organisation was dominated by Xhosas.

2. In addition to the ANC's official report on the Kabwe Conference, see *Searchlight South Africa*, No. 6, pp. 91–4.

Throughout the early part of 1985 Motshabi toured ANC camps in Zambia and Angola to canvass opinion, and even visited the surviving mutineers in Luanda prison. He was almost invariably accompanied on his tours of the membership by Chris Hani, who had a strong personal dislike of Motshabi as well as of his views on the Party and the ANC. Hani seems to have shadowed Motshabi as a way of keeping a watch on his activity. The Party leadership responded with an article in the ANC journal, *Sechaba*, penned by Jack Simons and attacking Motshabi's document, without mentioning its argument in detail or its author by name. Motshabi's outspoken opposition to open membership was to cost him his seat on the NEC, although his views were widely shared.

A typical case of the sort described by Motshabi was actually to take place next year, during the finals of the 1986 soccer World Cup. A group of white and Indian ANC members gathered to watch the games on television in an ANC Military Intelligence safe house in Lusaka whose existence was not even known to many African Military Intelligence officials. Some ANC members, ultra-sensitive to any suggestion of discrimination on racial grounds, felt moved to complain about this, since it seemed to confirm the widespread belief that some of the white ANC leaders generally felt more comfortable with Indians or with other whites than with blacks. Military Intelligence was widely regarded as being staffed by whites and Indians rather than black South Africans.

During the Kabwe Conference itself, opposition to the motion to open membership of the NEC to non-Africans came from several quarters, including inside the Communist Party, which once more demonstrates that, for all its rigidity, the Party was able to tolerate dissenting opinion on the part of at least some comrades within its inner core. The white communist Central Committee member Brian Bunting, a Party member since 1940 and the son of Sidney Bunting, opposed open membership of the NEC on the grounds that too many Africans still required an organisation of their own. He cited in evidence the three million people who had recently attended a rally of the reactionary and pro-government Zionist church in the Northern Transvaal and who had applauded an address by P.W. Botha. He was also, probably, rather more sensitive than most whites to the arguments put forward in extreme form by Motshabi, namely that African ANC members might be alarmed by the appearance of whites and Indians in the governing body of their organisation. Bunting's arguments were treated with acid contempt by conference chairman Jack Simons, who accused him of betraying his communist creed and of citing the activities of the most backward part of the population to condemn a whole sector of South Africa's people.

Among others who spoke, and eventually voted, against non-African membership of the governing body was Ruth Mompati, a non-communist who was regarded as a strong opponent of Xhosa domination of the ANC. Others included Johnny Makatini, the head of the International department, also a non-communist. Other leading figures who opposed the motion were Eric Mtshali, a leading figure in SACTU, and M.B. Yengwa, a prominent Congressman from Natal. Nevertheless, the proposal was carried and whites, coloureds and Indians were admitted to membership of the highest organ of the ANC, the NEC. Many of those opposed to the elimination of racial barriers to membership of the NEC were Tswanas, like Mompati and Motshabi, or Zulus like Makatini and Yengwa.

When the time came to vote for a new NEC, Oliver Tambo produced a list of candidates which included the entire list of members of the previous NEC with the addition of other names considered suitable for election. The conference included delegates from every section of the ANC, not only those from the camps in Angola and posts in Africa, but also people who had travelled from London, Eastern Europe and elsewhere. Each delegate was invited to cast up to 30 votes, one for each place on the National Executive Committee, but since not all candidates were known to all the delegates, Tambo considered it useful to draw up a list of possible appointees.

In the event, the top posts in the ANC were retained by their incumbents – President-General Oliver Tambo, Secretary-General Alfred Nzo, Treasurer-General Thomas Nkobi and Army Commander Joe Modise. Only one of these four, Nzo, was a communist. Newcomers to the NEC included one white (Joe Slovo), two coloureds (Reg September and James Stuart) and two Indians (Mac Maharaj and Aziz Pahad), all of whom were Party members. All the members of the Stuart commission which had investigated the 1984 mutiny in Angola were elected to the NEC for the first time. Not a single person was elected from outside the list of suggestions drawn up by Tambo, indicating the degree to which it was considered a list of recommendations. To the disappointment of those who had taken part in the Angola mutiny the previous year, the conference failed to discuss the mutiny or any of the subjects associated with it and the report of the Stuart commission into the mutiny was not tabled. So completely was the conference dominated by ANC office-holders and hand-picked delegates that it was not possible to put the matter on the agenda. However, it was generally conceded, even by very senior officials, that the mutineers' grievances were genuine ones and that they had lacked any formal channel by which to express them. The whole question was simply avoided.

Of the 30 members of the NEC elected in June 1985, only eight were non-communists: Oliver Tambo, Thomas Nkobi, Joe Modise, Joe Nhlanhla, Ruth Mompati, Johnny Makatini, Pallo Jordan and Mzwai Piliso. The latter was a former member of the Party but had resigned. Among Party members elected to the NEC were the Party chairman Joe Slovo, the Party General Secretary Moses Mabhida and Politburo members Chris Hani, Thabo Mbeki, Mac Maharaj, Dan

Tloome and John Nkadimeng. In fact, the opening of NEC membership to all races resulted in the entire Politburo of the Party entering
the NEC, with the exceptions of the veteran white trade unionist Ray
Simons and of Josiah Jele, who announced that he was not standing
for election to the NEC on the grounds that he wished to concentrate
on Party work and to attend a course in Moscow. It was widely known
that the Party General Secretary and effective leader, Moses Mabhida,
was terminally ill, and it was generally considered inside the Party
that Jele was clearing the way for an attempt to succeed him in the top
Party job. Mabhida and Jele were close, and it was believed that
Mabhida had been grooming Jele for the succession. However, late in
1985, after the Kabwe Conference, Jele was dropped from the
Politburo after being accused of chauvinism on account of his alleged
hostility to white and Indian colleagues, just as Motshabi had been
dropped from the Central Committee in 1981. In due course, after
Mabhida's death in 1986, it was Joe Slovo who was elected in his
place as General Secretary of the Party. Jele was then rewarded by
being co-opted by the ANC's National Executive. Any ANC member
aware of Party manoeuvres could not fail to notice that membership
of the NEC was being used as a prize to console a man disappointed
in his aspirations to the top job in the Party. It was not difficult to see
which was the more important and powerful of the two bodies – the
Politburo of the SACP, or the National Executive of the ANC. At
stake in the run-off between Slovo and Jele was not only personality,
but also political approach. Slovo was considered impeccably
orthodox, whereas Jele had Mabhida's streak of Africanism.

Mabhida's death, and his succession by Slovo rather than Jele, had
a marked effect on ethnic relations within both the Party and the ANC.
The opening of membership of the ANC's National Executive to
people of all races, which had been guided through the Kabwe
conference by the Party, in fact provoked widespread criticism. Many
of the most forthright critics, both at the Kabwe Conference and in the
ANC at large, were Zulu-speakers from Natal. The Zulus had a reputation inside the ANC for their exceptional pride in their own language
and traditions, and also for hostility to Indians in particular, perhaps
because most South African Indians also have their family roots in
Natal. Mabhida, himself a Zulu, represented this Africanist tendency
at the very heart of the Communist Party, and wished to pass on the
General Secretary's post to Jele, also a Zulu. The fact that the vote was
favouring open membership of the NEC at Kabwe in 1985, and that
Slovo rather than Jele took over the top position in the Party the
following year, combined to cause considerable dissatisfaction among
Zulu cadres particularly. It added to the ethnic tensions caused by
Hani's blatant championing of Xhosa-speakers from the Eastern Cape
to create an ethnic tension which persists to the present day.

There was however, a major debate concerning the prosecution of
the war. The conference believed that the long-planned People's War

was now at hand. Accordingly, there was another overhaul of the PMC, intended to restore the central control it had enjoyed in the old days of the Revolutionary Council. The thinking behind the innovation was that, since some areas of South Africa now hosted locally composed street committees, the PMC should put itself at the apex of a unified ANC command structure extending from Lusaka, through the Frontline States, to the street committees. Joe Nhlanhla, whom many communists had come to respect in spite of what they regarded as his suspect ideological positions, not to mention his eccentric personality, retained his post as PMC Secretary, having earned general respect for his efficiency. Under the PMC a second layer of command was created in the forward areas of Lesotho, Botswana, Swaziland, Mozambique and Zimbabwe. The second-tier command centres were known as Regional Political-Military Councils or RPMCs. This was of course done without the knowledge of the authorities in those countries. Pretoria soon learned of the plan and started applying pressure on the Frontline governments, who in turn protested to the ANC. Every RPMC except one was dominated by Party members. The exception was Zimbabwe, packed with Modise's placemen. But even the Zimbabwe RPMC was taken over by the Party in 1987, when it came under the chairmanship of Garth Strachan, a Lenin School graduate and the son-in-law of Ronnie Kasrils, the head of Military Intelligence.

The operation of the RPMCs provides a good illustration of the way in which, by the mid-1980s, overlapping Party and ANC member-ship enabled the Party to implement its aims through the ANC: but it also demonstrates how the Party's political aims sometimes blunted the effectiveness of the armed struggle. Any army's effectiveness rests largely on the efficiency of its command and control, sometimes referred to in military jargon as one-man command. In Umkhonto we Sizwe this crucial ingredient was often missing. Umkhonto we Sizwe did not have a unified command structure since it served two masters, the Party and the ANC. The upshot of this was that field commanders who were aware of the existence of the twin command structures learned to play one against the other, thus maximising their own autonomy.

A case in point was Lesotho. The military commander in Lesotho in 1983–5 was a non-Party man, Alfred Wana, a veteran of the Wankie campaign. His commissar was a member of the Party's regional committee, Skenjane Roji, also known as Isaac Makana. Under these two were the field commanders of Border command led by Party member Zakes Kulu; the Eastern Cape under Mzwandile Mabopane, also a Party member; Western Cape under Lizo Ngqumbane, also known as Sipho Kgosi, a Party member; and Transkei under Mazizi 'Pieces' Maqhekeza, a close friend of Wana, who joined the Party only in 1985. The three regional commanders who were also Party men were constantly faced with a dilemma about whom to obey: their military chief, Wana, or their political chief, Roji, who vied with one another in giving instructions. The three Party men could be reminded that they were communists first and foremost. To this end Skenjane, on the basis of the Industrial Principle of the Party which states that communists work for the interests of the Party in all circumstances, formed a Party corps inside the military structure, comprising all who were communists. Thus, communists in the military structure had two masters, but Roji always had an edge since he was a member of both chains of command.

In due course, the Party regional leadership issued a directive that all the structures – Security and Intelligence, SACTU and the Political Department – must establish a Party corps. This was rationalised as the Party's need to ensure the accountability of communists in ANC structures. This activity was, of course, kept secret from non-Party members. The Party Politburo dissolved the Party corps in 1985 out of concern that its existence might become known, thus causing embarrassment when non-members were allowed to see the existence of a secret Party command mechanism.

Thus, in the case of Lesotho, Alfred Wana did not have full control over his men. He was competing with a rival who was much more powerful in that he commanded a Party chain of allegiance. In many of the world's armies, Wana could have dismissed Roji for insubordination. In Umkhonto we Sizwe, though, commanders did not have that right. Wana would have had to recommend Roji's withdrawal to Military Headquarters in Lusaka if he had wished to assert his primacy, and such a move would surely be vetoed by Party chieftains who were also senior in Umkhonto we Sizwe such as Joe Slovo, Chris Hani, Ronnie Kasrils and Cassius Make. Roji was also fond of telling his Party comrades that Moses Mabhida had warned him that Wana was not a friend of the Party, a piece of information intended to convey the message that to obey Wana rather than his political commissar was in effect to work against the interests of the Party. Wana lost his long struggle and became frustrated. He was recalled in 1985 to be replaced by Party member Morris Seabelo. The three commanders who were forced to toe the Party line did so only grudgingly. They were aware that they were being manipulated but there was no recourse. The ethos of democratic centralism required that once a decision was made by the Party leadership, it was binding on all members. They could not challenge Roji's line whatever they might feel. This was the Stalinist method in action.

At the inter-structural level, a similar situation prevailed. The four structures – Security and Intelligence, Military, SACTU and Political Department – had each to delegate two people to the the RPMC.[3] Four of the eight who constituted the RPMC initially were Party

3. Called the Regional Political-Military Committee (RPMC) only after the Kabwe Conference in 1985. Previously it had been called the Coordinating Committee. For the sake of clarity we refer to it here as the RPMC.

members. Only one of the four, Kenny Jones, was actually the commander of a structure. The three others were deputies, with the title of either commissar or secretary. When there were elections for the positions of chairman and secretary of the RPMC, the chairmanship was won by Party member Wabert Gaba, also known as Nevo, and the secretaryship went to non-Party member Frazer Mafafa, a Robben Islander. A week or so after the election the Party regional committee decided to reverse Mafafa's election since it did not want to see a non-Party man in the job of RPMC secretary. Thus the Party arranged for the proposal and seconding of a motion to unseat Mafafa and to have him moved. Because the Party acted as a cohesive unit, the motion carried and Roji became RPMC secretary with Mafafa being moved to treasurer. Later, after a visit from Chris Hani in October 1984, it was decided that an eight-person RPMC was too unwieldy. A four-person working committee was set up, all four of them being Party members. In 1985, when the real RPMC was established, the PMC appointed five people, all of them Party members.

This meant that the most powerful body in the Lesotho region was an exclusive preserve of the Party. The fact that SACTU, the Military Department and the Political Department were headed by non-Party people was irrelevant since the Coordinating Committee (later, the RPMC) was the locus of power. It handled regional political and military strategy, budget appropriations, communications with headquarters and appointments of personnel. At all times Party members of a mixed body like this had a coherent programme and agenda. They acted in unison on behalf of the Party, adopting caucused positions, agreed beforehand in Party meetings. Because the Party operated in secrecy, non-Party members of mixed committees were unaware of the manoeuvres behind the scenes, or were even ignorant of the fact that the other four acted as one. They mistakenly believed that the four were individuals. This was merely a microcosm of how completely the Party controlled both the ANC and Umkhonto we Sizwe by the mid-1980s.

The task of the RPMCs was to set up Area Political-Military Councils (APMCs) in every locality of South Africa. The Umkhonto we Sizwe High Command would then be able to infiltrate men and material through this chain to the local commands. The Zimbabwe RPMC was intended to cover the northern Transvaal, although that never developed into a field of major conflict with the exception of a landmine attack on 16 December 1985. Swaziland RPMC, commanded by Ismael Ebrahim, consisted of two sections, one covering Natal, the other known as Transvaal (urban), to cover the crucial Vaal townships. The latter section came under the command of the Umkhonto we Sizwe commander for Swaziland, Siphiwe 'Gebuza' Nyande, the son of a wealthy Natal businessman. Lesotho covered the Cape and the Orange Free State. Botswana was to cover the Western Transvaal.

With the townships in a state of ungovernability and increased calls from the rank and file to carry the war into white areas, the ANC was aiming to have in every locality of South Africa highly trained organisers and commanders who would in turn train, arm and deploy their local sympathisers. The maturing of what Slovo called 'components of the people's army' with Umkhonto we Sizwe as its nucleus would be in place for a new phase of insurrection. With that scenario unfolding, the ANC intended to prove that a revolution can take place in a relatively advanced capitalist country without reliable rear bases in neighbouring countries, without jungles and mountains which are regarded as indispensable terrain in classical guerrilla warfare. This was the plan enunciated in the ANC Strategy and Tactics document adopted at Morogoro in 1969. It now seemed on the verge of coming to fruition.

Although some overseas journalists, especially, portrayed every young comrade in South Africa as an ANC sympathiser, it was far from being the case. In Port Elizabeth, one of the most radical areas of the country, some areas were under the control of people nominally loyal to the Black Consciousness-aligned AZAPO and led by the Reverend Ebenezer Maqina. Maqina's deadliest enemies in the fight for control of the townships were the numerous pockets of pro-UDF comrades. So vicious did the fighting become between these rivals that local ANC sympathisers in the Eastern Cape appealed to Umkhonto we Sizwe to come and help them fight Maqina's gangs. Hani was in favour of taking up the invitation on the grounds that by fighting the ANC youth, Maqina's men were in effect doing the government's dirty work. Slovo and Modise opposed the idea. The question was eventually put on the agenda for a meeting of the PMC. There, the decision went against deploying Umkhonto we Sizwe against Maqina on the grounds that the powerless should not be encouraged to fight the powerless. In fact, a local Umkhonto we Sizwe cell had already made its own decision to attack. Maqina was driven out of Port Elizabeth and eventually expelled from AZAPO, but went on to found the vigilante group known as Ama-Afrika, still active in the Uitenhage region of the Eastern Cape.

An even more serious conflict of similar type arose in the Cape Town squatter camp of Crossroads. Young pro-ANC radicals virtually took over the camp in 1985, and it became a no-go area for the security forces to the extent that ANC guerrillas were able to patrol the streets openly, gun in hand. But the dominance of the young comrades was not to the taste of everyone in Crossroads, including some erstwhile ANC supporters. The street committees organised by the comrades there gained a reputation for brutality and fanaticism in enforcing a boycott of white businesses, systematically stopping camp residents and forcing them to reveal the contents of their shopping-bags. There were cases of elderly shoppers being stopped by gangs of comrades and forced to eat soap powder or cooking oil which they had bought in white shops in contravention of the boycott. Excesses of this sort so sickened many among the older generation that there was a reaction, led by the unofficial 'mayor' of Crossroads, the autocratic Johnson Ngxobongwana. Ngxobongwana had previously been a UDF supporter, but, resenting his loss of control and realising that there was a backlash of revulsion against the comrades, now began recruiting his own gangs to oppose them. The white armbands or scarves sported by Ngxobongwana's men earned them the nickname *witdoeke*.

While it was true that the ungovernable townships represented a habitat in which Umkhonto we Sizwe guerrillas could move under cover, as Slovo had foreseen years before, even pro-UDF township groups were far from being under ANC command. In some areas the political labels adopted by youth gangs meant little, since local warlords fought for control of territory and used UDF, ANC, Black Consciousness or other political badges only for convenience. Elsewhere, feuds between pro-UDF and Black Consciousness rivals could turn murderous. In Soweto, rival gangs attacked each other with guns, knives and whips, killing dozens. AZAPO General Secretary George Wauchope had his house firebombed and several members of his family killed by UDF supporters. The authorities encouraged this feuding by circulating forged UDF leaflets urging UDF radicals to kill Black Consciousness comrades. The response of the security forces was often not to attempt to keep the peace, but to encourage fratricidal warfare between black groups.[4]

Although Black Consciousness activists generally dissociated themselves from the ANC, there was rather little ideological difference between themselves and the organisation. All but the most extreme Black Consciousness adherents had come to accept that a post-apartheid South Africa must be a multi-racial society, which was of course the ANC's fundamental position. Moreover, Black Consciousness groups had all adopted socialism of various brands, and indeed one of their main criticisms of the ANC and of the Communist Party was not that they were Marxist-Leninist, but that they were not radical enough in their application of socialism. The emphasis had changed since Biko's time.

The PAC, too, saw the township uprising as an opportunity to reassert its claims to radical leadership and to activate its long-dormant support. Since the collapse of Chinese interest in Africa, following Mao Ze-Dong's death in 1976, the PAC had been without a major international sponsor, and it had turned to anyone who might be willing to aid it with money and training. Some assistance had come from the Arab world, notably Libya, whose leader, Colonel Moammar Gadaffi, was widely admired among young South African radicals on account of his theatrical opposition to Western imperialism and capitalism. After the fall of the Shah in 1979, the PAC also acquired support from revolutionary Iran. A by-product of the PAC's support

4. Described in Rian Malan, *My Traitor's Heart* (Bodley Head, London, 1990).

in the Islamic world was that it began to acquire strong support in a new constituency, Cape Town's Muslim community. The PAC head-quarters in Dar es Salaam sent its military number two, Enoch Zulu, into the country in April 1986 on a secret mission to meet Muslim leaders. He was intercepted by the security forces and imprisoned. There has been no perceptible organisation of a PAC guerrilla army since his demise, although in the opinion of some, the PAC retains considerable potential support. But, ever since the early 1960s, the difference between the PAC's potential and the reality has always been widened by the PAC's chronic problem of leadership. The organisation in exile had a history of in-fighting which sometimes degenerated into murder and racketeering. Its adoption of ultra-radical socialist slogans, mixed with its closeness to Islamic fundamentalism, has convinced many intellectuals that it has no coherent identity or strategy. Africanist and Black Consciousness groups inside South Africa, lacking support from a superpower and having little appeal outside the continent of Africa, found it impossible to compete on the international stage, and it was this which left the ANC with the prime position.

The main exception to this was in Natal, where Buthelezi's skilful navigation left him with control of the most powerful of the township politicians and warlords. His abysmal relations with the ANC, especially following the murder of Griffiths Mxenge in 1981 and of his wife Victoria Mxenge in 1985 at the height of the township insurrection, increasingly set members of his Inkatha Central Committee and their followers against pro-UDF comrades. The townships of Durban and Pietermaritzburg especially became the scene of faction fights between rival groups, descending into a civil war which had claimed thousands of lives in Natal by 1990. Inkatha's local appeal was essentially to Zulu ethnic solidarity, but at the same time Buthelezi campaigned on the national and even international stage in an attempt to court moderate opinion. Received by President Reagan and Prime Minister Margaret Thatcher, he had some success in this venture.

That the ANC was able to maintain or enhance its popularity in the face of competition from Inkatha, AZAPO and the PAC may be ascribed to several causes. It had a long pedigree and could claim to represent all South Africans who were opposed to apartheid with a degree of consistency unmatched by others. It had significant international support, and it had Nelson Mandela, whom it had turned into an international icon. But most of all it had Umkhonto we Sizwe. In spite of its inability to transcend the limits of armed propaganda to wage a full-scale guerrilla war, Umkhonto we Sizwe served as a symbol of resistance for the youths who manned the barricades in the townships, and derived immense prestige as a result. The Kalashnikov rifle became a cult object and the guerrillas popular heroes.

For all the ANC's domestic popularity and international renown, it and the Communist Party, increasingly hard to distinguish in the later years of their exile, were always struggling to exercise their control over people and events. At its Sixth Congress in 1984 the Party had foreseen this difficulty in post-apartheid South Africa and hence had set its sights on recruiting more members inside the country. In fact, even during 1985, Umkhonto we Sizwe's most successful year, the small number of trained cadres who were able to liaise with the township activists were not able to impose their authority or their political line. The gruesome township mode of execution known as necklacing provided a good example of this. It was not an ANC invention, but for years ANC officials refused to condemn the practice. Winnie Mandela, who wasn't at that time an ANC official but who was known as an ANC supporter the world over, even praised it, shocking sympathisers with weak stomachs both inside South Africa and internationally.

The same difficulty of controlling from without what was happening within the country also applied to delicate ideological questions, such as the relative merits of the national democratic revolution and the socialist revolution. Ever since 1928, left-wingers inside and outside the Party had wondered whether the notion that the advent of socialism could be postponed until after the liberation of South Africa did not represent some sort of sell-out to the benefit of capitalists. It was possible to argue that, since the majority of blacks earn their living from the sale of their labour, the abolition of apartheid would not constitute a solution to their problems. If apartheid were abolished, black people would still have to contend with the problems of staff reductions, rising prices and falling wages. Only a small number of blacks would be able to enjoy the fruits of capitalism. What was needed, the left-wing argument went, was not just a national democratic revolution, as suggested by the Party, but a revolution which would introduce socialism at the same time. Inside South Africa this point of view gained ground among white radicals particularly and also interested some blacks in the UDF and the ANC.

The ANC and the Party in their exiled fastness rejected such analyses and stuck to their strategy of a two-stage revolution, but they occasionally experienced severe difficulties in transmitting their thoughts to their sympathisers inside South Africa. In 1985, for example, a congress inside South Africa of the Azanian Students' Organisation (AZASO) was dominated by a group led by its Vice-President, Blessing Mpela, which claimed to be representing the authentic ANC line but which adopted a distorted version of it. The ANC in Lusaka was hard put to prevent meetings inside the country from adopting heresies of this sort in the belief that they were genuine ANC policy.

Despite all these problems of command and control, there could be no doubt that the township uprising put the ANC in a stronger position than ever before. For the first time in decades, protest spread from the major cities of South Africa to small towns and rural areas, leaving the government in disarray and businessmen demoralised. But although the insurrection was a boon to the ANC, and shook the confidence of the government as never before by demonstrating the ungovernability of the townships, it also posed problems to the Party. Communist Party leaders could be satisfied that, by and large, the ANC in exile adopted policies and tactics to its liking. Umkhonto we Sizwe in particular was a Party fief. But the exiles did not control the UDF, even though the UDF was packed with supporters of the Freedom Charter. The UDF in turn did not control everything that was done in its name. Although in the heady days of 1985 and 1986 the Party really believed that the long-awaited popular insurrection was at hand, it underestimated the government's resilience and the fact that the exiles' control of the internal forces was perilously shaky. The Party, devoted to Lenin's technique of democratic centralism, and preoccupied with discipline, wished to assert its control of a solid structure of command extending through the ANC's external structures and into the country, as far as the street committees. And that was precisely what the securocrats in Pretoria wanted to prevent.

8
States
of Emergency
1986-7

The South African government was every bit as aware as the ANC of the relationship between the external front and the internal one. Fighting the enemy abroad was the job of the SADF, which had responded with its highly successful and awesomely destructive policy of destabilisation, whose main purpose was to prevent Umkhonto we Sizwe from organising proper channels of supply which would enable it finally to realise its ambition of fomenting a People's War, a popular insurrection under the revolutionary guidance of the Party.

Fighting the enemy at home was in the first instance the task of the Security Police, although P.W. Botha, transformed from prime minister to state president, with sweeping powers, by the constitution of September 1984, believed that repression had to be accompanied by reform. The strategy of counter-revolution held that the defence of the home front was a task for all departments of government, not just the police.

The Vaal uprising upset this division of labour, proving too big for the police to handle alone. The uprising effectively drove the police out of some townships and destroyed their informer network, making it impossible to identify and arrest suspected agitators and overstretching the resources of the 55,000-strong South African Police. The government had no choice but to call in the army. The deployment of 7,000 troops in Sebokeng in October 1984 marked a watershed in law and order operations.

The military chiefs were not unprepared for this turn of events, and indeed some of them seem to have taken a certain satisfaction in showing the police how the job should be done. Some of the more sophisticated army officers, who generally had better education and training than their police counterparts, despised the police for their crudeness. They regarded the police force, traditionally manned by poorly educated whites, as causing more problems than it solved with its thoughtless brutality. The military men had higher hopes for their more subtle hearts-and-minds approach, influenced by the latest theories taught in the staff colleges. And it is true that the army was often less unpopular than the police on the streets of South Africa.

It was the civilian government of the country which invited the army to police the townships and restore the control which had been lost in 1984, but nevertheless the soldiers were not freed from political constraints. Some civilian politicians, and occasionally, it was said, the police chiefs, resented the way that the military were now in charge of everything. There were stories of fierce rivalries behind the scenes as South Africa's securocrats discovered, as military men have done the world over when they have entered government, that politics does not cease just because it is soldiers who are giving the orders.

The final arbiter of power, P.W. Botha, was hampered by the hostile international environment. Foreign investment in South Africa had never resumed at the same level after the Soweto riots of 1976. The new uprising of 1984 shocked the world as never before. International banks led by Chase Manhattan lost their nerve and decided to call in their loans. In August 1985, Pretoria shut its foreign exchange markets and declared a moratorium on maturing loans, trapping over $14 billion of money owed to foreign banks inside the country. Senior government advisers and diplomats, as well as private sector businessmen, called on the government with renewed urgency to negotiate some sort of political solution which would persuade the world that South Africa had a bankable future. But after the failure of the 1984 constitution Botha had little taste for further attempts at reform. A notoriously bad-tempered man, he was bitter that the world had given him no credit for what he saw as his courageous exhortation to his white constituents to adapt or die and his attempts at dismantling some of the apparatus of apartheid legislation. He left the field to the SADF chiefs to experiment with their own theories on counter-revolutionary warfare, using all the latest techniques of psychology and social science as well as billions upon billions of rands to win the hearts and minds of the people.

Botha and the security chiefs decided, after the failure of the 1984 constitution and its three-chamber parliament to win either local or international support, that they would press on with reform not in the glare of publicity, which in many ways had done them nothing but harm, but by stealth. They would not proceed from the top downwards, as they had in the early 1980s by attempting to introduce a new national constitution, but from the bottom up, by improving living conditions in the townships and reforming local government. These would be the building blocks for another attempt at national reform at a later date.

To carry out its strategic task of restoring control while also winning popular support the State Security Council created what it called the National Security Management System. This was in effect a parallel system of government, controlled by the State Security Council and designed to coordinate every department of government, so that repression could go hand in glove with economic advancement. The securocrats hoped in this way to buy off revolution and win the support of the people with the provision of better housing, sewerage, electricity and so on.

The new nerve-centre of the civil service became the State Security Council secretariat, located in an eight-storey office block bristling with antennae in the business district of Pretoria. The secretariat coordinated the work of government departments, ensured implementation of State Security Council decisions, and oversaw the work of the various intelligence services. Its tentacles reached from Pretoria into every town and village in the country. Below the national level it set up regional Joint Management Centres in the main cities of South Africa, composed of government officials and military men. Below these were two lower levels of command. The whole system, about whose operations neither parliament nor the public were fully informed, was designed to coordinate the sticks and carrots of official policy more efficiently than anything which had gone before. Neighbourhood management centres drew up lists of local grievances and developed ideas for improving facilities at the same time that they were monitoring political opposition. They poured large amounts of money into the townships for upgrading. The SADF created a new Internal Security department to supervise the rebuilding of an informer network. Like so many of the departments responsible for fighting counter-revolution at home, it was headed by a former commanding officer in Namibia, in this case Major-General Charles Lloyd. Among military men, Namibia had always been regarded as a testing-ground for methods, men and weapons which might one day be needed in South Africa itself. All available means were used – informers, arrests and propaganda, as well as upgrading of services and infrastructure. All were coordinated by the securocrats. White businessmen and farmers, and even some blacks, were drawn into the network.

The new security chiefs held a number of advantages in their campaign to restore the control over local government which had been lost in 1984. First among these was the existence of numerous rival factions in the townships. The securocrats were not going to miss the opportunity offered by people like Ebenezer Maqina in Port Elizabeth and Johnson Ngxobongwana in Crossroads, and they encouraged these leaders to form gangs of anti-ANC vigilantes. In 1985 vigilante groups appeared in a number of urban and rural areas which had witnessed anti-government protest by the comrades. Their targets were primarily the leaders of civic and youth organisations, accused by the vigilantes of leading resistance to established black authorities. Undoubtedly, many vigilante groups were founded on authentic local interest groups within the black community. But they were able to flourish only because of protection from the security forces. Community councillors and conservative black businessmen formed the backbone of vigilante activity. One study[1] of 13 such

1. Nicholas Haysom, *Mabangalala. The Rise of Right-Wing Vigilantes in South Africa* (Centre for Applied Legal Studies, University of the Witwatersrand, Johannesburg, 1986).

vigilante groups concluded that official support for them ranged from passive support by the authorities to the active manipulation of divisions and the armament of those factions judged to be useful to the state in its battle against revolution.

Perhaps the best – or worst – example of this was at Crossroads. During 1986 the security forces promoted violence by black supporters of Johnson Ngxobongwana's *witdoeke* against young comrades who supported the UDF. They also exploited divisions between UDF radicals and their AZAPO rivals. Ngxobongwana's men launched a ferocious purge in Crossroads, burning hundreds of houses and driving out the young radicals. At least one senior security officer believed to have helped in the organisation of the Crossroads vigilantes flew in specially from Pretoria.

Vigilantes were devastatingly effective. Since they sprang from the local community itself, there was no place to hide from them. Since they were tolerated or even encouraged by the police and the army, it was impossible to defeat them. Community organisations and radical political groups which had survived police repression crumbled under the onslaught as vigilantes, operating under the banners of law and order and respect for elders, mobilised ill-feeling towards militant youth. The resulting bloodshed was represented in the press and on television as black-on-black violence, which offered an important propaganda advantage to the government. In late 1986, when the vigilantes had largely succeeded in breaking the grip of the young comrades, many of them were officially enrolled as special constables, and sent on duty with a uniform and a shotgun after only three weeks' training.

Combined with the vigilantes was a State of Emergency. First proclaimed on a limited scale in 1985, this was promulgated nation-wide in June 1986 and again proved highly effective. It permitted the security forces to detain suspected troublemakers at will without fear of legal recourse. Torture became widespread as over 24,000 people were detained in the second half of 1986. A few were eventually tried. The majority were detained, often assaulted, and released without charge. Some were held uncharged for over three years. Not least, the State of Emergency enabled the authorities to restrict severely the broadcasting of film of unrest and police action, which had proved so influential in undermining international confidence in South Africa.

At the same time as the government moved up a gear in the severity of its measures to deal with the home front, it continued to maintain pressure abroad. Mozambique had not hosted Umkhonto we Sizwe since 1984, but there was little or no reduction in South African support for RENAMO. Indeed, by 1986 it appeared that the intention of South African Military Intelligence had gone beyond neutralising Mozambique as an ANC base and had taken on a more ambitious geopolitical dimension, nothing less than the partitioning of Mozambique and the establishment of a puppet government in at least one part of the country. Some people saw South Africa's hand in the death of President Samora Machel in a plane crash in October 1986, although it was never demonstrated that South Africa was responsible, and even senior Mozambican officals have admitted in private[2] that they do not know whether or not Pretoria was involved. But the timing of the plane crash which killed him was remarkable, since it occurred just as RENAMO was making its biggest-ever push to reach the sea and set up a corridor of occupied territory from Malawi to the coast, splitting Mozambique in two and opening up a maritime supply route. Moreover, shortly after Machel's death there was a reshuffle in the senior ranks of South Africa's Military Intelligence directorate, suggesting that military men may have been judged to have gone too far in the destabilisation of Mozambique. In any event, the chaos in Mozambique drew in Zimbabwean, Malawian and Tanzanian troops acting either out of solidarity with the government in Maputo or to protect their own vital interests.

The anarchy in Mozambique also maintained economic pressure against both Zambia and Zimbabwe. In fact, in as much as RENAMO could be influenced by South African aid and advice, it was aimed at least as much at putting pressure on Zimbabwe, potentially a major foe of Pretoria, as at Mozambique. Zimbabwe's relations with the ANC improved as peace was restored between the nationalist rivals Robert Mugabe of ZANU and Joshua Nkomo of ZAPU. In January 1987, the ANC's National Excutive was invited to meet the ZANU Central Committee. This represented a breakthrough in relations between the old adversaries, who had never had formal bilateral contacts in the political sphere, as opposed to contacts with government officials. After the meeting, Oliver Tambo was invited to address the Central Committee, which received him warmly. It was the start of a closer ANC–ZANU friendship to replace the hostility which had lingered ever since the ANC, the South African Communist Party and their Soviet ally had backed the losing side in the competition between ZANU and ZAPU.

In Angola, the South African Defence Force continued to prop up UNITA while consistently denying that it was doing more than providing military supplies. In fact, South African forces were quite often deployed in support of UNITA, a task normally given to the 32 'Buffalo' battalion under Colonel Jan Breytenbach. Since this unit was staffed largely by Angolans recruited after the collapse of one of the parties in the anti-colonial wars before independence, it held tactical advantages over regular units of the South African army. Soldiers of the Buffalo battalion often wore UNITA uniforms; if they were killed, it was difficult for the enemy to prove that the corpse was in fact that of a soldier in the service of South Africa. Apart from being experienced and effective soldiers, men of the Buffalo battalion almost

2. In conversation with Stephen Ellis.

all spoke Portuguese and some of the African languages of Angola, making them effective in guerrilla warfare and scouting duties. If they were killed, the grief of their families would not embarrass the South African government. To use white soldiers of the South African army always carried the risk of having to explain casualties, and thus to reveal the extent of South African intervention in Angola.

Almost every year, Angolan government forces launched conventional, armour-led offensives against UNITA-held territory, and then the SADF was obliged to intervene with regular units if it wished to save UNITA from being overrun. Only South Africa had the armour and aircraft necessary to defend against this type of offensive. There were moments when it seemed as though the war was in danger of escalating to the point where South Africa would have to choose between intervening massively, which would be politically untenable, or abandoning UNITA. One such case was during a major Angolan government offensive in 1985, when an armoured column was advancing on UNITA headquarters in southern Angola. A disastrous oversight left the column unprotected against air attack, and South African aircraft were able to bomb it to a halt.

From a military point of view, the SADF continued to hold the Namibian border secure with relative ease, as SWAPO guerrillas were pinned down in central Angola and the SWAPO political leadership was paralysed by spy scares. But the long-term plan of SADF chiefs was to go beyond containment and to drive the ANC from all its sanctuaries in the Frontline States. After this had been achieved with respect to Mozambique in March 1984, and with Zimbabwe neutralised because of the poor relations between the ANC and ZANU until very late in the struggle, Pretoria could turn its attention to some of the other states which served as sanctuaries for Umkhonto we Sizwe.

Lesotho was in some respects the most worrisome of the ANC's host governments, as far as the South African government was concerned, because it is an enclave in the heart of South Africa. But Prime Minister Leabua Jonathan had made a large number of enemies inside his country, and there was an abundance of material to hand for Pretoria's strategists, who had been destabilising the country for some time through a proxy force called the Lesotho Liberation Army, attached to the Special Tasks Directorate of Military Intelligence.

On 20 December 1985, South African commandos staged a raid on an ANC house in Maseru, killing the Umkhonto we Sizwe regional commander Morris Seabelo, a Party member who had gained a reputation as a tough soldier during the UNITA campaign in Angola. From 1984 to October 1985, when he was posted to Lesotho, he had served as the head of ANC security in Angola. Among those killed with him was his chief of staff Joseph Mayosi, wanted in connection with the shooting of a South African Police colonel in the streets of South Africa's Gugulethu township. This was followed by the closure of the Lesotho-South African border on 1 January 1986. The resulting economic blockade led directly to a coup on 20 January, carried out by pro-Pretoria officers of the Royal Lesotho Defence Force. The new military junta was the first government to be installed by Pretoria in any independent country.

Thus began the retreat of the ANC from Lesotho, a condition demanded by Pretoria for the re-opening of the border. There was a sigh of relief in Pretoria as the new Lesotho military council under General Justin Meitsing Lekhanya expelled leading members of the ANC regional intelligence unit, regarded by Pretoria as critical to the ANC's survival in the country because of the contacts it had cultivated in Lesotho's National Security Service. Hard-core members of the ANC's RPMC stayed on, although some were soon arrested by Lesotho police, tipped off by South African Intelligence, by coincidence shortly after they had arrested and interrogated Marion Sparg, a member of the SACP and the first white woman ever convicted of membership of Umkhonto we Sizwe. She had been caught after failing to alter her pattern of attack, which was to call at a police station, ask to use the toilet, and then plant a bomb there while she was inside the building. Those who escaped the purge of ANC personnel in Lesotho, like Wabert Gaba and Tony Yengeni, the head of the RPMC, were subsequently arrested inside South Africa.

The new Pretoria-Maseru alliance gave no respite. With the help of two ANC men who had defected, Atiso 'Works' Kali and 'God-father' Manyai, there was a further offensive against ANC cadres remaining in Lesotho. One of those detained was an old ANC stalwart, Simon Makhetha, who was a naturalised Lesotho citizen. He had secretly taken over the task of disbursing funds allocated to ANC members in Lesotho by the Swedish government, together with Limpho Hani, Chris Hani's wife, an employee of Swedish International Development Aid. Curiously, it was at this time that the head of the Lesotho military junta, General Lekhanya, made a personal R20,000 donation to ANC funds. The ANC accepted the money, in spite of the controversy it aroused because of its source. Joe Nhlanhla and Chris Hani protested so strongly about the donation as to oblige Treasurer-General Thomas Nkobi to put the money into a trust fund, where it is believed to remain to this day.

In March 1988, a South African death squad killed another leading commander, the Umkhonto we Sizwe commander for Transkei, Mazizi 'Pieces' Maqhekeza, alias Mpilo, a law graduate from the Fort Hare University class of 1979. Maqhekeza was travelling with two colleagues when they were stopped at a Royal Lesotho Defence Force road block. One of the three was killed on the spot while another, a guerrilla named Khaya who had made headline news in South Africa by holding off a combined South African/Transkeian police force for 36 hours, again miraculously escaped. Maqhekeza was wounded and taken to hospital, where he was shot dead by an assassin as he lay in his hospital bed. He had been marooned in Lesotho for more than a year after retreating from the Transkei, where he had been based. Both Pretoria and Maseru had put a price on his head. Why the ANC did not withdraw him from Lesotho to a safer haven remains a mystery. At the same time as it committed such murders, the South African government showered Lesotho with inducements to cooperate against the ANC, including notably the lucrative Highland Water Scheme, which created thousands of jobs in Lesotho. Less publicly, South African security men offered inducements to the many car thieves and smugglers who worked between the two countries, proposing to them immunity from prosecution in exchange for information about the ANC.

Partly, the ANC had itself to blame for some of its losses in Lesotho. Hani's time there, from 1974 to 1982, was marked by bitter rivalry between himself and his deputy Lehlohonolo Moloi, a Lesotho citizen by origin and a protégé of Hani's rival Joe Modise. This split the ANC cadres in Lesotho into two camps even after Hani's departure to take up the post of political commissar of Umkhonto we Sizwe. The ANC Ordnance unit in Lesotho, which was pro-Hani, refused to arm ANC cadres at the behest of the Security organ, considered pro-Moloi. The Ordnance Department's argument was that arms were destined for caches inside South Africa and it rejected the idea that operatives needed to be armed while they were in the relative safety of Lesotho. Arms that were earmarked for use inside South Africa were stored in an abandoned house known as Moscow, which had been Hani's residence when he had lived in Lesotho. It was evacuated in July 1982 after it came under rocket attack from the Lesotho Liberation Army, a rebel movement run by South African Military Intelligence in the same way as UNITA and RENAMO. The Moscow house was the first target hit by South African intruders on the fateful night of the 9 December 1982 raid, when all the weapons stored there, including the latest bazookas, limpet mines and explosives, were destroyed. All twelve houses which were attacked offered no resistance as the occupants were unarmed. The only exception was at the Ordnance house occupied by the head of Ordnance, Faku Ntoyi, who used his access to the armoury to defend himself, but was nonetheless killed by the attackers. Another guerrilla, Mathabatha Sexwale, managed to save his entire family – three daughters, his wife and his sister – using a privately-owned AK-47. Mathabatha was later wrongfully accused by the ANC of having stage-managed the attack on his house, which was razed to the ground in the action. He was expelled from Lesotho and later detained by ANC Security in Tanzania. He managed to smuggle from his place of imprisonment a message to the Tanzanian authorities who intervened to secure his release. In a subsequent analysis of the raid, a general of the South African Defence Force attributed its success to the divisions and financial crisis inside the ANC, which was an accurate assessment indeed. Lehlohonolo Moloi escaped the December 1985 massacre of ANC personnel in Lesotho only because he was away in Lusaka trying to persuade the High Command to release funds that had been inexplicably withheld from the region. Internal divisions resulting from rivalry between rival barons of Umkhonto we Sizwe were all too frequent and reduced the army's effectiveness.

After dealing with Lesotho by means of the Lekhanya coup of January 1986, Pretoria moved on Swaziland. Its success here was the result of effective intelligence and espionage work. Two of the leading Umkhonto we Sizwe officials in the country were Sidney Msibi, a former bodyguard to Oliver Tambo who had been working underground in Swaziland since late 1983, and Glory Sedibe, the Military Intelligence chief for Transvaal, also known as Comrade September. Before 1983 he had been the commander of the Transvaal rural machinery. Msibi had also worked as the head of the processing unit under chief Intelligence analyst Dr Sizakele Sigxashe, and was effectively his deputy, prior to being deployed in Swaziland. These two had managed to recruit a black South African security policeman and were running him as an agent inside South Africa. The Security Police discovered this and detained the man. Instead of arresting him or killing him, they turned him into a double agent, sending him back to his ANC handlers. They told him that he must set up a meeting with Msibi where the Security Police would be lying in wait. Sure enough, the man arranged a meeting with Msibi in Manzini on 26 June 1986. The double agent subsequently claimed[3] that he was coerced into making the arrangement for Msibi's capture, and that he tried to alert Msibi by arranging a day-time meeting contrary to normal procedure. Msibi, however, failed to interpret the intended warning of impending danger. A squad of plain-clothes Security Policemen, lying in wait, pounced and arrested him. He was captured, abducted and taken to South Africa. The Security Police handlers repeated the operation in an attempt to abduct Sedibe, but it failed, and the double agent managed to escape in the confusion. Sedibe was later abducted from a Swazi prison in August 1986, when the police took him back to South Africa, got to work on him, and turned him into a double agent, too.

Sedibe gave the Security Police information enabling them virtually to wipe out Umkhonto we Sizwe in Swaziland. Later that year, they mounted a sweep on the guerrilla underground in the country, the targets of which included an office which channelled overseas funds to Umkhonto we Sizwe. On 12 December 1986 Grace Cele was woken up in her house in Swaziland by an explosion. She was dragged out of bed by three masked men and bundled into a van which took her to South Africa where she was kept in solitary confinement for 66 days with occasional beatings.[4] Acting on information provided by the 'turned' Glory Sedibe, the Security Police captured a most valuable

---

3. In a discussion with Tsepo Sechaba.
4. Karel Roskam and Boris Dittrich, *The Crime of Kidnapping. Abductions by South Africa from the Frontline States* (Anti-Apartheids Beweging, Amsterdam, 1990), pp. 13–20.

prize – Ismael Ebrahim, the chairman of the Swaziland RPMC and a leading communist. He was abducted on 15 December 1986 by two men who took him to a Security Police building in Pretoria where he was held in solitary confinement and tortured, as he testified at his subsequent trial, by being subjected to piercingly loud noises. Ebrahim's successor Siphiwo 'Gebuza' Nyande escaped capture or death by sheer luck when South African security men stormed his house in Swaziland while he was away in Lusaka, on 24 May 1987.[5] They kidnapped his wife, Sheila, and took Gebuza's BMW car. On 11 July 1987, a Security Police squad ambushed and killed Cassius Make, the chief of the Ordnance department in the Umkhonto we Sizwe High Command, and Paul Dikeledi, a senior commander for the Transvaal, while they were travelling in a taxi from Swaziland's Matsapa airport. Both were members of the Communist Party, Make being one of its brightest stars.

The destruction of the ANC-Communist Party underground in Swaziland was accompanied by further attacks on the machinery based in Mozambique. In December 1986, at Pretoria's request, the Mozambican authorities expelled six senior ANC members including Jacob Zuma, later head of Intelligence Operations and today Deputy Secretary-General of the ANC, plus Sue Rabkin, Farouk Salooje, Bobby Pillay, Indris Naidoo and Keith Mokoape, the deputy head of ANC Military Intelligence.

It gradually appeared to ANC Intelligence operatives that, even before Sedibe's treachery, their network in Swaziland had been riddled with spies. They eventually discovered what they believed to be firm evidence of this in 1988, when ANC Security became suspicious of a senior cadre known as Comrade Cyril, the Operations chief of the Natal Military Command and a member of the same RPMC as Sedibe. Cyril had occasionally been under suspicion of treachery in the past. One of his accusers had been Zweli Nyande, the brother of 'Gebuza' Nyande, but Zweli had been murdered by a South African death squad in December 1983 shortly after voicing these suspicions.

It is not clear in what circumstances Cyril was eventually detained, but he was held and interrogated by ANC security men. He confessed to being a career security policeman who had been ordered to infiltrate Umkhonto we Sizwe. If it was indeed true that he was a professional spy, then he had been stunningly successful in rising through the ranks of Umkhonto we Sizwe. ANC Security operatives were convinced of Cyril's guilt and believed he was on the verge of further revelations about his role when he died, either from poison, as some say, or as a result of a severe beating. Another suspected spy detained almost at the same time as Cyril had risen high in the ranks of the Party, and had even attended the Lenin School in Moscow. She was last heard

5. *Ibid.*, pp. 45–55.

of being detained in Uganda.

ANC security men under Joe Nhlanhla and his lieutenant Iscor Chikane – the brother of Reverend Frank Chikane – proceeded to make a thorough investigation of the activities of the Swaziland-Mozambique front. As a result of their inquiries, the Security department detained the man who had been the commanding officer of both Sedibe and Comrade Cyril. This was Thami Zulu, also known as Muzi Ngwenya, the head of the Natal Military Command. One of the 1976 generation of recruits, Zulu had risen rapidly through the ranks to become the first Chief of Staff of the Nova Katenga camp in Angola, where he had worked closely with the political commissars Francis Meli and Jack Simons. A Party member, he had attended the 1979 extended meeting of the Central Committee in East Berlin which had elected Moses Mabhida to the post of General Secretary. He had come close to joining the Umkhonto we Sizwe High Command, with strong backing from Chris Hani. At the 1985 Kabwe Consultative Conference of the ANC, Zulu had chaired some crucial sessions of the important Internal Reconstruction Commission. His arrest in 1989 by ANC Intelligence led to the final collapse of the Swaziland RPMC.

Although Thami Zulu was a senior commander of Umkhonto we Sizwe, and prominent in the Party, there were those who disliked him. The reasons for this dated back to his appointment to head the Natal underground machinery in 1983. Some ANC Zulus disliked his appointment to the post, since Thami Zulu came from Soweto and not from Natal. They would have preferred one of the Natal people to have got the job. His fate in detention led to scandal in the ANC. He was kept in such poor conditions, periodically beaten and starved, as to die shortly after his release. Today, few in the ANC believe that Thami Zulu really was a spy, but blame his death on the excessive zeal of the ANC's security apparatus. It shocked many that in 1989, five years after the Angola mutiny, the Security department could act with such impunity as to hound to death a very senior official without having to give any account of its actions.

Botswana was the only one of the former protectorates whose underground was not comprehensively smashed in 1986–7. As early as April 1978, one of the most celebrated Umkhonto we Sizwe operations had been mounted from Botswana, the Rustenberg skirmish. An Umkhonto we Sizwe unit led by Barney Malakoane, a legendary figure in the ANC's military wing, infiltrated from Botswana and encountered a combined SADF-Bophuthatswana Defence Force unit. In the ensuing six-hour fire-fight up to ten enemy personnel were killed, according to the ANC. Pretoria recognised the importance of Botswana as a military front by putting pressure on the Botswana government in 1979 to expel the ANC chief representative there, Joe Gqabi, who had recently left South Africa after being acquitted in the marathon trial of the Pretoria Twelve. Botswana's effectiveness was, however, crippled by espionage work by Pretoria's spies. It was, for example, a spy who had betrayed Joe Modise and Cassius Make into Botswana police custody in 1982. Another spy, a Security Policeman named Freddy Baloyi, is said to have been actually carrying his police identity card when he was arrested by ANC Security in 1985 and killed. Baloyi was only one of a number of agents handled by a Security Police colonel based in Protea, who persisted in sending more agents into Botswana even after Baloyi's execution. The ANC had no difficulty in spotting them, thanks to the information obtained from Baloyi.

The unravelling of the Umkhonto we Sizwe command centres in Lesotho and Swaziland took place in 1986–7, coinciding with the imposition of a State of Emergency in South Africa itself. For a few heady months before that, the ANC and the Communist Party really believed that the People's War had at last arrived. Expensive and difficult though it was to send cadres into the country one or two at a time, with enough money for their upkeep, there was a steady trickle of trained saboteurs infiltrating into the country. Cadres would fly from the camps in Angola to Lusaka, and from there to Lesotho or one of the other forward areas. They slipped across the border into South Africa and received weapons at a point pre-arranged by the Ordnance department. The average life expectancy of a guerrilla in the mid-1980s was very short, a few months at most before death or capture. But some succeeded in recruiting comrades from the street committees, sending them for training in Lesotho, and then spiriting them back into South Africa. The newcomers' weapon training was mostly in the use of hand-grenades, the easiest weapon to smuggle. Grenade-squads made their appearance in Port Elizabeth and Gugulethu, hurling their missiles at policemen during mass demonstrations.

In August 1986, an incident in the Soweto area of White City illustrated well the possibilities of People's War if sufficient guns were forthcoming. Council officials attempting to evict people for non-payment of rent were confronted by angry crowds, and the police were called in. Hidden in the crowds were trained Umkhonto we Sizwe soldiers armed with AK-47 assault rifles. Emerging to the edge of the crowd to fire a burst at the police, they then retired into the mass of bodies as the crowd closed ranks around them, a tactic highly effective in attacking the police while at the same time impressing the crowd. Any police retaliation was more likely to kill unarmed demonstrators than the gunmen.

According to government statistics, the 50 or so Umkhonto we Sizwe attacks recorded in 1984 rose to a record 230 in 1986. Moreover, some of the RPMCs in the Frontline States had succeeded in setting up local, autonomous Area Political-Military Councils (APMCs) inside South Africa. The Botswana RPMC oversaw a successful APMC in Sekhukhuneland, just across the border in South

Africa. Three such units were set up in the Cape, intended as the start of a home-based Umkhonto we Sizwe network. Perhaps the most successful of all was the Western Cape unit set up in 1984 which reached a high stage of sophistication and efficiency. Led by Jenny Schreiner, the daughter of a leading white liberal family and the direct descendant of the famous South African writer Olive Schreiner, it had been stiffened by the addition of Tony Yengeni, the commander of the Lesotho RPMC and a member of the Communist Party sent into South Africa to help establish the underground there after the Lesotho machinery had been smashed by General Lekhanya. But even such an efficient and effective unit as the Western Cape APMC could not survive long. Its members were arrested in October 1987. Official incident reports reveal just how frequently Umkhonto we Sizwe was able to strike in this period. The following sample of news reports for mid-1986 makes the point, and indicates the political climate in which the underground army was operating:[6]

16 June 1986: Soweto day, the tenth anniversary of the 1976 Soweto uprising. One and a half million black people stay away from work in commemoration. At least 11 people are killed in unrest-related incidents.

17 June 1986: A car bomb explodes in Durban, killing three people and injuring 69.

21 June 1986: A bomb explodes on the Durban beach-front. No one is injured. Elsewhere, Brigadier Andrew Molope, the Bophuthatswana police chief who commanded a unit which shot 26 people dead in Winterveld three months earlier, is assassinated.

24 June 1986: Nineteen people are injured when two bombs explode in Johannesburg city centre.

26 June 1986: Official figures reveal that an average of 40 whites a day have been emigrating because of the political situation.

27 June 1986: A European Community summit in the Hague deplores the impostion of the nationwide state of emergency and urges a national dialogue 'with the authentic black leaders'.

29 June 1986: A bomb explodes in the Queenstown shopping centre in the Cape. Three people injured.

30 June 1986: Official figures state that 161 deaths occurred in June as a result of the unrest.

1 July 1986: A bomb in Johannesburg injures eight people. Ten die in a car bomb blast in Bophuthatswana.

---

6. We are grateful to Jeremy Pope for compiling this list of incidents and for permitting its use here.

3 July 1986: A bomb explodes in the Mowbray police station in Cape Town.

4 July 1986: A bomb injures 20 people in the Pretoria suburb of Silverton.

10 July 1986: A bomb explodes outside the Johannesburg stock exchange.

31 July 1986: Official statistics record 90 deaths due to unrest in the month of July.

No one ever believed that Umkhonto we Sizwe was going to march into Pretoria with its banners flying and its guns held high from bases in the Frontline States. That was not the object of ANC military strategy. But the constant series of bomb, grenade and rifle attacks, coming as they did in such a climate of political and economic pressure on the South African government, had a marked effect. The key to the future development of the insurrection was for Umkhonto we Sizwe to be able to establish organised and armed squads like the Western Cape APMC which could operate autonomously inside the country. Only then could Umkhonto we Sizwe consider that the phase of what it termed armed propaganda had passed indisputably into the phase of People's War.

The catalogue of unrest, repression and misery represented by statistics such as those above marked the climax of the war for South Africa. While the level of violence inside the country remained high, it became clear in the second half of 1986 that the government was winning the struggle. The security forces, equipped with an effective licence to torture, had both the means and the will to prevent a popular insurrection by detaining any number of suspected organisers of anti-government agitation or violence and by setting black communities against one another by encouraging the formation of vigilantes. In the face of this many black people preferred to settle for peace. Moreover it was apparent that the government's resources and ruthlessness were far from diminished. Government death squads like the cynically named Civil Cooperation Bureau assassinated ANC personnel, or simply anyone they disliked, both inside and outside South Africa. One by one, the policy of destabilisation, which directly or indirectly led to hundreds of thousands of deaths in over a decade,[7] closed down Umkhonto we Sizwe's networks and bases within striking distance of South Africa.

Soon after the imposition of the nationwide State of Emergency in June 1986, it became clear that the government had gained the military initiative, even if it was bereft of political ideas after the failure of P.W.

---

7. Phyllis Johnson and David Martin (eds), *Apartheid Terrorism: the Destabilisation Report* (Commonwealth Secretariat and James Currey, London, 1989).

Botha's attempt at installing a tri-cameral parliament. The mobilisation of the entire resources of the state in a counter-revolutionary strategy in South Africa and the neighbouring countries, the Lesotho coup, and the effectiveness of Pretoria's espionage system added up to a comprehensive defeat for Umkhonto we Sizwe and the strategy adopted by the ANC and the Communist Party since the 1960s.

It seems likely that, had President F.W. de Klerk not unbanned the ANC, the Communist Party and other banned organisations in 1990, in time there may well have been another rising of even greater importance and ferocity than those of 1976 and the mid-1980s which Pretoria had contained only with great difficulty and at high cost in money, in international standing, and in morale. But what was also clear after Umkhonto we Sizwe had been beaten back from the Frontline States was that the ANC's long-term military strategy was in need of complete rethinking. There was to be no People's War in the sense that the High Command had conceived of it.

9
Soldiers and Diplomats
1987-90

Like army commanders the world over, the people at the top of Umkhonto we Sizwe always liked to claim in public that they were winning the war and confident of eventual victory. During 1987 and 1988 they could point to the increasing number of attacks by their guerrillas, even according to the government's own statistics, and to South Africa's problems in the international arena, handicapped as it was by diplomatic isolation, financial sanctions, and an arms embargo which prevented it from acquiring some of the Western arms which it needed, especially aircraft, for its war in Angola. They could be confident that, whatever setbacks the ANC might suffer, the long-term survival of apartheid was impossible.

The immediate prospect was considerably more alarming. Any Umkhonto we Sizwe member with a sense of perspective could see that the guerrilla war declared in 1961 was being lost. The Soviet Union, the supporting super-power, was losing heart, although that did not become fully apparent until 1988, and the South African strategy of total mobilisation for counter-revolution was successfully knocking out the Frontline States one by one and denying Umkhonto we Sizwe its bases. Morale inside the ANC camps was low. After June 1986, the imposition of a nationwide State of Emergency inside South Africa restored a degree of government control and eliminated the possibility that Pretoria might be forced to negotiate a wholesale transfer of power. In 1985 it was still possible to believe rationally that the strategy of armed struggle, as the ANC and the Communist Party conceived of it, would achieve its goal. By 1988, that was hard to believe. Nevertheless, to a startling degree the ANC's leadership was blinded to the realities of the situation by a tendency to believe rather dogmatically in its own slogans.

The war for South Africa was only one phase in a much longer contest, which long pre-dated the foundation of Umkhonto we Sizwe and the declaration of the armed struggle, for justice and freedom in South Africa. The ANC has been in existence since 1912 and the Communist Party since 1921, and both had four decades or more of experience before they turned to armed struggle. Losing the guerrilla war did not mean abandoning the contest. But it obliged the alliance to build a new strategy and new tactics for the phase emerging. On the whole, the military leaders of the alliance were slow to do this and, like any military men, reluctant to admit that their efforts had been less than totally successful. The unbanning of the organisations and the opening of a new phase in February 1990 came as a rude shock.

Still, the military phase of the contest for South Africa had been a close-run thing. When the Commonwealth launched a peace initiative in early 1986, and mandated a group of distinguished and not-so-distinguished politicians to try to bring the two sides together, the Eminent Persons' Group made surprising progress.[1] It seemed to be on the verge of receiving commitments to talk from all the main parties until the SADF brutally slammed the door shut with a series of coordinated raids on the Frontline States, calculated to sabotage the peace process. It was said by European diplomats that the raids were planned and executed by the securocrats under President Botha without informing the Cabinet, some of whose civilian members might have been prepared to argue in favour of peace-talks.

At the same time as the guerrilla war was reaching its climax, a fierce power struggle developed inside Umkhonto we Sizwe. The main protagonists were the two principal warlords, army Commander Joe Modise and the army's Political Commissar Chris Hani. Having led a near-mutiny against the army leadership in 1966, and having escaped drastic punishment for his rashness only narrowly, Hani had gone on to build himself a glittering career and to become a legend inside Umkhonto we Sizwe and in the townships of South Africa. He had led a unit into battle at Wankie in 1967. He had personally established the Umkhonto we Sizwe network in Lesotho, daring to penetrate South Africa itself. He had evaded arrest or death on numerous occasions. He had personally addressed the mutineers at Viana in 1984 and persuaded them to surrender without further bloodshed. His feats were legendary.

Hani had also risen to become one of the leaders of the Communist Party. He was considered close to the most orthodox of the Party barons, notably Joe Slovo. Despite his relative youth, Hani already had some seniority in the Party since he had joined at a very young age, and was staunchly committed to Marxism-Leninism. In 1974 he joined the ANC's National Executive Committee. In 1982 he was promoted to the post of Political Commissar of Umkhonto we Sizwe, ranked at that time as second in command of the army. Since he had also been elected to membership of the Party's Politburo the previous year, he had a position of unique and unassailable strength in the various organs of the ANC alliance. He strengthened his political position assiduously by surrounding himself with the best and brightest of army recruits, guiding the most promising to membership of the Party.

The rivalry between Hani and Modise, a factor since the 1960s,

---

1. *Mission to South Africa. The Commonwealth Report* (Penguin Books, Harmondsworth, 1986).

grew more serious once Hani had entered the High Command. After his 1982 promotion, Hani left Lesotho and was stationed in Maputo, where he worked alongside Joe Slovo and Moses Mabhida, respectively the Party Chairman (after Dadoo's death in 1983) and General Secretary. Through them he acquired the backing of the Party machinery. Modise, meanwhile, was not without his supporters. At their core were the 'Joburgers', a group of his contemporaries who had known each other in Alexandra during the 1950s, and who remained at the heart of the ANC leadership. Included among the 'Joburgers' were ANC Treasurer-General Thomas Nkobi, born in 1922, a leader of the Alexandra bus boycott in 1957. Alfred Nzo, another organiser of the 1957 Alexandra bus boycott, was sometimes considered part of the same group, as was Josiah Jele, who was elbowed aside in the contest for the top post in the SACP as Mabhida's health declined. After Jele was dropped from the Party's Politburo in 1985, he was ineligible for the post of General Secretary which all knew would shortly become vacant. Jele was hurt by his treatment, and took refuge in his post as Secretary of the PMC, where he could build up a new power base. Despite the fact that Modise was not a communist, whereas Nzo and Jele were, and despite the fact that all were of different ethnic origin (Nzo being a Xhosa, Jele a Zulu and Modise a Tswana), the comradeship of the old days bound them together. They resented the speed with which Hani, from a younger generation, had risen to the top. The real heart of the ANC's leadership continued to be the 1950s generation. Tambo, Mandela, Sisulu, Modise, Nkobi, Nzo and Jele had all been colleagues at a time when Hani was still a schoolboy. They had managed to absorb members of the class of 1976 into the ANC and into the Communist Party without ceding the top positions in the organisation, and there was a certain jealousy, on the part of some, about the swiftness of Hani's rise.

After the start of the 1984 township uprising, there was an influx of young fighters into the ANC on a scale not seen since 1976, especially from the militant Eastern Cape townships of Mdantsane in East London and KwaZakhele in Port Elizabeth. They formed a ready constituency for Hani, who played to the young cadres' instinctive loyalty to another Xhosa, building his personal following in the army. He added to his reputation with a display of his habitual courage during Umkhonto we Sizwe's 1983-4 campaign against UNITA in Angola, and was hailed for his quelling of the army mutiny which followed. He continued to enter South Africa in person on underground operations. Hani was a living symbol of the fighting leadership claimed by the Party. Modise, on the other hand, was not conspicuous in many of these situations, and this did not endear him to the young lions of the ANC camps.

Meanwhile the Tswana element in the ANC, although outnumbered by Xhosas, had also been strengthened by an influx of young militants from the Sharpeville, Alexandra and Mamelodi townships. They became aware of the predominance of Xhosas in the ANC and looked to Modise for leadership. Thus the struggle between the warlords came to assume an ethnic and regional dimension.

The use of the tribal bogey became a useful tactical variation in cases of in-fighting within the ANC bureaucracy. Any beleaguered officer, threatened with demotion for some fault real or imagined, had only to 'go back to his roots', claiming that he was the victim of ethnic conspiracies when confronted with the prospect of demotion. A good example of this occurred at the top of the ANC Intelligence and Security organ. Peter Boroko, a Tswana, was facing certain demotion as the chief of Intelligence Operations, second in command in the Intelligence hierarchy, after numerous complaints about his conduct, including his detention of a member of the ANC's NEC, Pallo Jordan. His chief, the head of the Intelligence and Security organ, was Mzwai Piliso, a Xhosa. Boroko, fighting to preserve his position, was able to mobilise a Tswana constituency in his support. He recruited onto his side Ruth Mompati, the ANC Administrative Secretary and a close friend of Oliver Tambo. The upshot of the rearguard action fought by Boroko and his supporters was that Tambo, himself a Xhosa and ultra-sensitive to allegations of tribalism, agreed to postpone Boroko's demotion. After more than a year of procrastination, during which much intelligence work was paralysed by the in-fighting at the top, a compromise agreement was reached. The entire directorate of the Intelligence and Security organ was dissolved in January 1987. A new provisional Intelligence and Security directorate headed by Secretary-General Alfred Nzo, and with an equal distribution of posts between Xhosa and Tswana, was established. Thus the ANC's response to the problem was to fire both Boroko and Piliso, despite the fact that Piliso's conduct was not at that point in question. The consequences were easily discernible in the weakness of the ANC's intelligence-gathering arm. The absence of a clear authority at the top of the intelligence service was sorely missed by officers on the ground.

Events in 1987 brought these feuds towards a head. Early in the year Joe Slovo, recently elected General Secretary of the Party to replace the late Moses Mabhida, resigned his post as Chief of Staff of Umkhonto we Sizwe in order to concentrate full time on Party work. In July, the murder by Security Police officers of Cassius Make, the Umkhonto we Sizwe head of Ordnance, opened up another vacancy in the High Command. This presented Hani with a problem. Slovo had been his ally, and the prospective candidate for the vacant chief of staff position, ranked third in the army hierarchy, was Siphiwo 'Gebuza' Nyande, an Umkhonto we Sizwe commander based in Swaziland. The problem was that Gebuza was regarded as a Modise supporter. Hani used all his contacts in the army, the Party and the ANC to pull off a major coup, by having himself appointed to the Chief of Staff slot and at the same time having the post upgraded to second in the hierarchy, quoting as justification the fact that the chief of staff was second only to the military commander in the new Soviet military model. He then arranged for the appointment of Steve Tshwete, a communist, former Robben Island prisoner and former President of the Border district of the UDF, as Political Commissar of the army. Tshwete had only recently fled from South Africa in disguise after he had been the victim of an assassination attempt by the Security Police.

Tshwete's appointment stunned ANC chiefs. They knew that he had only just been appointed to the post of ANC representative in Zimbabwe. Now Hani managed to get the Zimbabwe job given to Stanley Mabizela, also a Party member, who had previously been earmarked for Mozambique. The most shocking aspect was that Tshwete had no military training beyond a two-month crash course in East Germany in 1986. Nor were his personal qualities, especially his reputation for tactlessness, considered suitable for the third-ranking post in the army ahead of well-qualified veterans like 'Gebuza'. Hani was able to pull off this coup only because of the influence of the Party inside the ANC.

In August 1987, the new Military Headquarters hierarchy was announced. It stood thus:

Joe Modise	Army commander
Chris Hani	Chief of Staff
Steve Tshwete	Political Commissar (Hani loyalist)
Lehlohonolo Moloi	Chief of Operations (Modise loyalist)
Rashid	Chief of Ordnance (Hani loyalist)
Ronnie Kasrils	Chief of Military Intelligence (Hani loyalist)
Borgart	Chief of Logistics and Finance (Hani loyalist)
Jacqueline Molefe	Chief of Communications (Mother of Modise's two children)

Modise, outmanoeuvred by Hani in terms of support in the Military Headquarters, quickly appointed Keith Mokoape as Deputy Chief of Military Intelligence and another of his supporters, known as 'Manchecker', as Deputy Chief of Operations. But Hani still had the support of the military top brass, Tshwete, Kasrils and Rashid.

In only five years in the military hierarchy, Hani had substantially changed the balance of forces in his favour. He still faced the formidable 'Joburgers', though, in the PMC, the body which had political control of the army. There, Modise had secured the nomination of Josiah Jele, his long-term ally.

While Hani could use his position in the Party to strengthen his hand in the ANC, the 'Joburgers' were not without resources of their own. They attacked Hani's personal vanity and criticised his flamboyant life-style. They spread ugly rumours about his wife. The 'Joburgers' persistently criticised Hani for being too close to the whites, a reference to his close ties with Joe Slovo and other white

Party members, and took delight in referring to Hani as a *moegoe*, a country bumpkin, in reference to his origins in the Transkei.

As so often in rivalries of this sort, Oliver Tambo stood above the fray. He regarded his position in the ANC as that of a chairman, who should not side with different factions, but give a broad sense of direction and keep the movement together. Moreover, he had no taste for the politics of cabals and cliques. He was ageing, sick, and tired. He worked very hard and was frequently abroad, to the point that it was apparent that the power-brokers of the Party and the ANC in Lusaka kept him on a tight schedule of diplomatic work and foreign visits partly to keep him away from headquarters, and to allow them free rein for their intrigues. The President's office was staffed almost exclusively with Party members who controlled his schedule and filtered the flow of paper across his desk. The Administrative Secretary in the President-General's Office, Anthony Mongalo, was a senior Party member and a former ANC representative in East Germany, where he was sufficiently intimate with Erich Honecker and others of the elite as to have accompanied them on private hunting expeditions. Virtually all of the staff of Tambo's office were Party members.

The result of Tambo's hands-off approach was constant feuding among ANC chieftains and disaffection among young cadres, dismayed by what they saw above them. The in-fighting damaged the effectiveness of the army command and of intelligence work, and spread to the whole PMC. It was apparently because of this, for example, that eleven members of the Western Cape APMC under Jenny Schreiner, the most successful Umkhonto we Sizwe unit inside South Africa, were arrested by the Security Police in October 1987. Most members of this unit were also members of the Party's Cape Town regional committee, a unit composed exclusively of whites, which was serviced directly by Ray Simons in Lusaka on behalf of the Party's Politburo.

By June 1988, Hani was ready to go public in his challenge to the existing army command. The South African government was preparing to inaugurate new black municipal councils later that year, and it was essential for the ANC to ensure the lowest possible voter turnout. In June, Hani and his close friend and colleague Steve Tshwete, now respectively number two and number three in Umkhonto we Sizwe, gave a series of interviews to leading newspapers, including the *New York Times*. They spoke on the record about the need to take the war in South Africa into white areas and to adopt a harder and more militant approach. They threatened, with outrageous bluster, to turn South Africa into a wasteland. A spate of bomb attacks on soft targets, including Ellis Park sports stadium in Johannesburg, seemed to confirm that these were not mere words, but that Hani and Tshwete were taking Umkhonto we Sizwe strategy in a new direction. Although the ANC had frequently attacked soft targets in the past, it had always claimed that this was not official policy. The fact that two such senior military men now claimed it as ANC policy was a clear break with tradition. From then until October, bomb attacks continued almost daily, including indiscriminate attacks on restaurants and other public places.

Unusually for a man who generally refrained from internal quarrels, Tambo publicly repudiated the line advanced by Hani and Tshwete, rejecting the policy of soft targets, and saying that the two were speaking in their personal capacities only. In July he fired Tshwete from the position of Umkhonto we Sizwe Political Commissar, a post he had occupied for no more than a few weeks, but compensated him with appointment to the NEC, redressing the political balance of the Committee by naming a number of both Hani and Modise allies at the same time so as to appear even-handed in dealing with the two factions. In fact, in spite of the in-fighting at the top, and in spite of Umkhonto we Sizwe's logistical difficulties stemming from its expulsion from the Frontline States, the army was able to launch more attacks in 1988 than in any previous year – though only at the expense of losing large numbers of its trained guerrillas to action by the Security Police, and only by attacking undefended soft targets, which cost it dearly in terms of international support. Even the usually unquestioning Swedish government expressed concern.

The debate over hard and soft targets, and the power struggle between Hani and Modise for control of the army, diverted attention from the fact that there was a degree of desperation in the ranks of Umkhonto we Sizwe. Its leaders and soldiers were more than ever convinced of the rightness of their cause and of the historical certainty that apartheid would one day be overthrown, but in the meantime international events were once again turning to their disadvantage.

Their unease stemmed from a most unlikely source – the Soviet Union. In 1985, the Communist Party of the Soviet Union elected as its General Secretary Mikhail Gorbachev, a protégé of Yuri Andropov, the long-serving chief of the KGB who had died after only a few months in the General Secretary's office. During his years as director of the KGB, Andropov and the group of intellectuals he gathered around him had become convinced of the impending crisis of the Soviet system, stemming from economic stagnation and political inertia. Gorbachev, sharing his former patron's conviction of the need for profound reform, set about a complete restructuring of the Soviet government and Soviet policy. In order to implement his reforms and restore some vitality to the economy, Gorbachev was determined to end the Cold War, whose financial cost was ruinous. His priority was domestic reform, and in order to achieve this he first had to secure an agreement with the US government which would permit him to reduce military expenditure and to be sure of being able to proceed with his plans for political restructuring with a guarantee of US non-interference.

Gorbachev signalled this new approach from the start of his tenure as General Secretary and at the 27th Congress of the Soviet

Communist Party held in 1986. In October 1986, came his first, historic, summit meeting with President Ronald Reagan at Reykjavik in Iceland. The meeting set the groundwork for a comprehensive deal: the Soviet Union and the USA would agree on an arms reduction treaty which would permit both sides to reduce the colossal sums they were spending on weapons. They also agreed to adopt a joint approach to regional conflicts, effectively redefining zones of influence. The USA agreed to allow the Soviet Union to restructure its relations with its Eastern European allies without interference from outside. In a number of places where the Cold War was being fought by proxy – notably in Afghanistan, but also in southern Africa – the Soviet government committed itself to withdraw its forces or to refrain from seeking the overthrow of the existing order, leaving the field to the USA and its allies on the ground. Although the exact content of the discussions between Gorbachev and Reagan remained a secret between the two men and their senior aides, many African diplomats believed that they had briefly mentioned South Africa, including it in the category of countries where the USSR would henceforth refrain from aggression. Whether or not they explicitly reached some measure of agreement on South Africa at the Reykjavik summit, the terms of their discussions implied that the Soviet Union would no longer throw its weight behind the effort by the ANC and the SACP to foment a revolution in South Africa. It also meant that the Soviet Union would lend its weight to negotiating a solution to local problems, such as the status of Namibia.

The implications of the new Soviet thinking introduced by Gorbachev were not immediately foreseen in southern Africa. Joe Slovo attended the 27th Congress of the Communist Party of the Soviet Union and, impressed by the commitment to renewal and restructuring, pronounced it the most remarkable he had ever attended. Like every other observer and commentator, he could not know the turn events were going to take over the rest of the decade and the implications for South Africa. It was almost a reflex action for the SACP to welcome any new approach coming from Moscow, so closely was it aligned to the Soviet version of Marxism-Leninism. South African communists had followed the various twists and turns dictated by the Comintern in the 1920s and 1930s. They had embraced Stalinism unreservedly, including the 180-degree turn involved in switching to the Allied side in the Second World War after Hitler's attack on the Soviet Union in 1941. Thereafter, the Party had fully accepted Krushchev's criticisms of Stalin but had gone on to endorse the Soviet invasions of Czechoslovakia in 1968 and Afghanistan in 1979, the latter the subject of a well-known difference of political opinion between Slovo and his wife, Ruth First, who had consistently and even publicly opposed the positions of the SACP on international matters. The Party had been unstinting in its criticisms of communist parties which had broken decisively with the Soviet model of communism, and had a strong distaste even for Swedish social democracy, in spite of consistent Swedish support for the struggle in southern Africa. In 1985, it was natural for the SACP to endorse reform and the policies of *glasnost* and *perestroika* announced with such élan by the Soviet leadership. Unlike the communist parties of Eastern Europe, which were far more reserved in their reception of the new doctrines, the SACP did not have to defend a record in government. It was in the comfortable position of being able to welcome the attractive new policies, while continuing its own practice of intense secretiveness on the grounds that it was still fighting a war against a ruthless enemy.

As far as southern Africa was concerned, the main testing ground of the new international line-up was Angola. This theatre of the Cold War at first appeared unaffected by warmer relations between the two superpowers. Throughout 1986 and the early part of 1987, the Soviet Union continued to send massive supplies of weapons to its ally, the Angolan government. The sophisticated material shipped from Eastern Europe included, most alarmingly for Pretoria's military chiefs, large quantities of armoured vehicles and modern technology for air combat, including sophisticated radar systems and Mig-23 fighter aircraft, superior to anything in South Africa's arsenal. The Angolan armed forces, with help from Soviet advisers and technicians, were busily building a line of air-bases and radar facilities from Lubango across southern Angola, gradually extending control of the air and restricting South Africa's ability to launch conventional offensives or counter-offensives as it had done on so many occasions since 1975. There was, moreover, no sign of any Soviet pressure on its Cuban ally to withdraw the 35,000 or so troops which it deployed in Angola, and whose numbers were to increase to over 50,000 by 1988.

For its part, the USA continued to maintain its traditional stand in Angola by supplying military aid to the UNITA rebel movement, affirming that it would continue to do so for as long as the Soviet Union and Cuba gave help to the Luanda government. The US government refused to extend diplomatic recognition to Luanda, despite the fact that US oil companies were represented in Angola in government-controlled areas and did good business there. The world contemplated the truly bizarre circumstances in which US oil companies relied on Cuban troops for protection against a guerrilla force armed by the US government. In private, oil industry executives lobbied for the Cubans to stay in Angola while the US government publicly called for their withdrawal.

By June 1987, there were unmistakable signs of preparation for another massive offensive by the Angolan armed forces, led by armour and with air cover, aimed at the main UNITA bases in the south-east of the country. The offensive was launched in September, supervised in part by a Soviet general, Konstantin Shaganovitch. Government armoured columns headed towards Mavinga, a UNITA-held town which was crucial to the rebels' supply-route to their guerrilla forces in the centre and north of Angola. The government's aim was to take Mavinga, restrict UNITA in its ability to infiltrate forces further north, and build an air-base there which would complete its line of air facilities right across the south of the country, preventing South African incursions further north than a thin strip along the Angola-Namibia border. South Africa responded to the offensive against Mavinga in its usual manner, by sending in the 32 'Buffalo' battalion and other units to stiffen UNITA's defence. It was shortly to send in regular units of the SADF too, including tanks.

In October 1987, the Angolan government offensive ground to a halt on the banks of the Lomba river. Combined UNITA and South African forces inflicted very heavy casualties on the advancing Angolans, but in spite of their success in stopping the offensive, there were signs which Pretoria tried hard to disguise that all was not well for the South Africans. Above all, the SADF was hampered by the improved performance of the Angolan air force. In the last week of September, for the first time an Angolan MiG fighter shot down a South African aircraft in aerial combat, a sign of the changing balance of conventional forces. Angolan planes ruled the skies over Mavinga. In a terse announcement in November 1987, the SADF announced the loss of 12 white personnel in one incident, believed to have been a bombing attack by Angolan aircraft.

Although the full story of the Angolan war remains to be written, it is apparent that, after the victory of combined South African and UNITA forces in the battle of Lomba River, there were differences of opinion in Pretoria about what to do next. The cautious approach would have been simply to rest after the battle and to withdraw SADF units to their Namibian bases, leaving UNITA to make good the losses it had sustained in repelling the Angolan government offensive. That course of action, however, would have left the Angolan government forces and their Soviet and Cuban allies free to regroup and re-equip in time to launch another offensive a year later. And with every month that went by, Angolan air power became stronger, and Pretoria became correspondingly less able to intervene with impunity. Moreover the financial cost of mounting increasingly sophisticated campaigns in Angola, and maintaining a large army of occupation in northern Namibia, was becoming ruinous. The prospect of annual Angolan offensives with increasingly sophisticated material, and annual South African interventions at increasing human and financial cost, was not one which appealed.

One faction in the South African armed forces, which appears, to judge from public pronouncements at the time, to have been led by the Minister of Defence, General Magnus Malan, advocated a strategy of hot pursuit, following the defeated Angolan army from the battleground on the banks of the Lomba River to its main logistical base at the town of Cuito Cuanavale. Using the initiative and pursuing a defeated enemy, the South Africans would aim to take Cuito Cuanavale and destroy its air-base, thus postponing completion of the Angolan line of air-bases which was gradually extending from west to east across the country. Military hawks in Pretoria had been warning for months of the growing threat posed by Angolan air-power, and had been calling for pre-emptive action. Until now, they had always been overruled by the arguments of civilian colleagues, and notably officials at 'Pik' Botha's foreign ministry, who feared the diplomatic effect of a major South African offensive in Angola and cautioned against aggression. Now, the victory of Lomba River gave the hawks the chance they had been waiting for. They had the ear of President Botha, whose notoriously aggressive character inclined him to favour military action in such circumstances, and were flushed with their victory at Lomba River. Having deployed thousands of troops in Angola to defend UNITA's bases from attack, they wished to press home their advantage, knowing that if they returned to their bases in Namibia it might be months before they were again authorised to enter Angola in strength.

But the South African and UNITA counter-attack against Cuito Cuanavale, while it may have made sense in military terms, made less political sense. If South Africa and its ally were to succeed in taking Cuito Cuanavale, it would enable UNITA to expand its supply-lines from its headquarters at Jamba near the Namibian border to areas in the centre of Angola. But it was out of the question for the SADF to occupy Cuito Cuanavale itself, and UNITA too would be unable to occupy the town permanently since it would make the rebel forces vulnerable to air attack and present them with problems of supply. From UNITA's point of view, therefore, an assault on Cuito Cuanavale was of strictly limited value. It would provide a useful propaganda advantage but would cause heavy casualties to the UNITA army, already badly mauled by the fighting at the Lomba River. There was already a faction inside UNITA which estimated that the movement had become too reliant on South Africa and was increasingly being drawn into becoming purely a South African surrogate force, fighting battles that were more important to South Africa than to UNITA. There was a sharp public exchange of words between Jonas Savimbi, the UNITA leader, and South African military spokesmen, in which the unusually harsh and cutting remarks made by both sides indicated some disagreement.

Nevertheless, it was the forward faction in Pretoria, led by General Malan and apparently accepted rather less than wholeheartedly by the chief of the SADF, Lieutenant-General Jannie Geldenhuys, which won the argument. A combined force of UNITA, South African irregulars including the Buffalo battalion and black Namibian troops, plus SADF regular units, advanced to Cuito Cuanavale in December 1987 and laid siege to a town then defended by only a small garrison of Angolans and Cubans, well dug-in, well-equipped with anti-tank weapons and having the benefit of air cover. Over the next few months, Angolan government sources were to claim that South Africa had deployed as many as 11,000 men in southern Angola, plus hundreds of vehicles and artillery pieces. South African government spokesmen insisted the figure was never more than 3,000 men. The difference in the size of these figures may have been explained partly by the deployment on South Africa's side of units, such as those of the South-West African Territorial Force, which were excluded from the official total, enabling South African military spokesmen to reduce their figures.

Over the next six months, Cuito Cuanavale settled into a state of siege. South Africa's formidable long-range artillery, especially the G–5 and G–6 howitzers, which were able to project a shell over 40 kilometres with great precision, pummelled the town. On some days they landed as many as 200 shells. Closer to the town itself were UNITA fighters, who sustained heavy losses attempting to invest its outer defences. On several occasions combined South African and UNITA forces launched assaults which got stuck in barbed-wire entanglements and minefields and came under fire from the Angolan and Cuban defenders of the town, who, although heavily out-numbered, were soon able to secure fresh supplies and reinforcements. The South Africans found themselves fighting under heavy political restrictions, being under orders to eliminate the enemy presence in Cuito Cuanavale without using the entire strength of the SADF and without sustaining casualties. This was a quite impossible demand to satisfy when fighting against a well-armed enemy. South African military estimates in early 1988 were that Cuito Cuanavale could be taken with an infantry assault, but at the risk of losing up to 300 white troops and much greater numbers of black Namibian troops and UNITA guerrillas. This was politically unacceptable since it meant that, even if the SADF was correct in thinking that Cuito Cuanavale could be taken, the town could not be held for long. Hundreds of white South Africans, and thousands of black South Africans, Namibians and Angolans would thus have died, and UNITA would have been badly mauled, for no permanent gain. It did not make sense. By May 1988, the South Africans had decided to withdraw and lift the siege, having been out-fought and out-thought.

South African military spokesmen were later to claim that it had never been their intention to take Cuito Cuanavale, and that their sole aim was to clear the surrounding areas of enemy forces. That version smacks of a rationalisation after the event, designed to explain South Africa's failure to achieve its desired objective in the Angolan war. For the SADF, it was of the utmost importance to save face, just as, for the forces combined against it, it was essential to puncture the myth of South African invincibility. Thus, the siege of Cuito Cuanavale, after the fighting there had finished, became the subject of a major propaganda campaign by both sides. Cuba and Angola claimed Cuito Cuanavale as a major success and the turning-point in their long campaign, the Angolan equivalent of Stalingrad. A Cuban-made video of the battle, some three hours long, was soon compiled and shown to appreciative audiences in Harare, throughout the Frontline States, in Europe and elsewhere. Copies were smuggled into South Africa and Namibia. The South African government, on the other hand, dismissed with contempt claims that Cuito Cuanavale had been a defeat, claiming it as a victory achieved at minimum cost to itself, insisting that the Defence Force had withdrawn in good order and with no more than a few dozen white South African lives lost by comparison with the enemy's thousands of casualties.

There can be no doubt that throughout the campaigns of 1987–8 in Angola, the Angolan government forces suffered very heavy losses and failed to achieve their initial objective of overrunning UNITA positions in the south-east of the country, taking Mavinga and opening the way to UNITA headquarters at Jamba. However, South Africa, too, failed in its objective of taking Cuito Cuanavale and also suffered comparatively heavy losses in men and material. South African forces were operating in exactly the political context which soldiers instinctively dislike, being required to take military action in pursuit of rather unclear objectives, and being prevented by constantly changing political considerations from fielding their maximum strength. They were running up against the political limits of the Angolan situation.

For the first time too, South Africa lost aircraft in numbers, indicating the extent of Angolan air supremacy. The number of whites killed during the siege of Cuito Cuanavale was officially put at 31, although there are grounds for thinking the true total was higher, since official South African announcements of deaths were often couched in terms which made it difficult to keep a tally day-by-day. In any event, the number of white casualties was sufficient to cause alarm among the South African public and to provoke questions about what was really happening in Angola, and why South Africa was sending its sons to fight and die there. Moreover the type of warfare employed in the Angolan theatre had become highly sophisticated and expensive. The days were gone when South African troops could simply climb into armoured vehicles and drive into Angola with little resistance. They were fighting a high-technology war, with computer-guided artillery, pilotless 'drone' spotter-aircraft, the latest radar and all the paraphernalia of modern, conventional warfare. It was too expensive for a government squeezed by financial sanctions and disinvestment, and attempting to win the hearts and minds of black South Africans by a programme of intensive investment in social amenities at home. For all these reasons, the SADF chiefs and the politicians decided that the only sane course was to withdraw without taking Cuito Cuanavale. They did not, of course, want to admit failure and claimed it publicly as a victory.

While Cuito Cuanavale lay under siege, Cuba had raised the stakes considerably. In December 1987, President Fidel Castro took personal control of military affairs, overruling the commander of the Cuban expeditionary force in Angola, the hero of many a revolutionary war, General Arnaldo Ochoa Sanchez. Later, shortly after returning to Cuba, Sanchez was to be convicted of corruption during his service in Angola and executed. Castro decided to send the first of an eventual 11,000 reinforcements across the Atlantic to Angola. These were the best units in the Cuban army, including elements of the Presidential Guard. It was a high-risk strategy indeed. The Cubans even dismantled many of the air defences of Havana city to transport them across the ocean, leaving Cuba exposed to risk of attack by any neighbour which should feel inclined, and exposing the flower of the Cuban army to the risk of battle in a foreign country where it was operating at the end of over-extended lines of supply. Having landed in Angola, the Cuban expeditionary force proceeded to advance from west to east along the Namibian border, setting up missile batteries which menaced towns and military bases inside Namibia, and threatened to cut off the South African besieging force at Cuito Cuanavale. The South Africans turned and headed home, and there were even reports, denied by Pretoria but confirmed by US intelligence sources,[2] that as many as 300-400 South African troops were for some time trapped in southern Angola, cut off from their home-bases in Namibia by the Cuban expeditionary force. The Americans, for once, were not unhappy at seeing South African forces in difficulties in Angola, since it increased the pressure on Pretoria to submit to the US wish to achieve a diplomatic settlement there in line with the superpowers' desire to terminate regional conflicts.

It was at this juncture that the two superpowers, the USA and the USSR, attempted their first exercise in regional peace-making in conformity with their new global understanding. Both Moscow and Washington sponsored a series of negotiations which began in London on 3 and 4 May 1988. At a small and discreet hotel in London's West End, delegations from the Angolan and Cuban governments met under the chairmanship of the Assistant Secretary of State for African Affairs at the US State Department, Dr Chester Crocker, with his Soviet opposite number in attendance. The Soviets and Americans made it clear that they wanted peace in Angola and a political settlement in Namibia, and that they were agreed on the need to bring pressure on their respective allies to bring about that solution. Also present was an important South African delegation including Lieutenant-General Jannie Geldenhuys, the head of the SADF; the head of Military Intelligence, Major-General Cornelius van Tonder; the head of the National Intelligence Service; Dr Lukas Neil Barnard, plus senior diplomats and foreign ministry officials. It was the first

2. *The Independent,* 10 August 1988.

official, publicly announced, high-level meeting between the governments whose armed forces had fought each other to a stalemate at Cuito Cuanavale and elsewhere in southern Angola. Excluded from the peace talks were representatives of the main non-governmental forces involved on the ground, UNITA and SWAPO.

During the next six months there followed a series of meetings as the negotiating parties met in a variety of locations – Geneva, Cairo, Brazzaville, New York and elsewhere. A game of poker for high stakes was in progress. On the military front, both South Africa and Cuba were committing their full resources to the Namibian-Angolan border, such that if direct fighting were to break out between them, the casualties would have been very heavy indeed. South Africa had the ability to attack the supply lines of the cream of the Cuban army and to mount a full-scale attack on Havana's finest. But if the South Africans had done so, they would have been subject to Cuban and Angolan air and missile attack since Cuba now had the ability to target South African bases in northern Namibia with ground-to-ground missiles. South Africa's armed forces would have been faced with a conventional battle against the highest-quality conventional forces they had ever faced.

In Pretoria, there were, to judge from official statements as well as from private conversations with military officials, divisions between hawks and doves as to whether to press ahead with a full-scale military confrontation, with the prospect of confronting the Cubans in an all-out battle, or whether to succumb to intense US diplomatic and Cuban military pressure to make a comprehensive deal on Angola and Namibia. As the various delegations faced each other across negotiating tables around the world, the armies eyed each other nervously on the ground. Foreign diplomats, soldiers and journalists were uncertain which would prevail, a comprehensive peace or an all-out war.

On 27 June 1988, a Cuban-Angolan air attack at Calueque killed twelve South African soldiers in one incident, providing another reminder of the potential of Angolan and Cuban air superiority. In July, Cuban forces had occupied the Calueque dam in southern Angola, threatening to cut off water supplies to northern Namibia and rumours spread that a party of South African soldiers heading back to Namibia had been trapped on the banks of the Cuito River. Pretoria called up as many as 50,000 troops to positions in northern Namibia in preparation for the worst. These pressures convinced the South African government that a continuing war was too risky, and could only result in either a pyrrhic South African victory, achieved at great and unacceptable cost in men and money, or a South African humiliation. On 22 August 1988, South Africa, Cuba and Angola signed a security treaty committing South Africa to withdraw its forces from Angola and establishing a joint border monitoring commission under US supervision.

With this shaky ceasefire holding, both sides waited to see what would happen in Washington, where the presidential election campaign was pitting Vice-President George Bush, the candidate favoured by the US military and security establishment, against Michael Dukakis, a liberal who had promised that the USA would recognise the Luanda government and withdraw support from UNITA in the event of his election. Once Bush had won the election, on 8 November 1988, it became clear that the calculations in southern Africa remained unchanged and that there would be no radical realignment of US policy. As soon as this much had become clear, all sides were prepared to sign a comprehensive treaty on Angola and Namibia, which they did in New York, in December 1988.

The New York accords changed the landscape in southern Africa. They represented the recognition by all the major players that no military solution was possible in Angola now that both the USA and the USSR were intent on working towards peace, and that South Africa had no option but to decolonise Namibia, holding free and fair elections under United Nations' supervision. This would inevitably bring SWAPO into power, although in conditions which were helpful to South Africa. There were many in South Africa, in the SADF especially, who resisted this process, wondering why their political masters should hand over Namibia to SWAPO, when it was South Africa which was winning the bush war against SWAPO's armed wing, the People's Liberation Army of Namibia. But it was the politicians and diplomats whose arguments won the day. They could see that the agreements signed in New York offered white South Africa the best opportunity it was ever likely to have to withdraw from the government of Namibia while continuing to control the main financial and security levers, thus ensuring that white South Africa's vital interests would remain unscathed, even under a SWAPO government. In the meantime, the conditions created by the United Nations and the international community for Namibia's decolonisation were such that Pretoria had ample opportunity to promote opposition parties in an attempt to minimise the impact of the SWAPO victory which the vast majority of observers believed to be inevitable. Some South African officials even believed it would be possible to promote the opposition, especially the South African-backed Democratic Turnhalle Alliance, so effectively as to deny SWAPO a simple majority of votes cast on polling-day.

Thus the battle of Cuito Cuanavale was a defeat for Pretoria not in the sense of smashing the SADF but on the strategic level. Pretoria had failed to achieve its objective and the rulers of South Africa came to realise that there was no hope of a military victory in Angola. This weakened the hawks in the government and strengthened the doves, and prepared the ground for the presidency of F.W. de Klerk and the new thinking which he articulated. And the battle of Cuito Cuanavale led directly to the decolonisation of Namibia. In the history of South African militarism, it was a watershed.

The retreat from Namibia implied that the South African government, having normalised its political relations with the last of its neighbours on broadly acceptable terms, was now under irresistible pressure to tackle its major internal problem and address the delicate subject of relations between itself and the black majority of its citizens. The lack of political freedom in South Africa, or the continuing existence of apartheid, was the single most important cause of war and disruption in the region, and failure to address it now would mean that the fighting and enormous suffering inflicted upon southern Africa in the previous twenty years had been to no avail. As soon as the decolonisation of Namibia had begun in earnest, in April 1989, it was foreseeable that the Pretoria government would wish to renegotiate its relations with the main forces in black South African politics. Although there may have been some who believed that it would be possible to do this without including the ANC, realists knew that the ANC's support both inside South Africa and internationally was such that there was no prospect of normalising South African politics without making room for it.

For the ANC and the SACP, the New York accords were a bitter pill indeed. As a by-product of the deal, the ANC was required to close down all its Angolan bases and to move out of the country where it had concentrated its armed forces since the late 1970s. From December 1988, the ANC began moving several thousand guerrillas from Angola to camps in Zambia, Tanzania and Uganda. For the Soweto generation, teenagers who had left South Africa in 1976 determined to come home with guns to fight for their freedom, it was a heavy blow. They were now further from South Africa than they had been ten years earlier. Some had already experienced a similar expulsion from Mozambique, and now they were on the move again, always one step further from home. If negotiations were offered, there could be no realistic option of continuing the armed struggle since the conditions for doing so successfully were gone.

Some of the survivors of the 1984 mutiny, who had spent periods of up to four years in prisons in Angola, were released from prison in late 1988 and transferred as free men and women to Dakawa camp in Tanzania. Other ANC prisoners, however, were simply transferred to Mbarara in Uganda, including some survivors of the mutiny. In Dakawa the former mutineers re-entered the life of the ANC community, and in elections for a Zonal Youth Committee at the camp in March 1989, five ex-mutineers were elected, including three survivors of the Committee of Ten, which witnesses considered an indication of the continuing spirit of disaffection in the camps.[3] Later in the year Sidwell Moroka, once the security chief of the Committee of Ten, was elected to membership of the ANC's Regional Political Committee for Tanzania. The return of the remaining veterans of the mutiny into

3. *Searchlight South Africa*, Vol. 2, No. 1, p. 61.

the life of the ANC represented an attempt at reconciliation by both sides, although ANC officialdom displayed a continuing nervousness about the former mutineers, banning some of them from holding office in the ANC after they had criticised the continuation of the thoroughly Stalinist practice of subordinating the elected political bodies to the control of the administration.[4]

The retreat from Angola led to further trouble in ANC ranks. The Security Department continued to act with little restraint. On 5 August 1989, five ANC members who had complained about poor food and conditions and who had tried to resign from the ANC were detained by ANC security personnel in Lusaka. Unusually, news of the incident surfaced in the local press and the Zambian government, nervous of the growing lawlessness of the South African exiles, issued an unprecedented public rebuke to the organisation. There were further reports of detentions and beatings by ANC Security of people accused of disciplinary offences. A bombing at Andrews Motel, just outside Lusaka, claimed the life of Zakithi Dlamini, a member of Mbokodo, the ANC security organisation, who was investigating corruption within the ANC. In the previous months there had been a scandal after a case of corruption had implicated a senior Communist Party cadre working in the Treasury. It has been speculated that the investigation had led Zakithi towards the higher echelons, and that the bombing was an inside job designed to silence him. It was officially attributed by the ANC to South African agents, who had indeed carried out innumerable such murders of ANC personnel over the years. Many of the grievances of the rank and file remained the same as they had been five years before – frustration at their inability to engage their true enemy inside South Africa, poor living conditions, the restriction of freedom of expression, corruption in the senior levels of the ANC, and brutality on the part of the Security Department.

The privileges enjoyed by the ANC leadership, and the petty restrictions imposed on ordinary members, were a source of bitterness to people in this frame of mind. Over the years, the Party had introduced to the ANC a number of disciplinary practices which were intended to increase control, but which smacked of petty tyranny. ANC members wishing to marry had to apply to the Secretary-General for permission. Cadres were not allowed to communicate with their relatives in South Africa for security reasons. But in all these matters, many in positions of leadership openly flouted the code. They drank in the best hotels, had free communication with South Africa, and, in the cases of some male officials, made free with the wives and girl-friends of ANC members, who felt powerless to complain. The ANC and the Party had their own privileged elite, whatever they might say to the contrary, and the rank and file knew it, and resented the fact.

At the same time, members of the ANC and the Communist Party

4. Public address by Amos Maxongo, London, 26 April 1991.

at all levels continued to be targets for assassination by agents of the South African government. Some of the incidents which wracked the ANC in Zambia at this time, such as the poisoning of Jackie Mabuza, an official of the ANC's Department of Information and Publicity, were almost certainly the work of enemy agents. Mabuza was a member of Mbokodo and the nephew of a top security man, Joe Nhlanhla. A karate expert, he had been a bodyguard to Oliver Tambo. To add to the ANC's considerable difficulties, in August 1989, Oliver Tambo, the man who had held the ANC together through thick and thin, suffered a stroke and was taken to a London clinic on a jet belonging to the British Lonrho company, whose chief executive, the extraordinary 'Tiny' Rowland, was always ready to do favours for any African political party which seemed to be going places.

By January 1990, the atmosphere among the rank and file of ANC members in exile was not far short of mutiny once more. When Walter Sisulu and other veterans newly released from Robben Island made their first visit to ANC headquarters in Lusaka in the middle of the month, they were shocked by the virulence of criticisms made by rank and file members at an open meeting intended for the ANC to welcome back its heroes. Sisulu, apparently forewarned about the mood, sounded the keynote on his arrival at Lusaka airport by calling upon the movement to accept criticism and on members to express themselves frankly. Frustrated members, who had for years been prevented from expressing their opinions, responded with open denunciations of corruption and inertia at the top. They spoke of sexual abuse by some male senior office-holders, who stole wives and girl-friends with impunity, personal enrichment, and abuse of power by the Security Department especially. A widespread opinion in the ranks was that it was the task of the historic leaders of the ANC, on Robben Island for over twenty-five years, to restore the tradition of openness in the ANC which had been eroded during the years of exile. But, as on previous occasions when ANC members had criticised their leaders, there were no specific complaints about the role of the Party. In fact, many of the ANC leaders most frequently criticised were not Party members. The Party still had a reputation for having the best and most dedicated cadres. Few rank-and-file critics attributed the ANC's failings to Party influence, although there was a small number of nationalist intellectuals who had deeper reservations which they kept to themselves. To criticise the Party head-on in ANC circles was to invite defeat. In any event, so complete was the secrecy surrounding the Party and its membership that few outside the higher circles of the ANC were aware of the true extent of the Party's influence.

Taking a long-term view, and remaining unshakeable in its belief in the ultimate victory of its cause, the SACP could afford to be stoical about the low morale in the ANC camps and even to remain composed in the face of the expulsion of Umkhonto we Sizwe from Angola. In the strictest secrecy, senior Umkhonto we Sizwe commanders including Mac Maharaj, who had gone underground inside South Africa, were planning what was in some respects the most sophisticated and ambitious plan yet, known as Operation Vula. Although many details of Vula have not yet been made public, the aim appears to have been to set up a network of arms caches and underground personnel, almost all members of the Communist Party, inside South Africa. Planning for this began before the ANC had been unbanned in February 1990, and before the suspension of the armed struggle. To avoid leaks, the plan was known to few beyond those involved, a select group under the chairmanship of Oliver Tambo, who seems to have been one of only a handful of non-communists informed of the operation. Even Joe Modise, the Umkhonto we Sizwe commander, appears to have been in the dark about the plan. Much of the communication was entrusted not to South African operatives but to foreign sympathisers recruited through the Party's international contacts, again to avoid using circuits which may have been penetrated by Security Police spies. So complete was the secrecy surrounding the operation that even senior ANC members believed that Maharaj was undergoing medical treatment in Eastern Europe and that Siphiwo 'Gebuza' Nyande was attending a military academy in the Soviet Union. In fact, both were living underground in South Africa. The plan was exposed only in July 1990, apparently as a result of bad luck rather than any lapse or treachery.

The hardest blow to bear was that the Soviet Union had given up its commitment to the armed struggle and to revolution in South Africa. In fact, it was forming a steadily closer relationship with the Pretoria government. *Perestroika* had had the effect of bringing the Soviet Union and the USA closer together, and at the same time it had persuaded Moscow's policy-makers that since there was to be no revolution in South Africa, it was in the Soviet interest to be on good terms with those in power. It was against this background that in June 1989 the SACP held its Seventh Congress in Havana, Cuba, one of the last surviving centres of Marxist orthodoxy. Many Party members were privately alarmed about the course of events since diplomatic manoeuvres concerning Namibia and Angola the previous year. The realisation that international support was slipping away and that the armed struggle was failing led some to see that the Party had for too long put its faith in the armed struggle, and had concentrated on recruiting a relatively small elite of members, especially from within the ranks of Umkhonto we Sizwe. But the Party had never stopped recruiting new blood inside South Africa, and the principal duty of the Party regional committees in forward areas such as Lesotho was to set up Party cells inside the country. Such prominent trade unionists as Sidney Mufamadi, Chris Dlamini and Zola Dabula, all of them relatively young men who had never gone into exile, were all recruited before 1986.

The delegates to the Havana Congress, reportedly no more than a hundred or so, though this was nevertheless the largest congress since 1953, learned with satisfaction details of the Party's growing strength among the trade unions. Overall membership had increased by no less than 90 per cent since 1984, most of the new members being inside South Africa itself, and a large proportion of them in the labour movement. The Party was now able to boast as members respected trade unionists, senior officials of the Congress of South African Trades Unions. Although many trade unionists continued to show hostility to the Party, often because they saw in it an attempt to curtail union freedoms at the expense of a political programme, and sometimes because they objected to Party tactics which they considered authoritarian and bullying, it was nevertheless the case that the Party was able to recruit new blood inside South Africa itself on a larger scale than at any time since the 1940s.

Delegates to the Seventh Congress also proceeded to elect a new Central Committee and Politburo. After the election, only the names of the Party Chairman and General Secretary – Dan Tloome and Joe Slovo – were announced. The names of other successful candidates were withheld in the interests of security, so that even senior Party members might not know the identity of their own leadership. An interesting aside was that, for the first time, the Party revealed the fate of three members who had died at the hands of Stalin's secret police – Lazar Bach and the Richter brothers – and rehabilitated Sidney Bunting, who had done such sterling work for the Party in its early years and who had been so shabbily treated.[5] Although the SACP was still dominated by people who had learned their politics in Stalin's time, a new generation of militants, many of them Sowetans who had joined the ANC in 1976 and been recruited to the Party shortly afterwards, were pressing for inclusion in the senior levels of the Party. They included 'Che' Ogara, a senior Umkhonto we Sizwe official in Botswana who had trained at the Lenin School; Peter Mayibuye, a brilliant intellectual who worked for the secretariat of the ANC's PMC; Klaus Maphepha, chief of the Party's Swaziland regional organisation; Tebogo Mafole (also known as Dan Cindi), the ANC representative to the United Nations and son-in-law of ANC and Party chieftain Mark Shope; and others. Although all of these were loyal Party members, the mere fact that they were of a younger generation, and that most of them were black South Africans, subtly changed the balance of power and of ideas in the Party as they rose towards the level of the Central Committee and the Politburo.

At a lower level of seniority, there were black communists who had grown disillusioned by what they had seen of Eastern Europe while they were training there, and who were less hostile to the USA or to the West generally than their colleagues of the older generation. There

5. *Umsebenzi*, Vol. 5, No. 2, 1989.

were some who regarded with alarm the fact that the Party, fearing that there might be an eventual reaction on the part of ANC nationalists, had captured many top positions in the ANC, including all the main positions in the President-General's office, permitting them to control Tambo, and the RPMCs. The office of the ANC Secretary-General, too, was a Party fief. The head was Alfred Nzo, while his second in command was Henry 'Squire' Makgothi, a member of the Party's Central Committee groomed to take over from Nzo. The Administrative Secretary of the office was Sindiso Mfenyane, who also headed the secretariat of the ANC's National Executive Committee. Mfenyane, a Party member, had studied in the Soviet Union and married a Soviet citizen. Only the Treasurer-General's Office was not a Party preserve, since it was headed by Thomas Nkobi, a non-communist. But this was more a reflection of lack of interest than weakness on the part of the Party. The Treasury was mostly involved with technical matters, paying bills, running farm projects and so on. It was not at the cutting edge of the struggle.

There had, in fact, been a shift in the dynamics of the inner party since Slovo's election to the position of General Secretary in 1986. His cautious predecessor, Mabhida, had been acutely aware of the depth of nationalist feeling in the ANC and the liberation movement at large, and had always taken care not to risk flooding the ANC with Party placemen. Mabhida himself headed an Africanist tendency within the Party, largely composed of Zulus like himself, who tended towards caution about the extent of white and Indian domination, just as Moses Kotane had done in earlier years. Others of this persuasion included middle-level Party cadres such as intelligence chief Jacob Zuma, Kingsley Xuma, the representative in Maputo, Dan Cindi and Klaus Maphepha.

After Mabhida's death, and his replacement by Slovo, those who shared this way of thinking found themselves in a position of diminished influence. One of Slovo's deepest fears was of the potential threat from black South African nationalism, which could derail the Party's strategy of working towards a socialist revolution beyond a nationalist one especially in the crucial period when the ANC might have achieved some form of majority rule in South Africa and might be tempted to turn away from what the Party defined as socialism. Slovo's response was more than ever to encourage the appointment of Party members at senior levels in the ANC. Mabhida's protégé Josiah Jele, removed from the Politburo for his alleged chauvinist tendencies in 1985, lost influence.

On the theoretical questions which have always loomed large in the debates of the SACP, although the Seventh Congress paid lip service to developments in the Soviet Union, in its heart the Party continued to side with the most conservative elements in international communism. The new manifesto approved by the Congress, entitled *The Path to Power,* devoted its first chapter to 'The World Revolutionary Process', maintaining that 'more and more peoples [are] taking the path of social progress' and referring to 'the growing instability and internal crises of modern capitalism'.[6] This programme was adopted before the fall of President Nicolae Ceausescu in Romania, and, above all, before the fall of Erich Honecker in East Germany and the opening of the Berlin Wall.

It was the latter event which finally caused the Party's leaders to realise that there was no hope of holding to the traditional line. Of all the Eastern European states except the Soviet Union, and then only until the advent of Gorbachev, East Germany had been the Party's closest friend, providing material support, training, and other services including the printing of Party and ANC literature and the provision of forged bank-notes. Joe Slovo was eventually to acknowledge these changes by the publication of a personal reflection on the history of Eastern European communism in the form of an essay which he entitled *Has Socialism Failed?*, a document later adopted as the Party line. In it he acknowledged the lack of democracy in Eastern Europe, the failings of Stalinism, and the necessity of maintaining a multi-party system in a future South Africa. This pamphlet initiated a debate which continues at the time of writing.

By the time of the Party's Seventh Congress there was increasing talk, including in ANC and Party publications, of the role of negotiations, which all knew were on the agenda. It was an open secret that for some months there had been substantive meetings between Nelson Mandela, in his prison cell, and officials or ministers of the white government. This culminated with Mandela's reception by President Botha at his official Cape Town residence, Tuynhuys, in July 1989. When a new state president, F.W. de Klerk, was elected in September 1989, he set the government on a political initiative to negotiate what he called 'a new South Africa,' a process which is still in its early stages. Under intense pressure from the United States in particular, and realising that the government now had the historic opportunity to address the internal political problems which the securocrats had always insisted was the only lasting counter to revolution, de Klerk continued the process of sounding out the imprisoned Nelson Mandela on the possible normalisation of South African politics. That would involve scrapping all the legislation which prevented free political expression by blacks, and an amnesty for political prisoners and exiles. It was in order to promote this process that, on 2 February 1990, President de Klerk rose before the parliament in Cape Town, and informed members of his decision to unban certain proscribed political organisations, including the ANC and the SACP.

6. *The Path to Power. Programme of the South African Communist Party as Adopted at the Seventh Congress, 1989* (no place or date of publication).

CONCLUSION

The unbanning of the SACP and the ANC on 2 February 1990 came as a surprise to the exiled leaders of both organisations. Although they were aware that the nature of the struggle in southern Africa was changing, and that it was becoming more of a political and diplomatic competition than a military one, they underestimated the tactical skill of President de Klerk and his government and the National Party's ability to adapt and to survive.

The fact that the Communist Party was caught unawares threw it off balance. It was faced with going home from exile, a joy to any South African living abroad for years, but requiring the learning of new political habits associated with the freedom to operate legally inside the country for the first time in 40 years. The surprise with which the Party received this news to some extent indicated a failure in its political assessment. It had not got the true measure of the new de Klerk government, just as in earlier years it had consistently underestimated the sophistication of the government's security apparatus. To some extent this was no doubt because of lack of resources, but it may also be attributed to the strength of the Party's belief in the Soviet model of socialism. Its dogmatic pursuit of the Soviet line for so long had blinded it to certain realities and deprived it of some obvious assets. A good example of this is the strong dislike of the USA engendered by the Soviet connection, which caused the ANC to miss many opportunities to promote its cause in the world's most powerful country over three decades. It did not even maintain an office in Washington until 1989, and outside United Nations circles was practically inert on the political and diplomatic front.

More than a year after the unbanning, it still remains to be seen what use the Party may be able to make of its unaccustomed freedom and new status. Some trends were clearly apparent within months of the unbanning. It is clear, for example, that the Party has a base of support and popularity among black South Africans, no doubt largely on account of its reputation for being at the cutting edge of the struggle against apartheid. The red flag of the Party has been prominent at ANC meetings and rallies, and ANC delegations and committees have continued to contain communists sitting side by side with non-communists in the organisation in apparent harmony. At the same time, there can be no doubt that relations between the two organisations have changed as a result of their legalisation. For the first time it has become possible for leading members of the ANC to debate publicly the nature of socialism and of the SACP without being accused of disloyalty. Pallo Jordan, a prominent socialist and non-communist who heads the ANC's Department of Information and Publicity, and is a prominent member of the National Executive Committee, has published some thoughtful and searching comments on the subject. Above all, the conditions which enabled, or even encouraged, the Party to dominate decision-making in the ANC during the years of exile have now altered. The leader of the ANC is now Nelson Mandela, who has a taste for leading from the front rather than for the careful attention to collective decisions which characterised Oliver Tambo's leadership.

The ANC, too, has returned from exile to its true home. The millions of ANC supporters who have spent their whole lives in South Africa, and who never went into exile, are already changing the character of the organisation by their free participation in its activities. They are people who never knew the conditions of the Angolan camps or the frustrations peculiar to exile, and who have acquired, in the democratic movement inside South Africa, habits of open debate and public criticism which were not the hallmarks of the ANC in exile, where the less pleasant characteristics of democratic centralism gained the upper hand. Now, the vast majority of ANC members are people accustomed to having leaders who must account for their actions in public. The new conditions have reduced the Party's influence over the ANC.

There is now a real prospect of there coming into existence, within the next three years, a South African government which can be said to represent majority opinion, to some degree at least, and in which all people have equal political rights enshrined in the constitution. This will fall far short of the sort of socialist revolution which has always been the Communist Party's ultimate ambition. If majority rule indeed comes about, then it remains to be seen how the Party and the ANC will proceed, and what relations they will have with one another. The SACP has a whole new struggle in prospect.

It is not the function of the present book to debate what may happen in the future, but the Party will at least be able to embark on the next phase of its struggle in the knowledge that it is able to function openly and legally, and that it has a popular constituency, although exactly how extensive that is remains unclear. In that sense, the 'Road to South African Socialism' and the 'Path to Power' described in the Party's two manifestos since 1962, could be very long and tortuous routes indeed. Nobody seriously believes that the socialist revolution to which the Party's aspires is close at hand.

In all these ways, the Party's journey continues. In one sense, though, it has ended. It has come home, and its leaders are no longer obliged to travel the world contemplating and analysing the situation in a country which is theirs but where they are not permitted to live.

For all of the period of exile, the Party put its faith in armed struggle, believing not merely that this was necessary for its success, but, really, that it was at the heart of its strategy. The Party and the ANC used to list the four pillars of their strategy as international support, mass action, underground activity and the armed struggle, and yet in practice the armed struggle was the central one of these four pillars. It conformed to the Marxist-Leninist tradition, established in 1917, of seeking power by force rather than other means. Successful guerrilla wars in Angola, Mozambique and Zimbabwe seemed to indicate that the same formula would succeed in South Africa. And it seemed to be what many of the people of South Africa wanted, to judge from their efforts to take up arms in 1976 and 1984. The mystique of Umkhonto we Sizwe, of the fighting Communist Party and of the armed struggle, were maintained by the policy of armed propaganda, which was intended to be the prelude to People's War. The Communist Party, which throughout the years in exile played the dominant role in ANC theorising and strategising, transmitted its views on the armed struggle to the ANC in exile, especially after the Morogoro Conference in 1969, when the ANC adopted a version of the Party's own political and military strategy. The Party received the full support of the Soviet Union in the importance it accorded to warfare, at least until the mid-1980s. And until its Sixth Congress in 1984 at least, the Party continued to concentrate its recruiting efforts among Umkhonto we Sizwe cadres, turning the army largely into its own fief. Although it never ceased to recruit inside South Africa, that was a most dangerous and difficult task which became easier only in the circumstances of the 1980s.

Since the armed struggle was so central to the strategy of both the Party and the ANC, it is necessary to ask why it failed. For fail it did, at least in the sense in which the revolutionary alliance of the Party and the ANC defined it. Apologists may argue that the war succeeded in keeping alive the spirit of resistance, and in forcing the enemy to the point of negotiation. That is true, but it was hardly what was intended. The blunt fact is that Umkhonto we Sizwe failed to provoke the overthrow of the South African state by force, which is the purpose for which it was ultimately intended.

With the advantage of at least a short period of hindsight, we can say that the Party went on for too long promoting the armed struggle above other forms of activity in conditions which made this inappropriate. This was apparent to many of the ANC rank and file from an early period. One of the main causes of the 1984 mutiny in Angola was the perception of ordinary ANC members in exile that, having been trained for war and instructed in the correct political-military strategy, they were in fact kept inactive for years. When they were finally deployed for action it was less often in South Africa than in Angola, in a war for which they had little enthusiasm and for which they had never enlisted. By 1987, even before the ANC's expulsion from Angola had removed Umkhonto we Sizwe from its main military base and obliged it to seek refuge far from South Africa's borders, there were loyal ANC and Party members who regretted that the two organisations seemed to have put the maximum effort in the wrong direction. Critics pointed out that they were confronting the enemy primarily where he was strongest, in the military sphere, and not where he was weakest, in the political arena. Such was the support for the ANC–Communist Party alliance both nationally and internationally, that whenever the allies confronted the government on a political matter, such as on non-recognition of the 1984 constitution, they were victorious. Within a short time, other commentators who were broadly sympathetic to the democratic movement were wondering aloud whether the guerrilla strategy had not effectively cut the ANC and the Party off from their natural base of support inside the country, where underground operatives, wary of the attention of the security forces, were obliged to take their distance from the people.

To raise these questions is not to contest the logic of the view taken in 1961 that, once the main popular organisations in the country had been banned and many other forms of political expression muzzled, there was little alternative but to fight. But it is to suggest that the Party, and the ANC which looked to the Party for strategic direction, placed too much importance on the armed struggle for too long. Moreover, the Party at times seemed most intent not on prosecuting the war, but on maintaining the leading role in the revolutionary alliance which it acquired after Morogoro. Exile politics are always fraught with difficulty, and the danger of splits and factionalism is ever-present. But the Party was almost obsessed with control, opposing and rooting out dissident opinions in the ANC and, in the process, transforming the exiled organisation from a broad-based nationalist movement – which is what it was from 1912 to 1960 – into something more closely resembling a socialist party. In Tanzania, the syllabus and the teaching staff of the ANC's school, the Solomon Mahlangu Freedom College, provided an example of the Party's concern to remake the ANC membership in its own image. The Communist Party's insistence on training ANC recruits both politically and militarily, instilling in them its own political line in pure or diluted form, caused specific grievances in the Angolan camps. The mutineers complained bitterly of the excesses of security men and political commissars, and the leadership recognised this by subsequently abolishing the post of National Commissar of the ANC.

In conformity with its vision of an armed seizure of power, the Party worked intensely on the military front. Military leaders of the stature of Joe Slovo, Cassius Make and Chris Hani were Party members who did more than anyone else to lead the military struggle. But because the Party had another item on its agenda, to maintain effective control of the ANC, the effectiveness of the military command structure was diminished. The same people who were spearheading the military assault on South Africa were also attempting to pursue the Party's ideological and political interests. An illustration of the consequences of this is the obstacles preventing 'Gebuza' Nyande, a non-communist, from assuming the post of Chief of Staff in 1987, and the promotion of Steve Tshwete to the position of army Commissar. The dilemma of whether to make appointments on the grounds of technical expertise or political correctness is not, of course, unique to South African communism. The long-standing rivalry between Chris Hani and Joe Modise also came to assume an ideological dimension and adversely affected the war effort, as the two chieftains sought to neutralise key Umkhonto we Sizwe commanders, units and operations which were perceived as belonging to the other camp.

The Party's practice of democratic centralism, which it inculcated in the ANC, may also have contributed to the ineffectiveness of the armed struggle. In the end both the Party and the ANC in exile came to be run by a *nomenklatura,* an elite which, whatever its original merits may have been, grew distant from the mass of its supporters, lost their confidence, and did not listen to their voices. Demands for an ANC conference were heard from the mutineers of 1984. The Kabwe conference of the ANC of 1985 was top-heavy with Party members and ANC bureaucrats to the point of being unrepresentative of the ordinary members, whose voice was not heard. Demands for election of a new leadership were still to be heard from the ranks when Walter Sisulu visited Lusaka in January 1990. There was no really free conference of the ANC between Morogoro in 1969, when the Party encouraged popular criticism of the leadership for reasons of its own, and 1990, when the ANC's first conference back in South Africa saw delegates speak their minds unrestrainedly. In the intervening years, the real politics of the ANC and the Party in exile were fought out within the factions of the relatively small elite which ran both organisations. Their feuding did little to improve the army's efficiency, and there is a good case to be made for saying it hampered it by paralysing control and command in some cases. The Party also has a case to answer in any examination of the 1984 mutiny. The Party's role in creating a culture of intolerance, intellectual thuggery and simple repression of unacceptable ideology was a direct cause. The chief target of the mutineers was Mbokodo, not the Party as such. In fact the rank and file of Umkhonto we Sizwe, including the mutineers, generally commended the Party, its philosophy and its leaders. What they did not know was that Mbokodo in Angola was a Party fiefdom. Security chiefs in Angola over the years were all Party members, such as Lentsoe 'Captain' Moeketsi, the nephew of the famous musician Kippie Moeketsi and sometime Deputy Chief of Military Intelligence, who was expelled from the Party in 1984; Morris Seabelo, who was killed in Lesotho in a South African army raid; and Vuki Jacobs. The man most often blamed for the mutiny, and who was sidelined at the

1985 Kabwe conference as a result, Andrew Masondo, was a Central Committee member. None of this was known to the mutineers because Party membership was secret. Had they known it, they may have been more sceptical about the Party.

While the Party's conduct of affairs, methods and judgement may all be questioned, one accusation that could never be made against the leaders of the SACP was that they were lacking in intellectual ability. The Party has always been run chiefly by intellectuals, often capable of penetrating analyses of the South African condition. They were fully aware of the connection between the international and domestic dimensions in the struggle for South Africa. So too, for that matter, were their enemies in the South African government. There was a constant interplay between the two spheres throughout the years of exile. The Sharpeville massacre of 1960 contributed greatly to awakening the world to the true nature of the South African government. Fifteen years later, the liberation of Angola and Mozambique from colonial rule inspired the Soweto rising of 1976 and subsequent political unrest. And, in the end, it was largely in the international arena that the armed struggle was won and lost, putting the initiative back with the internal forces which are currently struggling to determine South Africa's future. Decisive in this respect was the South African policy of destabilisation or undeclared war, which forced the country's neighbours to moderate their anti-Pretoria stand and to deny bases to Umkhonto we Sizwe. Also crucial was the end of the Cold War between the USA and the USSR, and its consequences in Angola and Namibia. It created conditions which persuaded Pretoria that, taking account of its financial plight and international isolation, and knowing that the greatest cause of instability in the region was the existence of apartheid, it could make peace with its neighours, since the Marxist influence in their governments was now diluted.

The New York accords of December 1988, which set a timetable for the departure of Cuban troops from Angola and committed South Africa to decolonise Namibia under United Nations' auspices, was the starting point for a new political logic which would lead inexorably to the unbanning of the ANC, the SACP and other organisations. A faction remained in the South African military and security forces which resisted this point by point, since, in their view, it not only threatened the future of white South Africa, but also their own pre-eminence in government. So pervasive were the clandestine networks for assassination, smuggling and intelligence-gathering set up by the security services during the period of armed struggle and international isolation, that there are also powerful financial incentives to motivate some of those opposed to President de Klerk's programme. Some in the government and security establishment retain a personal interest in instability which is not really political in nature. Quite simply, normalisation and the rule of law threaten lucrative rackets which were tolerated or encouraged during the period of war and destabilisation.

These represent a highly dangerous element, capable of sabotage but not of construction.

On the other hand, military strategists motivated by security concerns and intellectual analysis, no matter how tough, militaristic or downright reactionary they may be, are thwarted by their own logic. The securocrats always maintained that counter-revolution was eighty per cent political and twenty per cent military, and that only a political solution could ultimately answer South Africa's problems. Continuous war could not. They could not convincingly deny that South Africa under F.W. de Klerk had a historic opportunity to escape from the corner which it had been defending for many years. The end of the Cold War, above all, meant that the SACP and the ANC no longer had the backing of a superpower intent on supporting a revolution. The Frontline States were ready for peace, and the decolonisation of Namibia, eventually leading to the adoption of a multi-party constitution and the election of a government which did not fundamentally disturb white interests in the country, all pointed to the urgency of unbanning the ANC and the Communist Party, releasing political prisoners and eventually normalising South African politics. In this they would have the tactical advantage of surprise and control of the state during the period of normalisation.

That this course was eventually taken owed much to the fact that South Africa had at least two exceptional leaders at its service, who also led the most important political organisations in contention. Frederik de Klerk, who became state president in September 1989, had a previous reputation as a skilful if somewhat faceless and highly orthodox, National Party man. He has since demonstrated that he is possessed of consummate political skills and considerable courage and nerve. Nelson Mandela, the other dominant figure in South African politics, is arguably one of the great figures of the twentieth century, who has not only dedicated his life to a cause, but has demonstrated a depth of historical vision which has allowed him to dispense with such sentiments as personal bitterness at the treatment meted out to himself, his family and his people. It must be added, though, that these qualities are not necessarily those which make for an effective politician.

The debate on the influence of individuals on history is never-ending. But, while it is clear that President de Klerk has shown rare qualities of political skill and courage, it would be wrong to over-estimate his personal contribution. The fact is that even his irascible predecessor, the Great Crocodile P.W. Botha, regularly encouraged some of his ministers to visit Mandela in jail, and even to invite him to their homes. Botha himself publicly received Mandela for tea at his official Cape Town residence. Botha, generally regarded as a man little endowed with patience, tolerance or tact, went further than he has generally received credit for in opening the way for the unbanning of the ANC and the Communist Party. In that, he was voicing the consensus of opinion in the white political establishment. De Klerk, too, for all his undoubted gifts and virtues, is a spokesman for the mainstream of South Africa's political and business establishment.

Nelson Mandela is both more and less than that. Revered by the younger generation in the ANC as the man who had dared to begin the armed struggle, seen by exiled ANC members disillusioned with their leaders as the man who could restore internal harmony and a sense of direction to the organisation, he is a figure of national and international stature. Like de Klerk, he recognised relatively early that the time for armed struggle was over, and that South Africans had to resolve their differences by political means. Unlike de Klerk, he does not have a well-oiled political machine at his disposal and therefore is less effective as the leader of a party. But considering the short time that he has been out of prison, he has already gone a long way to persuade the ANC, Umkhonto we Sizwe and their supporters of the logic of his point of view. It is impossible to imagine any other person who would have had the authority and the vision to have accomplished this, so deeply is the notion of armed struggle ingrained in South African political life.

Both the ANC and the Party have had difficulty adapting themselves to legality. This was entirely to be expected. Any organisation condemned to clandestinity for three decades or more, whose members have lived in fear of assassination, and who are still not always safe from attack, unsure of adequate police protection, would find it difficult to adapt. They are short of the funds required to mount conventional political campaigns. Their leaders had been so long abroad that, even when they began to come home, they had only an incomplete understanding of the society they found. There were differences of outlook and opinion between the various generations and layers of leadership, the old generation which had spent years on Robben Island, the young militants who had never left South Africa, and the leadership which had run the armed struggle from Lusaka and elsewhere.

The Communist Party has its share of these problems, although its penchant for organisation, its small size and its habits of discipline and authority make it a far more manageable organisation than the ANC. Some observers consider that the Party might be able to capitalise on these assets and build a strong Party able to play a leading role on its own account in the politics of a free South Africa. The National Party, on the other hand, appears confident that it can take on the Communist Party and win on the political terrain where the National Party has so many advantages: control of the police and the army, overwhelming international support, an experienced and well-oiled political machine, abundant finance, control of jobs and patronage, control of state broadcasting and influence over other mass media.

The Party faces other obstacles. It still has to negotiate a new relationship with the ANC. Party control of the ANC in the past depended not just on packing ANC committees with Party members, but on a culture of secrecy and collectivisation reinforced by the threat of infiltration and assassination by the Security Police. That changed with their unbanning. Although Umkhonto we Sizwe retains a mystique out of proportion to its real achievements, guerrillas returning from exile have not spared their leaders from criticism and have given South Africans a different view of the real nature of the ANC and the Communist Party. Their leaders are revealed not as gods, which many in South Africa had come to think they were, but as human beings, fallible like everyone else.

The Party, unlike the ANC, has a deep ideological problem which it has hardly begun to address. Precisely what do socialism and communism mean after the collapse of communist governments in Eastern Europe? It is one thing to admit, as the SACP has done, that socialism in the Soviet Union was deformed from the 1920s by the stifling of democracy, setting a thoroughly tyrannical precedent for communists elsewhere. But can the SACP assimilate this admission truly into its own behaviour, shrugging off a long tradition of democratic centralism, as this brand of tyranny is known? And if the Party accepts the necessity for democracy defined in terms of multi-party politics and open debate, then will it become just a social democratic party? To South Africans, socialism has traditionally meant the workers controlling the means of production. But if nationalisation is now admitted to be limited as a future economic policy, because of its inherent inefficiencies and because it frightens away investors, then what other mechanism can be found to satisfy the demands of workers? To date, South African communists have tended to underestimate the importance of these questions. Party spokesmen suggest rather glibly that they have learned from the mistakes of Eastern Europe and are ready to build a really democratic socialist party in South Africa. They have yet to provide a modern definition of South African socialism.

APPENDIX I
Acronyms

ANC	African National Congress. The premier African nationalist organisation in South Africa, founded in 1912, banned in 1960, and unbanned in 1990.
APMC	Area Political-Military Council. A local subordinate of the ANC's central organ for coordinating political and military activity.
ARMSCOR	The Armaments Corporation of South Africa. Established in 1964 to make the country less dependent on foreign armaments suppliers.
AZAPO	Azanian People's Organisation. Founded in 1978, it is now the leading Black Consciousness organisation.
AZASM	Azanian Students' Movement, nicknamed 'zim-zim'. Formed in 1983 to supersede the Black Consciousness students' organisation AZASO, which had moved into the ANC camp.
AZASO	Azanian Students' Organisation. Formed in 1979 as a vehicle for Black Consciousness, in 1981 the organisation aligned itself with the ANC and dropped out of the Black Consciousness camp but kept its original title.
BOSS	Bureau of State Security. The main organ for South Africa's external security, from its foundation in the 1960s until its suppression in 1978. It also undertook some internal security work. It later evolved into the National Intelligence Service, its modern successor.
CCB	Civil Cooperation Bureau, a death-squad under the command of South African Special Forces. Formally dissolved in 1990.
CIA	Central Intelligence Agency. The US external intelligence service.
CIO	Central Intelligence Organisation, the Rhodesian and Zimbabwean intelligence and security service.
Comintern	Communist International. The grouping of national communist parties.
CPSA	Communist Party of South Africa. Founded in 1921, suppressed in 1950, and reformed as the South African Communist Party in 1953.
FAO	Food and Agriculture Organisation. An agency of the United Nations Organisation.
FNLA	*Frente Nacional para a Libertação de Angola*, National Front for the Liberation of Angola. A nationalist party founded in 1962, it was backed by the USA during the 1975 civil war between rival nationalist parties and subsequently collapsed. Many former FNLA fighters were subsequently recruited into South Africa's Foreign Legion, the 32 Buffalo battalion.
FRELIMO	*Frente de Libertação de Mozambique*, the Mozambique Liberation Front. The premier Mozambican nationalist movement, founded in 1962. The ruling party in Mozambique since 1975.
KGB	*Komityet Gosudarstvyenoyo Biesopasnosty*, Committee of State Security. The foremost Soviet intelligence and security organisation.
IRA	Irish Republican Army. The principal nationalist organisation committed to the use of violence in order to achieve the unification of Ireland and complete independence from the United Kingdom.
ISL	The International Socialist League, formed in Johannesburg in 1915.
MK	Umkhonto we Sizwe, the Spear of the Nation. Founded in 1961 by members of the ANC and the SACP to launch a guerrilla war, it became the armed wing of both organisations.
MNR	See RENAMO.
MPLA-PT	*Movimento Popular para a Libertação de Angola - Partido do Trabalho*, Popular Movement for the Liberation of Angola - Party of Labour.

	Founded in 1956, the MPLA has constituted the government of Angola since independence in 1975 but has never been recognised by the USA. Having fought against Portuguese colonial rule since the early 1960s, it was engaged in fighting against UNITA and its allies, the USA and South Africa, from then until May 1991.
NATO	North Atlantic Treaty Organisation. The military umbrella of Western European countries and the USA, designed to defend Europe against the Soviet Union and its allies in the Warsaw Pact.
NCL	National Committee of Liberation.
NEC	National Executive Committee. The governing body of the ANC.
NUSAS	National Union of South African Students, the main English-speaking students' union.
PAC	Pan Africanist Congress of Azania. Established in 1959 by a group of former ANC supporters, the PAC was banned in 1960 and its leadership went into exile.
PLAN	People's Liberation Army of Namibia. The armed wing of SWAPO during its guerrilla war against South African occupation, between 1966 and 1989.
PMC	Political-Military Council. Established by the ANC and the SACP in 1983 to coordinate political and military strategy as a replacement for the Revolutionary Council.
Politburo	Political Bureau, the governing body of a political party operating a Leninist system of democratic centralism.
RPMC	Regional Political-Military Council, a regional subordinate of the ANC's central organ for coordinating political and military activity.
RC	Revolutionary Council. A joint committee of the ANC and the SACP set up in the 1960s and formally recognised in 1969 to oversee political and military strategy. It was abolished in 1983 and replaced by the Political-Military Council. The old Revolutionary Council building in Lusaka, still known as RC, was later used as a detention-centre by the ANC.
Recce	Reconnaissance regiment, one of the components of South African Special Forces.
RENAMO	Mozambican National Resistance or *Resistência Nacional Moçambicana*. Established by the Rhodesian intelligence service and former employees of the Portuguese security and intelligence services in the mid-1970s to combat nationalist organisations in Rhodesia and Mozambique, it later developed into the leader of a rebellion against the Frelimo government, receiving help from South Africa after 1980.
SACP	South African Communist Party. Established in 1953, illegal until 1990.
SACTU	South African Congress of Trade Unions. The communist trade union organisation, founded in 1955, having few members inside South Africa after the banning of the ANC in 1960, and dissolved in 1990.
SADF	South African Defence Force. It includes four commands: army, navy, air force, and medical service.
SAS	Special Air Service. A Special Forces Unit of the British Army, founded in 1941.
SASO	South African Students' Organisation, the main organisation for black students of Black Consciousness persuasion from 1969 until its banning in 1977.
SASOL	South African Coal, Oil and Gas Corporation. Founded in 1950 as a subsidiary of the Industrial Development Corporation, it manufactures oil from coal and refines imported crude oil.
SWAPO	South-West African People's Organisation. The principal Namibian nationalist organisation founded in 1960, it has been the ruling party of Namibia since 1990.
SWATF	South-West African Territorial Force. The South African colonial force in Namibia.

UDF	United Democratic Front. Founded in 1983 as a federation of political and community associations opposed to the government, it was broadly aligned to the ANC and included some veteran ANC members among its leaders.
UNITA	*União Nacional para a Independência Total de Angola*, National Union for the Total Independence of Angola. An Angolan nationalist organisation led since its foundation in 1966 by Jonas Savimbi. From independence in 1975 until May 1990, it fought the MPLA government with assistance from the USA and South Africa.
USA	United States of America.
USSR	Union of Soviet Socialist Republics.
ZANLA	Zimbabwe African National Liberation Army, the armed wing of ZANU.
ZANU	Zimbabwe African National Union. A Zimbabwean nationalist party led by Robert Mugabe. Founded in 1963, in a split from the older ZAPU, it has been the ruling party in Zimbabwe since 1980. It reunited with ZAPU in 1989.
ZAPU	Zimbabwe African People's Union. A Zimbabwean nationalist party founded in 1962 and led by Joshua Nkomo. Merged with ZANU in 1989.
ZIPRA	Zimbabwe People's Revolutionary Army, the armed wing of ZAPU.

APPENDIX II
Glossary
of African Words

dagga	Marijuana.
impi	A Zulu regiment
Koevoet	'Crowbar', a South African counter-insurgency unit in Namibia.
mbokodo	'The boulder which crushes'. The name of the ANC Security organisation.
mgwenya	A veteran of the 1967-8 Wankie campaign.
mkatashingo	The 1984 mutiny.
moegoe	A derogatory name, especially used by city dwellers of people who come from the countryside.
Nkosi sikelel' i Afrika	'God bless Africa', a hymn used as the national anthem by the ANC and the Communist Party.
tsotsi	A gangster.
Ukungena	A custom among some Xhosa people, whereby a widow must sleep with the brother of her dead husband in order to purge any guilt for his death.
Umkhonto we Sizwe	'The Spear of the Nation'. The armed wing of the ANC-Communist Party alliance.
witdoeke	'white scarves'.

INDEX

Note: Some organisations are listed under the acronym by ahich they are best known (e.g. KGB). Others are listed under their full titles (e.g. African National Congress).

Index

Index